THE MONKEY IS THE MESSENGER

THE MONKEY IS THE MESSENGER

MEDITATION AND WHAT YOUR BUSY MIND IS TRYING TO TELL YOU

Ralph De La Rosa

FOREWORD BY SUSAN PIVER

Shambhala
Boulder
2018

Shambhala Publications, Inc.
4720 Walnut Street
Boulder, Colorado 80301
www.shambhala.com

We hope the resources and practices in this book will be helpful to readers.
Those in physical or mental distress, however, should seek professional
care rather than relying on any self-help information provided in this work.
Please seek professional help immediately if you have thoughts of killing (or
otherwise harming) yourself or others, if you are gravely disabled (unable
to care for yourself), if you are abusing substances, or if you or someone
else is in any danger of harm. Neither Ralph De La Rosa nor Shambhala
Publications shall be responsible for the use of the information provided.

9 8 7 6 5 4 3 2 1

First Edition
Printed in the United States of America

♾This edition is printed on acid-free paper that
meets the American National Standards Institute z39.48 Standard.
♻This book is printed on 30% postconsumer recycled paper.
For more information please visit www.shambhala.com.
Shambhala Publications is distributed worldwide by
Penguin Random House, Inc., and its subsidiaries.

Designed by Gopa & Ted2, Inc.

Library of Congress Cataloging-in-Publication Data
Names: De La Rosa, Ralph, author.
Title: The monkey is the messenger: meditation and what your busy mind
is trying to tell you / Ralph De La Rosa.
Description: First edition. | Boulder: Shambhala, 2018. | Includes
bibliographical references.
Identifiers: LCCN 2018012459 | ISBN 9781611805840 (pbk.: alk. paper)
Subjects: LCSH: Meditation. | Meditation—Buddhism.
Classification: LCC BL627 .D395 2018 | DDC 158.1/2—dc23
LC record available at https://lccn.loc.gov/2018012459

For Sally Real Johnson (1966–2018)
For kindnesses I can never repay.
You handed down to me the gift of irreverent humor.
You awoke in me an obsession with music.
And without these two, I simply would not have survived.

To my teachers
Countless as the stars in the sky and yet
irreplaceable and precious, each one.
Though it's impossible to do you justice, alas I have tried.
May the work continue. May the teachings spread.
May the clear dawn rise, illuminating all.

Perhaps all the dragons in our lives are princesses
who are only waiting
to see us once beautiful and brave. Perhaps everything
terrible is in
its deepest being something helpless that wants
help from us.
—Rainer Maria Rilke

Contents

List of Practices

The practices in this book have a guided audio companion that can be found online at www.shambhala.com/themonkey isthemessenger.

Foreword

IT IS WONDERFUL that meditation is receiving so much attention for its proven ability to enrich our lives. It has been shown to regulate blood pressure; reduce the stress hormone cortisol; help with chronic pain, insomnia, and depression; and even to thicken the good parts of the brain and shrink the bad. In short, it has been scientifically proven that meditation is awesome.

Which is fantastic. However, there is a danger. To use meditation purely for its prescriptive capacity is to miss the point of the practice altogether. Though it is indeed a powerful medicine (my friend and fellow meditation teacher Jonathan Foust says that if meditation were a pill, everyone would take it), it is far more than that.

Meditation is not a life-hack. It is a spiritual practice.

In the pages of this book, Ralph De La Rosa points us over and over again to the practice of meditation as a doorway, not to self-improvement, but to liberation. Our life is the path, says Ralph, and we are already completely whole, worthy, and brilliant.

As Western meditation teachers, we see three big misconceptions about the practice, all of which are clearly dispelled by *The Monkey Is the Messenger.*

The first misconception is the most important to clear away. It is that in order to meditate, we have to stop thinking. "Monkey mind" is seen as the enemy, something to shut down. But where did we ever get the idea that meditation was about "clearing" the mind of thought? The mind exists to make thought, just as the eyes exist to see and the ears to hear. Trying to make yourself stop thinking is like trying to get your eyes and ears to stop seeing and hearing. Ludicrous! And even if you could do it, so what? That would not bring much benefit to you or your fellow humans. To try to stop thinking means to enter into a giant battle with yourself, one in which part of you is telling another part of you to shut up. In the vast canon of Buddhist wisdom on meditative practices, I'm pretty sure no one ever included the instruction to "zip it." Instead of telling the monkey mind to freeze, the great adepts tell us, we make space for it to be exactly as it is. In so doing, we find that our endless thoughts are simply one part of what is happening in the inner world, and there is no need whatsoever to expel them. Instead we meet the monkey as a friend with wisdom to share, not an enemy to be vanquished.

The second misconception about meditation is that it is a form of self-help. Okay, it is enormously helpful. It has fantastic applications in a variety of therapeutic settings. But to use meditation for self-improvement does not work. It is not like going on a diet or resolving to work out more often. It is far more radical than this—a proven method for jumping off the self-improvement treadmill to instead see our natural perfection and wholeness. Meditation is a journey, not a tactic. The journey unfolds when we divorce it from all agendas. This is quite radical and, at least for myself, hard to imagine. Stop trying to get somewhere? Relinquish all my strategies? No more beating myself up for not being more awesome? These have been my full-time occupations! However, when I enlist spiritual practice in service of conventional aims, all the mojo dissipates. When I can let go of my agendas and simply let the process develop, I find what practitioners have discovered over millennia: meditation is a gateway to the three qualities of the awakened mind—wisdom, compassion, and power. Such qualities far outweigh my conventional aspirations and concerns. When I allow myself to be exactly as I am, the monkey becomes a source of love.

Countless images of blissed-out meditators in yoga pants notwithstanding, the third misconception about meditation is that

the practice will make you more peaceful. (Sorry!) Actually, meditation is far more interesting than that. Rather than teaching you
how to convert the vast spectrum of human emotion into an equal
tone, meditation points you toward the wisdom contained in your
present experience. All emotions are invited to the party. When
you sit to meditate, you place attention on breath and then simply
allow yourself to be as you are. Period. That is the entire practice.
Whether you are easeful, cranky, vicious, delighted, bored, or
frustrated, it is all included. You stop trying to mold yourself into
this or that and instead let down your guard. You soften toward
yourself. The power and consequence of this action cannot be
overstated. A wall begins to come down, and you stop being afraid
of your own life. It is quite extraordinary. You see who you really
are, and because you are not viewing everything through hard-
ened lenses of hope and fear, you also see more clearly into the
hearts and minds of others. Your life touches you because you
are actually living it. Everything, then, is heightened: joy, sorrow,
love, the whole nine yards. This is not exactly a prescription for
peace—but it is a path to something better: authenticity. In this
way, the monkey becomes a source of courage.

The Monkey Is the Messenger blends Ralph's work as a therapist,
Buddhist teacher, and perfectly imperfect human being to present a nuanced view of this powerful, transformative, magical, and
exceedingly ordinary practice. It is a much-needed entry into the
Western literature on this mysterious practice, one that honors
its past and brings it into the present.

—*Susan Piver*

Prelude

Thinking within the Myth

EMPIRICAL DATA AND peer-reviewed, evidence-based findings are important and they form the foundation of what I have to say within these pages. I remember the day, in my second semester of a research methods class in graduate school, this type of knowledge became an inspiration to me. I felt empowered when, having prepared a meta-analysis of a dozen or so studies on mindfulness-based interventions, I noticed so many commonalities between studies. For example, different researchers studying different applications of mindfulness consistently found that participants continued practicing mindfulness meditation long after the study was over. In one journal article after another, I read comments about participants having found the practice to be so beneficial that they had integrated it into their daily lives indefinitely. This not only validated my own predilection toward practice, it fostered a desire in me to deepen it.

Contrarily, my first neuroscience class began with our professor holding up the course textbook and announcing, "In twenty years this will be obsolete." She was pointing to how rapidly we are making discoveries about the brain and how quickly various scientific theories about the brain were being proven wrong. After all, there was a time when scientists thought that all our brain's wiring is set up in childhood, and after that we are stuck living out whatever has been programmed into us. This is why we used to lock alcoholics in asylums and throw away the key; addiction was considered irreparable. Today, we're able to observe that the brain is plastic, constantly changing with every experience we have, and that this process continues throughout our entire lifespan.

Here's another interpretation of what my neuroscience professor meant: We tend to consider scientific findings as definite knowledge, and this can be dangerous. All knowledge is potentially a trap if we cling to it too tightly. What we "know," regardless of its source, is constantly being upended and updated. Those who become inflexible in their current understandings of things tend to end up on the wrong side of history. Consider those who persecuted Galileo as a heretic when he proclaimed his heliocentric (Sun-centered) model of the solar system. Thus, mainstream science has grown to be careful about framing things as *theory* in all of its claims. It's far wiser to hold what we "know" lightly and continue to question everything. Keep the conversation open.

Thus, I ask that you consider what I have to say as a *theoretical lens*. A theoretical lens is a set of ideas, observations, and views that we can pick up and look at the world through. We can actually think of theoretical lenses as myths or childhood stories. Childhood stories and fairy tales, after all, were the first place we ever received meaningful information about the world beyond our own homes and families. They are where we first picked up meaningful insights and life lessons. What's similar about stories, myths, and science are that they ask us to suspend both our belief and disbelief for the sake of discovery, so that we can earnestly question in pursuit of evolving our understandings and perceptions. That is what I'm asking you to do here. To suspend agreeing and disagreeing in the name of trying on a lens, seeing how it fits after some time, all while knowing that we can (and will) put the lens down later. After all, no lens will ever be a complete and final representation of reality. Lenses are templates of experience, but experience is the point.

As the work of the great Joseph Campbell has shown us all myths are truth bearing in some way. That is, all myths, no matter how fantastical, have something meaningful to show us, and theoretical lenses are very much like ancient myths in this way. I had another professor who referenced this thought of Campbell's often and urged us to develop a skill he called "thinking within the myth." That is, if we can think according to the logic put forth by a myth, we can extract its insights without having to adopt it as a belief system.

What matters most about all theory and knowledge boils down to the question of whether or not it functions. Does the lens function to bring about a useful result in some way? Does an insight advance the conversation, push us toward clearer understanding? The sole function of all empirical knowledge, theory, philosophy, reasoning, and mythos is to lead to *experiences* that are in some way liberating—to bring about ease, strength, and resilience in our lives. After all, it's one thing to know about freedom and yet another to experience it.

Experiences that are liberating in nature are always rooted in compassion. We will see ideas and processes in this book that have the power to help us resolve our repetitive thoughts and compulsions, become more skillful with difficult emotions, and achieve more fluency in identifying and navigating our patterns in relationships. But it is only when such processes begin to be coupled with the quality of emotional warmth that results come about—a point I will be discussing at length. To borrow an analogy from a Tibetan Buddhist teacher, Lama Thubten Yeshe, we need flour to make a cake, but it's the butter and sugar that make the cake enjoyable and desirable. Here, knowledge as well as psychological and somatic processes (including meditation) are that flour. They're essential, but on their own they're pretty bland. Compassion, then, is the butter and sugar—the richness that makes the flour delicious, and the endeavor of consciously evolving our life worthwhile. If evidence, theory, myth, insight, and meditation advance the experience of compassion, growth, and resolve in our life, then they have served a great purpose. I invite you to "think within the myths" offered in this book in the hope that you will taste the sweetness of life more richly and more frequently.

THE TECHNICAL STUFF

Beyond offering new ideas regarding some of the most confusing aspects of our existence, the intention of this book is to be utterly practical in helping you address such matters. For this reason, all ideas in this book dovetail with meditation practices that are interspersed throughout. I recognize that this book will attract readers with varying degrees of meditation experience. To be as inclusive as possible, I provide information addressing the very basics all the way up to more nuanced aspects. After some twenty years of exploration within various traditions, both Eastern and Western, what I am offering to you here is what has worked best for me—in many cases, techniques and ideas I wish I had been exposed to from the beginning. As with anything, please take what works for you and leave the rest behind.

Because having access to guided meditations on audio is extremely helpful for internalizing both the technique and the spirit behind meditation instructions, an audio companion to this book has been created for you. It can be found at www.shambhala .com/themonkeyisthemessenger.

The information and practices presented herein are systematically interlocking in nature and intended to be approached in sequential order. If you are new to meditation or to these practices in particular, I strongly suggest that you move methodically through the text and meditations, stopping to spend a good number of days or even weeks doing each new meditation—every day or as often as your schedule allows—before moving on to the next. The Tibetan word for meditation is *gōm*, meaning "habituation," or "to make familiar." Stay with each of the guided practices until they begin to feel familiar. The timing will be different for each person reading this book.

For the seasoned meditator, if you wish to skip ahead in the book, I can condone that approach as well. You might find the material in chapter 8 and onward to be of most use to you. This book can either offer you a thorough system for practicing or serve as a supplement to a practice that's already relatively working for you. Choose your own adventure. May it inspire you to continue in your practice and deepen your daily engagement.

The more experienced practitioner may feel that this book offers a contrasting approach to what they are accustomed to. Especially for meditators who have been taught to ignore or try to shut off their thinking minds, practices designed to skillfully *engage* parts of the monkey mind may seem odd or uncomfortable. I encourage you to be adventurous and to assimilate new ways of harnessing the body and mind's vital energies to see what benefits may be there for you. If in the end what I've offered does not stick or prove beneficial, please abandon it and return to what works best for you.

We live in the age of "I read five books at once and finish none of them." It's a phrase I've come to hear often. In all honesty, this tends to be my habit with books, too. My hope is that *The Monkey Is the Messenger* will break through the glass ceiling here. This book is meant to take you on a journey, starting at the surface of what is observably true for all of us and going down the rabbit hole to truths and realities present at the depths of your very being. My wish is for you to extract every bit of clarity and well-being made available here.

In the words of my first teacher, Amma, "There are as many spiritual paths as there are spiritual seekers." Whether you relate to the practice of meditation as being spiritual or not, the essence of this statement remains vitally relevant: each of us has a unique life in every regard, and thus no two meditators' practices could or should be identical. It is your energy you are investing, and it is you who will live with the result of that investment. The path of meditation, however one defines it, is one of personal empowerment, a celebration of our unshakable uniqueness.

THE MONKEY IS THE MESSENGER

Introduction

Write one true sentence. Write the truest sentence you know.
—Ernest Hemingway

THE TRUEST SENTENCE I know: There's always more to the story. That is, despite our tendency to act as if our perceptions are objective, as if our senses are telling us how things really are, this is almost never the case. And so our trouble begins.

Human experiences are layered and complex. They have a rich subtext that, when uncovered, is often surprising. Our perceptions of people and things and situations merely scratch the surface, only tell us a fraction of the story. If this book is about anything, it is about how things are often about more than they appear to be about. Thus, our conversation with experience in this examined life is an ongoing one. It's a dialogue rife with commas, colons, semicolons, and endless parentheses—but never a period.

If we accept this as true—that there's almost always more to things than what we're privy to—then we must accept some other possibilities. We must also accept the possibility that everything and everyone deserves much more compassionate consideration than they're usually given, including ourselves. We must accept the possibility that there is more to the story when it comes to all that we struggle with in this life: that meaning might be found in what we take to be random; that something worthwhile, some human goodness just may belie what we are certain is difficult and cruel. Might it be possible that there is brilliance hiding in the shadows of life waiting to be discovered? Perhaps it is the case that the frustrations and fears we strive to vanquish are actually the doorways to the rich and satisfying life we sense we are meant for. Perhaps we were born with brains that compel us to shut down our conversation with life too soon. Perhaps our brains tend to construe perceptions so loud that we can't hear what is being whispered in our ear. Perhaps we can learn to listen in a new way.

Matters of the brain, belief, and behavior always come down to matters of perception. And perception, highly limited in nature, is always worthy of further examination.

This Layered Life

In the summer of 2000, I got rid of most of what I owned and followed the world-famous Indian guru, Amma, from city to city across the United States. I traveled by Greyhound bus and rental car to experience blessings and teachings delivered to swaths of spiritual seekers gathering in convention centers. At the time, I believed I was motivated by feelings of rapturous devotion to this being who lived like an embodiment of love. On one level, that much was true: it was a beautiful summer. But deeper down I was on a sophisticated mission to escape myself. It was an exotic alternative to actually dealing with a mind wrecked with relentless, wounded narratives. It was my *Eat, Pray, Love* moment long before that book was conceived of, and with a far less born-for-the-movie-screen ending. Which is to say, when Amma delivered the final blessing of the tour and I had to peel myself away from her, I found myself on the opposite end of the country without a home to return to. I had failed to plan for what would happen next.

I ran into an old friend, also following the tour, who offered me a room in Colorado. A few days later, I found myself living in the Rocky Mountains with horses in the yard and miles between myself and the nearest neighbors. The land was so removed that

I felt I could finally replace the damaged version of me with a freshly spiritualized adaptation. Clearly this was the setting in which my new devotional life would take root.

I had with me only what would fit into my thrift store Samsonite suitcase; there was no room to pack any music or a radio. This was a huge deal. I grew up punk-rock and had played in hardcore and metal bands since my preteen years. Rebellious music had always been my refuge, but that refuge was now closed for remodeling.

Imagine the irritation I felt when I could not get Madonna's "Like a Virgin" out of my head. Every morning I would rise with the sun, do my hatha yoga, chant the various mantras and prayers in my repertoire, and sit quietly with the intention of falling into a deep stillness, when . . . *"Touched for the very first time! Like a vir-ir-ir-ir-gin . . . when your heart beats . . . next to mine . . ."*

I encountered this experience every single day for two months, and I hadn't a clue what to do about it back then. Nor did I think for a second that this experience might be connected to the nature of human evolution and the dynamics of personal development, some of the key topics we'll be exploring in this book. At the time, I was quite certain that my experience was really about what it seemed to be about: my brain was torturing me, skewering me on a bed of hot nails otherwise known as the Top 40 music of my childhood. I took my troublemaking mind to be evidence of life's unfairness.

I'm certain you can relate in your own way. It's been estimated that the average person thinks 12,000 to 70,000 thoughts per day (of course, the validity of measuring something so ephemeral and subjective is contested).[1] There's even more going on if we consider the thought *fragments* that rumble beneath the surface of our conscious mind but don't quite cohere enough to emerge as fully formed thoughts—what the Tibetan meditation master Chögyam Trungpa Rinpoche referred to as "subconscious gossip." I've heard other Tibetan Buddhist teachers estimate that we have sixty such fragments per snap of a finger.[2] Each one of those rumblings correlates with any number of our 100 billion neurons firing, many of which are firing at speeds nearing 200 miles per hour. It's so much activity that our brains are responsible for about 20 percent of our daily calorie burn even though they only weigh about three pounds, less than 2 percent of the average person's body weight.[3] Add to that how terribly stuck we get: 70 to 90 percent of our thoughts are ones that we've thought before, and we're especially likely to land on the higher end of that scale if the majority of our thoughts are unpleasant.[4]

Imagine a nuclear reactor being used to power an army of hamsters running on treadmills—and then every so often those hamsters, much to your surprise, turn to you and say something meaningful. It can seem like that's what we've got going on upstairs. Or perhaps this is a better analogy: that nuclear reactor is powering the most magnificent record player in the cosmos— one that was built to play the most exquisite, transcendent, and celebratory music ever heard—and yet the needle is stuck on a scratch. We keep hearing the first two and a half seconds of the intro but never quite get to the song.

I've come to call the universal experience of repetitious thought "broken-record consciousness." The Buddha called it "monkey mind," as our thoughts tend to behave just like little mischievous monkeys: jumping about from place to place, nearly impossible to catch hold of, caring little about the mess they leave behind. It is the part of our mind that is restless, random, sometimes speedy, sometimes cloudy, unwieldy, and untamable. It is the mind-current that can feel like a raging river, or like six rivers trying to carry us in six different directions. To "monkey around," according to Merriam-Webster, is "to do things that are not useful or serious; to waste time."[5] Also, the words *monkey* and *ape* are slang for mimicry. This connotes that what we encounter at the surface level of perception and cognition is a mere facsimile of life—or an absurd carbon copy of realities extant on a much deeper plane of consciousness. Or both.

My friend Ambyr tells the story of being in a restaurant in India that actual monkeys would routinely invade. It was such an issue that the restaurant had a man whose sole job was to stand near the doorway and slam a big stick on the ground every time a monkey tried to walk in. There Ambyr sat, trying to enjoy lunch amidst the periodic cartoonish "THWACK!" of yet another unwanted patron being run off, when a monkey finally broke past the defense. Every hand in the restaurant, cooks and all, emerged to corner the monkey and chase it off, following the creature right out the door. Without any staff to keep watch, another monkey casually drifted into the establishment, took the seat opposite Ambyr, and proceeded to beg for a bite of her chapatis.

Whether sneaking in through the front door or the side door, a crafty and indefatigable force—sometimes a bully, sometimes a class clown—seems to have taken up residence within the complex tissues and neural pathways of our brains. Is it any wonder that the monkey mind is the scourge of meditators across the globe? For those attempting to find respite in contemplative practice, thoughts are often regarded as an irritating nuisance, a primitive agitator sneaking in through the side door. Interestingly enough, the experience of the monkey mind drives people toward meditation practice *and* away from it. In my decade of teaching I've heard two competing stories about the discursive mind more than any others:

1. "My mind is so busy, I really need to meditate."
2. "My mind is so busy, there's no way I can meditate."

For some of us, this broken-record consciousness fosters graver matters. The inability to regulate repetitive thoughts and ruminations is associated with the clinical diagnoses of anxiety, depression, obsessive-compulsive disorder (OCD), acute stress disorder, and post-traumatic stress disorder. Each of these are risk factors for suicide.[6] I have a client who, prior to seeing me, had recovered from the most pronounced dimensions of her OCD. In every situation she'd find herself in, her brain would generate a fantasy of the worst thing that could possibly happen and put those thoughts on an infinite feedback loop. This debilitating tendency followed her like a shadow.

Consider Ken Baldwin, whose depressed ruminations led him to believe everything in his life was "unfixable." Such thoughts led him to walk halfway across the Golden Gate Bridge, climb over the railing, and jump 220 feet to the water below. In his own telling, the very second he let go of the railing he realized that all of his problems "were totally fixable—except for having just jumped." Somehow, midair, he had the presence of mind to flip around (he was falling head first), point his toes, and make his body as streamlined as possible to minimize the impact. Ken Baldwin shattered almost every bone in his body, but he lived to tell his story. He lived to become an advocate for suicide awareness and prevention.[7] The central role his thoughts played in his suicide attempt is clear. He got stuck in an inaccurate mental narrative of hopelessness, and it nearly took his life.

Of course, it's not always so bad. We do pass through moments when the claustrophobia of the monkey mind abates and allows us states of being that feel much more open, warm, connected, even transcendent. We touch another capacity within ourselves, often without noticing, when taking in a brilliant sunset, when we are transported by a performance, in moments of playing sports, when making art, or in engaging in any project wherein it all seems to connect and flow. We touch this more natural state in sexual climax, in moments of accomplishment, in moments of earnest compassionate action—in any moment when our usual sense of self falls away and we are left with pure, present-time experience. We could go so far as to say that we glimpse a true (or at least tru*er*) self in such instances. A self that is quietly yet enthusiastically present to the true vibrancy of things. These moments reveal a capacity beyond managerial or defensive modes of being, beyond living in autopilot mode.

It might seem like we have to generate the sense of openness, freshness, joy, revelry, or stillness we touch in such moments. From the Buddhist perspective, however, such a state of being is already there within us and has been so since the beginning. It's tantalizing to think that perhaps expansiveness lies waiting to be uncovered within us while we go searching for it everywhere else. It's not something we go toward so much as it is what we are left with when all our running around ceases. Our deeper nature is simply what's left when we put down the endless task of trying to be somebody.

Thoughts of suicide began for me at age eight. They continued almost daily until I finally found competent treatment at age twenty-eight in 2004. By then, my father had disappeared on my family—twice, I had been bullied and publicly humiliated, physically assaulted to the point of developing PTSD, and I had experienced all kinds of death (including the death of my father, deaths of close friends, and a woman who died while sleeping right next to me). I came close to fitting the diagnostic criteria for borderline personality disorder by the time I landed in treatment. There was nothing "crazy" about that, either, it was simply the manner in which my monkey mind had been conditioned by things that weren't my fault. I tried everything to shake off the depression and rage: LSD, MDMA, Special K, drum circles, Hare Krishna, Amma, Reiki, Christianity, Wicca, wanderlust, whiskey, punk, politics, dancing in nightclubs. I also tried the more conventional method of taking it out on everyone around me and leaving a trail of grievances behind me. With each attempt at getting relief, the incessant and painful thoughts I lived with would only temporarily abate, if at all. I came to hate everything and everyone. I came to hate myself most of all. I spiraled downward until I reached a point where putting $150 worth of heroin and cocaine in my veins every single day seemed like the only way I could pacify the war going on inside me.

Like Ken Baldwin, I got lucky. In addition to having people in my life who didn't give up on me, I found a residential substance abuse treatment facility, Walden House, where I could check in for six months, free of charge. Simultaneous to this, I discovered mindfulness-based meditation. I started practicing within a community called Urban Dharma (now known as Against the Stream), under the tutelage of Vinny Ferraro of Mindful Schools. Meditation, in tandem with the work I was able to do with my therapist at Walden House, helped me to disentangle the roots of my inner chaos. Here I was, in this state-funded rehab—a place in which I slept next to ex-cons straight out of the penitentiary—experiencing authentic, lasting transformation for the very first time. Despite my experiences with enigmatic gurus and ashrams and the like, genuine spiritual life began in the lowest place I had ever found myself. I woke up while at the depths, not on a mountaintop.

It's a story for another book entirely, but everything I took in during those six months at Walden House provided the inspiration for who and what I am today. After rehab, I moved to New York with two suitcases, a few hundred dollars, the generosity of a few friends, zero college credits, and a clear desire to give back to the world exactly what had saved me: psychotherapy, meditation, and yoga.*

Given the nature of the predicaments the thinking mind puts us in, it makes perfect sense that we tend to demonize it. And, there's more to the story. After all, our brains and bodies are the most sophisticated things in the known universe. They're more complex and enigmatic than nebulas and supernovas;

---

*The rehab I went to was free and paid for by the State of California through disability benefits granted to addicts. No question: I would be dead or flailing on the streets this very day save for this good fortune of living in a state with a robust social safety net. Because I was offered a chance when on the brink of despair, I now have a life centered on giving back tenfold. If you receive any insight or benefit from this book at all, kindly consider that the next time you vote.

with the capacity for things we used to call miracles before the advent of science. Picture your brain for a moment like Marlon Brando in the opening scene of *The Godfather*: raspy, pleading, "What have I ever done to make you treat me so disrespectfully?" After all, despite the fact that the monkey mind, the untamed and undomesticated aspect of our mental experience, may seem like the star of the show, it's only one character—and a character that deserves much more compassionate consideration than it's usually given.

Welcome to the guiding principle of this book: radical non-pathology; the notion that there is ultimately nothing wrong with any of us. That is, when we apply compassionate attention to our lives, even the most troublesome parts of ourselves begin to reveal hidden layers of satisfying wisdom, spontaneity, purpose, and transformative potency. Radical nonpathology acknowledges that those hidden layers were there from the beginning. They are never lost, though we certainly lose our experience of them. In part one, we will see that the monkey mind actually has a perfectly good reason for existing. The monkey mind is not random, it's not the product of life's cruelty, it's not evidence that we are failures in some way, and it does not exist in a vacuum. Rather, our patterns of cyclical thought are but one of many repetitive patterns in our lives that interlock with one another, definitely have an origin, and are trying to get our attention. Our monkey mindedness is a matter that goes much deeper than our experience of cognition; it's bound up with our evolution as a species and our very survival—from the personal all the way up to the global. Straightaway I will offer you time-tested, evidence-based practices that go beyond mindfulness as it is commonly taught, methods that eloquently address a fundamental mismatch between our biology and the lives we lead.

In part two of this book, we will take those methods deeper and start to unravel why there are too many frustrated meditators out there. We'll dig into how we can move beyond the noise of our mind in practice without resorting to hostility toward parts of ourselves. We'll also move into trauma theory as it relates to every single one of us. How we tend to internalize adverse experiences accounts for how our monkey mindedness manifests, and insight regarding this deepens our understanding of what meditation is really for. Part three offers an exploration of the layer directly beneath our thoughts, the not-so-coded message staring us right in the face but that we don't tend to see. I will give you science-backed ways to respond that have been shown to increase well-being at the physical, emotional, cognitive, interpersonal, and societal levels.

In part three, we will unpack and clarify one of the most confusing aspects of the human experience: our strong emotions and the dynamic web of how they function. Here, I will introduce a unique blending of Western psychotherapeutic modalities and Eastern approaches to meditation designed to give you a direct experience of everything our discussion is pointing to. Through the lenses of evolutionary psychology, neuroscience, trauma theory, Tibetan Buddhism, radically nonpathologizing Western psychology, and reason, we will move toward a new understanding of ourselves.

It is my aspiration that the intelligence hidden within each and every one of our neurotic patterns might be laid bare for you in some way. The jury may still be out regarding this possibility while you gather further evidence within these pages and within yourself, but I will tell you what my two-decade journey has made plain as day for me: it is as if our deeper nature has sent the monkey mind as its emissary—a wonderful beast of a being who has resorted to haranguing us in hopes that we might finally hear its true message.

Part One: Body

THE MONKEY IS A MEDITATOR

1

Taking Responsibility
for Your Own Happiness

*Your present circumstances don't determine where
you can go; they merely determine where you start.*
—NIDO QUBEIN

THE EMOTIONAL EXPENSE OF DISTRACTION

GOD BLESS THE American educational system. And by that, I
mean our overworked and underpaid teachers. It seems they have
become the sole fuel source of the "Little Engine That Could" of
U.S. society, fighting its way uphill like none other. Believe that
teachers have my respect as I point out the absurd fact that most
of us attended school for at least a decade and a half only to walk
away without having learned about the most fundamental aspects
of our lives. We trained our minds to remember multiplication
tables and history lessons, but were we ever taught to train our
attention, the very thing that makes learning and memorization
possible? We spent heaps of hours in biology labs, but were we
ever taught about the importance of *body-mind awareness*? We
studied the wonders of the respiratory system, but were we ever
taught how to *use the breath* to positively impact the state of our
nervous system? We were corralled into our seats for an unnatural
number of hours each day, but were we ever taught how to *corral
a wandering mind*?

"A wandering mind is an unhappy mind." So says the title of a
study by Matthew Killingsworth and Daniel Gilbert.[1] These Har-
vard psychologists found that, when our minds are out of tune

with the present moment, it's corrosive to our emotional state. If we are doing one thing and yet thinking about another, our spirits drop—even if what we're thinking about is something pleasant. It's not that what we think about doesn't matter, though. Gilbert and Killingsworth found that the emotions of their participants correlated more strongly with the content of their distractions than with what they were actually experiencing in the observable world. Put succinctly: being distracted makes you feel worse, and if what you're distracted by is negative, you'll feel even worse still. Furthermore, this "emotional expense" of mind wandering comes about regardless of whether we're thinking about the past, the future, or pure fantasy. In other words, our busy brains eat away at our enjoyment of life over things that we can't do anything about, that haven't happened, or that will never come into being at all.

The busy beehive of the brain exhausts us. It buzzes endlessly, sapping our resources. We might manage to find an "off" switch, but it always turns out to be a snooze button leaving us to wake up to the same buzzing ten minutes later. That is, if we even sleep. The same broken record that exhausts us during the day also has the power to keep us up at night. The American Academy of Sleep Medicine estimates that 30 to 35 percent of us experience insomnia, and it lasts three months or longer for an unlucky 15 to 20 percent of us.[2] The main cause of insomnia is a mind activated by stress—an overabundance of concerns and thoughts about work, family, school, finances, and so on.[3] And then we medicate our untamable mind just to get some sleep. Nine million Americans are now taking prescription sleep medications.[4] Most of these medications are habit forming and don't resolve the underlying source of the problem, leaving insomnia to reemerge once the meds are stopped.

It doesn't help at all that the contemporary situation for many people, especially in the West, places unprecedented demands on us. We are expected to wear more hats, be adept in more roles, be increasingly flexible in our careers, keep up with an ever-growing number of people and events via an infinite array of social media platforms (the very same platforms that are shrinking our attention spans, no less), ad infinitum. Did the generations preceding us have laundry lists like ours to keep up with? At the very least, they weren't reachable when they were away from home or not at their desk. They couldn't be "pinged" on any one of twelve apps on their phone by someone who is expecting a response within hours, if not minutes. (Fun fact: Every time our phones go off, our blood pressure spikes. The buzzing and bleeping of our phones put our bodies on a small but significant emotional roller coaster all day every day.[5]) Yet, the issue of overstimulation and continual distraction is as old as they come. The Buddha could have told you about Killingsworth and Gilbert's findings 2,500 years ago: "Nothing can hurt you more than an untrained mind, and nothing can help you more than a well-trained mind."

Psychologists and clinicians know that our cognition impacts our well-being, which is why we have so many modalities of therapy that attempt to intervene at the level of thought. I myself was trained in one of the most recognized evidence-based trauma treatments for children and adolescents, Trauma-Focused Cognitive Behavior Therapy (TF-CBT). This modality riffs off traditional Cognitive Behavior Therapy, which identifies thoughts as the primary source of our suffering and thus engages clients in a process to change their thinking. The goal of TF-CBT is to diminish the most overwhelming symptoms of traumatic stress, in particular by teaching kids and teens how to reframe and rewrite their thoughts and perceptions, whatever adverse and overwhelming experience they've had. I think it's an excellent methodology for helping young people find their way out of self-blaming, avoidant, hyperemotional, and hypervigilant thinking (which, for kids, is all expressed through behavior). TF-CBT gives them a means to construct a coherent, positive narrative out of an otherwise fragmented traumatic experience.

However, there is a difference between coping and healing. While it is entirely possible to bend our thoughts toward happiness, this strategy merely manages the content of our thoughts and does little to address the deeper root of the issue. In the freight train of the mind, our thoughts are only the caboose. If we are to truly address that which drains our days and usurps our nights, we want to find our way to the locomotive, where we can deal with the steam engine.

Where psychologists might help someone reframe and rewrite their thinking—to train the monkey, so to speak—meditators often have an equally one-dimensional approach: they try to kill the monkey. In meditation circles, some unintended connotations of the Buddha's monkey metaphor prevail: that the thinking mind is a dirty, primitive, lower life form of no real value to us; it's just a bunch of garbage on repeat. (Take out the trash, already.) Yet this viewpoint contradicts a key tenet of neuroscience: The brain can't *not* be doing something. Its very nature is to be in perpetual motion. Imagine standing in front of a fire and judging, shaming, and resenting it for being hot. Sounds both ridiculous and futile, right? Yet this is exactly how many of us meditators try to deal with our monkey minds.

THE ANSWER LIES IN THE SPACE BETWEEN THINGS

"The space in between things" is a theme that comes up in many arenas related to working on oneself. It's something we'd do well to get curious about. In the context of this discussion, the space between things offers a key that can unlock the mystery of how we experience the mind and how we might even bring it under our own auspices. It's sometimes even called the "third thing." We know that an experience always entails a subject and an object (e.g., me and Led Zepelin's *III*). The third thing is what lives in the space between subject and object: their relationship (in this case, my undying adoration of that record). It can be much subtler though, so subtle that we hardly even notice it (e.g., such is often the case with us and our emotions). But we have a relationship to everything we experience, and the quality of that relationship determines the nature of everything we think, feel, say, do, and take in from the world around us.

Say you go to a workshop with a friend. Your friend is excited for you to hear the facilitator. He's been to many of her classes before and has told you how brilliant she is and how much her workshops have changed his life. You take a seat at the workshop, and the moment the speaker begins, you realize that you knew her in high school, and she used to bully one of your best friends pretty severely. You find yourself triggered: angry, resentful. You try to accept that maybe this person has changed, but it's no use. You can't help being upset. Every word out of her mouth is like fingernails on a chalkboard. You want to leave, but it would be too conspicuous. Halfway through the talk you resort to mentally revisiting your favorite scenes from *Seinfeld* just to cope. When the workshop ends, your friend turns to you and says, "Dear god, she is just so *insightful*. That was life changing. I think I'm gonna sign up for her immersion course." You turn to your friend, irritated. You ventilate all the feelings that you had been stuffing down by thinking about Elaine dancing at the company party and the time George Costanza got caught eating a pastrami sandwich during sex.

You and your friend experienced the exact same workshop, the exact same ideas, the exact same words, and yet what you perceived couldn't have contrasted more. There was only one variant present: your respective relationship to the teacher.

Now let's say you go home and, still fuming, you look up the teacher online. You write her an e-mail and let her have it about all the harm she's caused. To your surprise you get an e-mail back from the teacher an hour later. She apologizes profusely and asks if you'd have coffee with her. You agree to it. At the café the teacher apologizes again for the person she used to be. She tells you about the abuse she used to experience at home and how she had taken out her pain and confusion on your friend. She admits how wrong she was. You learn that the teacher has since gone on a healing journey and has radically changed her life, and that's why she teaches now. (I swear this is not autobiographical.) She asks if you have the contact information of your friend from high school whom she used to bully, because she'd really love to make amends. It strikes you that this woman really is profound after all. Your relationship has shifted, and now you wish you had participated in the workshop. You may even attend the next one.

What if I told you that your relationship to your own mind is not so different from your relationships to other people? What if the parts of your monkey mind are just like the speaker in this story? Various aspects of ourselves may have caused us pain in the past and we may want to punish or shame them—but all without taking the time to develop a relationship with our minds in the present moment. Generally, once we understand where a person is coming from and what they've been through, suddenly they're more human to us, which makes it so much harder to pass judgment on them. It is entirely possible to get to know the monkey mind in a similar fashion. The same goes for the anxieties, compulsions, resentments, misunderstandings, fears, urges, and desires that fuel it—something we will discussing with increasing depth and specificity as we go.

THE THREE TYPES OF RELATIONSHIP

Yongey Mingyur Rinpoche is a young and rather charming Nepalese-born teacher in the Tibetan Buddhist tradition who comes from a family of well-respected gurus. Enlightenment is sort of the family business. Despite growing up around high lamas, Mingyur Rinpoche was born with a panic disorder, which he overcame with meditation. He likes to talk about three categories of relationship we can have to our experience. When we allow our experience to dictate what we feel, think, and do, it's become our *boss*. When we fight against our experience or try to blot it out in some way, it's become our *enemy*. When we meet our experience with curiosity, allowance, and even kindness, the experience has become our *friend*, or an *ally*. Mingyur Rinpoche is suggesting that we have a say in the quality of our relationship to our experience. Hang on to this idea, as we'll be revisiting these types of relationship over and over again as we proceed.

The suggestion that we can consciously shift our relationship to our experience is deceptively simple and has far reaching implications. Psychologist Carol Dweck advocates a similar idea that she coined "the growth mindset."[6] Dweck's phrase points us in a useful direction here. The growth mindset is a perspective that intends to reframe adverse life experiences as opportunities for learning, insight, and development. It's an approach to living that acknowledges that just about every situation in life can either lead to us to clarity and satisfaction or confusion and misery; the difference lies not in our circumstances but in our attitude toward them. I call this *taking responsibility for your own happiness*. Ordinarily, we live in a mode in which, if something good happens, we're happy; if something bad happens, we're upset; if someone is kind to us, we feel worthy; if someone disregards us, we feel unworthy; if someone disrespects us, we get angry; and so on. Now go back through that last sentence and look for which of the three relationships is framing each experience. These are all examples of allowing our experience to be our boss or our enemy. This might make perfect sense according to conventional logic, but living in this way is exactly like having a remote control with buttons on it for happiness, upset, worthiness, unworthiness, and anger—and then handing that remote control to the world. When our emotions are hitched up to our circumstances without our consciously mediating them, it's a recipe for anguish.

By a similar tack, happiness is more likely to result from a positive orientation toward our experience than because of what's happened to us. For example, 55 percent of lottery winners say they're no happier as a result of becoming rich overnight.[7] Meanwhile, most of us have seen testimonials of people like Tyler Curry, a man who says contracting HIV is the best thing that ever happened to him. "It makes me value life, to make each moment one to remember and take the time to enjoy the journey . . . it is the catalyst that continues to push me out of the safe and into the incredible,"[8] Curry states.

"The growth mindset is like taking that remote control and replacing all the buttons with ones that say 'learning,'" says my friend Anna Lindow, founder of the cutting-edge opioid treatment clinic, Brave Healing. When we reframe our approach to life as if everything were designed to help us grow and heal and evolve, as if our experiences are here as our teachers and friends, doors open up before us. We can shift our relationship to the monkey mind by getting to know its reasons for being the way it is or, by extension, applying a growth mindset to our experience of it. When we do so, a door opens that leads to the settling of the monkey mind. From there, further doors open—ones that beckon us toward self-actualization and clarity. No matter how frustrated or stuck we might feel, we can come to embrace the goings-on of our minds and lives just like Tyler Curry. We can shift out of habit and enmity and into the incredible.

2

The Magnificent Mismatch

The universe is not short on wake-up calls.
We're just quick to hit the snooze button.
—BRENÉ BROWN

ON PRIMAL RAGE AND . . . WORD PROCESSORS

I HIT a roadblock the very moment I sat down to start working on this book. I opened my laptop, double-clicked my word processing app, and found myself mysteriously locked out of my account. An hour-long phone call with a small army of inept customer service agents ensued, mostly spent on hold. Set adrift on an odyssey set to smooth jazz and prerecorded sales pitches alternating with fake-nice quasi-human interactions, I wanted to scream. *Don't they know I just sat down to write my first book?* Had they no clue the self-inflicted difficulties fledgling authors such as myself face? How could these people be so blind to the personal resistance I had to cut through to get to this moment of finally, finally sitting down with the blank page? I had alphabetized my record collection and color coordinated my closet into precise gradients to avoid this intimidating moment. And now this.

My heart rate shot up, my shoulders and fists clenched, my legs began to fidget under my chair, and maintaining my inside voice was a challenge. Of course, my thoughts began to race as well. I became paranoid, wondering if this was a sign. Maybe the book wasn't "meant to be." Maybe it was all a cosmic joke. *Is mercury in retrograde?* More than anything, I was concerned that after all this I'd be in no mood to write. Permutations of "why me?" "why today?" "why do I give these people my money?" ran laps inside my head. I'm not proud to report that maintaining civility required a valiant effort on my behalf.

Sound overly dramatic? It was. I realized later that my body and mind were behaving as if I were under attack. The cardinal biological markers were all there. A surplus of energy had shot out to my arms and legs, becoming tight fists and tapping feet. This automatic and involuntary biological response is something that would've come in handy if I had needed to run away or retaliate with a punch or a handy weapon. The thoughts I experienced all assumed a tone of victimhood, replete with themes of fighting or fleeing—products of my limbic system. As there was no actual person to fight against or flee from, my thoughts turned to wondering if I was jinxed or if astrology had something to do with it—probably the work of my insular cortex, a region of the midbrain that is involved in construing meaning out of uncertain experiences.[1] At the biological level, even the anger and outrage I felt was due to the famous fight-or-flight stress response that has evolved over eons to mobilize our bodies against harm in these exact ways.

The matter was one of perception. That there was no actual threat present made no difference to my brain. It's true that something related to my livelihood (and, by logical extension, my survival) was at stake, but during that phone call the only threats that were actually present were wasted time, mundane experiences, and the discomfort of being treated like an insignificant consumer (as opposed to a person). I was experiencing an emotional reaction that was disproportionate to the severity of the situation, most likely exacerbated by the fact that I'm a trauma survivor who hates feeling restricted by others.

Maybe drawn-out phone calls with customer service agents don't feel as sadistic and draconian to you as they do to me, but I guarantee you've had your own versions of this situation. I know without ever having met you that you sometimes pass through activated, high-octane, survival-oriented states of mind that are mismatched to the actual reality you are faced with. Road rage is a common example. Or how triggered we get when our partner or spouse does or doesn't do the thing that we've talked to them about *three damn times.* I'm quite sure that there are times when emotionally activated states of mind cause you to do and say things that another part of you knows are a terrible idea. It's as if that other part of you takes over while you are forced to watch, helpless.

I know this happens to you because it happens to all humans. No matter how much work on ourselves we've done, how much we meditate, or how many times we try to tattoo "positive vibes only" onto our brains, at some point we all suffer some form of involuntary inner tempest. There's a reason for this, and it's not our fault.

Tortoise Evolution, Hare Evolution

What we know about the evolution of our species offers some key insights about such mismatched experiences. Consider the immense gap between our biological and social evolutions. Biological evolution is a staggeringly slow, incremental process. Current science suggests that it's taken us between five and eight million years to evolve from apes into the tremendously complex beings we are now. Five to eight *million* years. This is because it takes generations for a gene to mutate in adaptation to an organism's environment. For example, it took approximately 364,000 years for eyes like ours to develop from mere light-sensitive patches into the camera-like organs we have today.[2]

Human social evolution is another story altogether. The human species has existed for about 100,000 to 200,000 years (just half the time it took for eyes to develop). Our early societies were nomadic and hunter-gatherer until just 12,000 years ago, when agriculture was developed. Do the math: it took us 188,000 years just to figure out how to grow crops and herd cattle. Now, flash forward only about 11,800 years from the advent of agriculture to the industrial revolution, when we suddenly developed an ability to rapidly produce and transport goods. On the timescale of our physical evolution, human civilization became globally connected in a heartbeat. Our social worlds began to evolve at an exponential pace. Less than 200 years after the industrial revolution, we have smartphones, which have only existed since around the time President Barack Obama took his seat in the White House and Katy Perry's "I Kissed a Girl" was topping Billboard charts. From that moment and with unprecedented speed, literally everything about how we interact and get things done changed.

Societal evolution has sped up to the point that radical reorientations like this are taking place in the span of a few years. Meanwhile, our biology is bound to continue crawling along at tortoise pace. It's like trying to install Instagram on a flip phone: our ancient hardware is a terrible match for our societal software and its ever-increasing complexities. Our brains, nervous systems, and sense faculties are set up to deal with situations that are much more primal and far more threatening than the world most people in developed countries live in—especially those of us with the advantages society confers on people with lighter skin, dominant gender traits, able bodies, heterosexual orientations, and sustainable financial resources.

With this in mind, hopefully it's less shocking to you that I (*gasp!* a *meditation* teacher) went into the fight-or-flight stress response while on the phone in my quiet apartment. Over and over again, each of us are fated to experience our nervous systems working much harder than they need to, and putting us in painful circumstances as a result. It's simply the context we were born into, and the implications are far from just personal. Our outdated and overactive biological hardware plays an enormous role in fostering war, environmental degradation, greed, and violence. We instinctually sense that we live in a world of "dominate or be dominated," "get ahead or get left behind," and "survival of the fittest." This is an outdated mentality, a product of our mismatched biology, that continues to perpetuate itself in spite of how much unnecessary disaster it creates. We don't actually have to live in a dog-eat-dog world as a society, and yet our overactive defensive structures create the feeling that we do. This has played a great role in the establishing of systems of poverty and oppression that marginalize people and too often thrust them into *actual* life-threatening situations. It might take some time, but it is utterly possible for us to put ourselves in the driver's seat of our own evolution and recalibrate this mismatch. And although such work is individual and personal in nature, it is my belief that it can happen—and is starting to happen—on a mass scale.

We human animals are still a part of nature, and everything in nature has its place and purpose (not that there aren't exceptions to the rule). When the leaves of a tree die and fall to the ground, they decompose and turn into nutrients for the soil. As winds blow, they scatter seeds of various flora to locations where they stand a better chance at taking root. As predators hunt, they unknowingly regulate the population of the species they prey upon, which maintains the balance of resources in the ecological environment. Just about every aspect of every organism in nature has evolved to function systematically in this interlocking manner. Our brains and minds are no different. Our primitive biological hardware is definitely out of step with the modern situation we find ourselves within, and yet I must argue that everything about us continues to serve a purpose. The thing is, we won't be able to see that if we're too busy demonizing ourselves, or if we are certain that "this is just the way it is," with no room for taking another view.

Taking the self to be an ecosystem invites the growth mindset. With regards to the monkey mind, it poses the question: What purpose could it possibly be serving? What is it trying to tell us? We will explore this question in three different contexts throughout this book, and we will find three variations on a single answer:

The monkey is asking you to go deeper with your life. The monkey is showing you what a life lived on autopilot looks and feels like, and it's asking you if you're really content with that. At this leg of our journey in this book, the monkey is asking you to address your mind wandering, to begin training your attention, to have a more wakeful relationship with your experience.

The monkey is asking you—nay, begging you—to meditate. As William James, godfather of modern psychology, wrote, "The faculty of voluntarily bringing back a wandering attention over and over again is the very root of judgment, character, and will. . . . An education which should improve this faculty would be *the* education *par excellence*."[3] What William James didn't know at the time of writing this is that he was describing the basic instructions for mindfulness meditation. And the faculties of judgment, character, and will are indeed germane to matters of taking responsibility for our relationships to things—what to speak of taking responsibility for our own evolution.

MAYA AND THE MONKEY

In Hinduism, Maya, the goddess of illusion, is the personification of deceit—a trickster force of nature who bedevils us humans into living in *samsara*. The word *samsara* points to the cyclic, repetitive way things seem to work in the material world (e.g., the cycle of the seasons in each year). Samsara is fueled by our blind belief that material gain and hedonic pleasure will satisfy us in some lasting way (which is also the subliminal message of every advertisement you've ever seen). The problem is, lasting happiness can never come from a world in which all things are temporary. Thus, the end result of chasing samsara is frustrations, disappointments, and tragedies that we seem to revisit again and again.

Maya is by and large considered the enemy by Hindu spiritual practitioners. This is particularly true of the *Vaishnavas*, members of a sect that sees devotion to the god Krishna as the goal of human life. For them, Maya is a little like the Satan of the Bible: an agent of temptation to be on the lookout for. Yet there's a catch: Maya is actually a devotee of Krishna; she's just playing the long con. Yes, her job is to get us humans to expend enormous amounts of effort competing with each other and chasing frivolity, but as we face repeated heartbreak something in us shifts. As we continue to face old age, disease, death, and human disregard for one another; as we exhaust ourselves chasing after self-centered and superficial rewards; and as we start to see the impossibility of our quest to avoid pain and maintain an unbroken continuum of good feelings, we become fed up with the status quo of things. We tend to start to ask deeper questions about life's meaning and purpose. At the end of the day, Maya's deceptions are for our own good. Her service to the divine is to drive us to disillusionment with the material world so that we might develop higher aspirations, which in this particular tradition means becoming blissed-out devotees of Krishna, the symbol of achieving life's true purpose.

In the Buddhist traditions, our wild and relentless minds, which very much work in a circular fashion, are considered a manifestation of samsara. In an identical way, it is the very nature of such a mind—sometimes filled with creative genius, sometimes manifesting as a painful inner critic, oftentimes permeated by banal chatter—to drive us to seek meaningful methods of relief. We might try yoga, therapy, self-help books, cleanses, 12-step programs, making more money, acquiring more comforts, going on more vacations, and medications in attempt to abate the problem, and yet we remain stuck. If we are fortunate, we might start looking beyond quick fixes and begin questioning things. If we are fortunate, we might begin to look toward the path of meditation.

Meditation not only addresses the evolutionary mismatch between our biology and our social world, it does so poetically.

The science on mindfulness-based meditation confirms that it benefits us in myriad ways: it settles the mind, helps us be less reactive, improves our ability to discern our experience accurately, increases emotional and behavioral self-regulation, enhances our social lives, slows aging, prevents sickness, prolongs life, and even impacts the DNA we pass down to the next generation.[4] That meditation is being embraced *en masse* in Western society is no accident. That it is happening right at the very moment when our planetary crisis has reached fever pitch is even more to the point.

To be clear, there is a difference between secular meditation for stress relief as a stand-alone method and secular meditation as a path. Mindfulness has been thoroughly popularized as a method that merely provides immediate benefits such as lowering blood pressure and increasing creative output. While I embrace this development and everyone it has attracted to the practice, we must admit to ourselves that this approach falls ultimately into the "quick fix" category described above. To take meditation as a path, rather, is to sign on for the heart opening and emotional processes it inevitably entails, which then impacts our ethics, our understanding of how reality works, and how we show up in our relationships and work. To break this down in another way, we can engage meditation as a way of paying attention or we can engage it as practice of cultivating empathy and a radically liberating, holistic understanding of things. Pick your path.

Our wild and relentless minds serve the purpose of driving us toward methods of relief. Like Maya, the monkey mind is both an agitator and an ally. Thus, we are faced with the deep irony that the monkey is both asking us to meditate but also making meditation difficult. Why would the messenger that compels us to sit down and turn inward be the biggest obstacle we meet with once there? Why would the thing we are trying to get free of be the very thing we run right smack into the moment we sit down?

Over the course of this book, we will explore this matter within the context of the three main families of meditation in Buddhism:* *shamatha* (mindful presence), *maitri* (lovingkindness), and compassion meditation. We will see that our mind's workings and overworkings serve distinct purposes that intertwine seamlessly with each of these practices. We will see that such practices are made for us to address the true, hidden causes of overthinking. Starting from our most salient concerns—the busyness of our minds—we'll explore a terrain of increasing depth as we go.

In chapter three, we'll begin exploring meditation practices centered on embodiment—the most direct way to encounter and overcome the initial hurdles presented in meditation. Before we go there, however, I'd like to look a little bit more deeply at the dynamics of our inner worlds as they are reflected in our outer worlds. When the monkey decides to be a DJ playing Madonna on repeat, it's annoying but kind of funny. But having a mind that's out of control can have serious consequences—for ourselves, our relationships, our society, and for planet Earth.

At the end of the next chapter, we'll start exploring the meditation practices rooted in the principle of connection: these serve as a basis for growth and well-being, and can actually function to relax the noise of the mind. I'll begin by offering further insights

---

*A few things must be stated about the *B* word here. First of all, one does not have to be Buddhist in order to practice these meditations. They are utterly nonreligious in nature, especially in my particular presentation of them, and they do not conflict in any way with any belief system that I am aware of. To be honest, I am not always comfortable with the label "Buddhist" myself, as I find it to be a misnomer and inherently limiting in many ways. The Buddha taught what's possible for the human person to realize, not a path of following him or anyone else. Finally, it is of the utmost importance that I state clearly that I am not a Buddhist teacher, and I do not represent any Buddhist tradition or community whatsoever. I am proud to call myself a student of these practices who has been asked to share my experience. I have enjoyed the privilege of doing so for some ten years now, yet I am ten times more uncomfortable with the label "teacher" than I am with the *B* word. My aspiration is to highlight the cross-section of secular meditation and psychotherapeutic thinking and practice, and to push forward the current discourse regarding this cross-section in the mainstream culture. As such, the presentation of the practices we will explore does tend to depart from the traditional forms and methods.

about how we're fundamentally good just as we are, a truth we often overlook because it is literally closer to us than our own skin.

As we're about to see, when the monkey mind finds its home in the body—the *soma*, the physical apparatus that is inherently connected to and supported by the earth—our psyche begins to untangle itself quite naturally.

3

Befriending the Body in Meditation

The body is no dumb thing from which we struggle to free
ourselves. In proper perspective, it is a rocket ship,
a series of atomic cloverleafs, a tangle of neurological
umbilici to other worlds and experiences.
—CLARISSA PINKOLA ESTÉS

SO OFTEN the answers we seek are right in front of us, in the very things we have been taking for granted. This is true of the body and its role in meditation. The body is arguably the most primary thing about our existence; it is the basis for our being alive in the first place. Yet, the tendency toward disembodiment is not only widespread; it's encouraged, even championed. We've grown to embrace busyness as a value. For example, a feat made possible by an individual's ability to shut down their body's need for sleep, rest, and play. The ability to handle the workload of four people is practically considered a virtue. We have come to feel little to no empathy or appreciation for the body, taking for granted all that it does for us and all that we put it through. When we disconnect from the body in this way, we treat the body as if it were a mere object, a machine as opposed to a living organism. This disconnection has a direct correlation with mind wandering. Genuine mindful presence always has a tone of empathy and warmth to it, and empathy and disconnection are mutually exclusive. Mindful presence entails a shift toward the end of all such objectifications, a matter we will be discussing at length soon enough.

Objectification is what allows us to push our bodies beyond their limits to keep up with the demands of work, family, and our ever-growing social circles. Tired? Drink more coffee. Don't have enough time to finish the work? Sacrifice sleep. Had a bad day? Reach for a drink or prescription medications. Don't like the way your body looks? Punish it with workouts, diets, cleanses, and supplements. Think of the last time you did any of those things. At some point, you felt the body "whisper" to you; it sent a quiet signal that said, "I'm full," or "I'm exhausted," but that whisper was probably ignored. Some of us have built such a habit of ignoring those signals that we don't know how to feel them anymore. I would venture to say those whispers are more important than we might realize.

I have nothing against (and often everything for) using medications, being career-focused, staying up late, and intense workouts, but so often such behaviors are rooted in something more than cultural habits. Quite often these are driven by pervasive beliefs we have regarding our worthiness and fears that we might not be good enough. The possibility of being a failure or unlovable in some way can form a subconscious sense of threat that drives us toward self-judgment; endless comparisons to others; perfectionism; substance abuse; working in overdrive; and myriad forms of overcompensation, anxiety, paranoia, and depression. Such beliefs and fears (as well as the compensatory impulses they give rise to), whether we are conscious of them or not, correlate with a felt-sense of contraction in the body. These beliefs and behaviors are present in the knots in our shoulders, our lower back pain, our tense jaws, our heavy limbs, our chronic illnesses. All of this forces us up into the head, into the monkey mind. This mode of living is so commonplace that we're not even aware of our own self-abuse—and then wonder why we sometimes feel so stuck.

The Relaxation Response

The good news is, the very nature of the human soma and psyche is one of healing, growth, clarity, and calm. When not in the presence of perceived threats but rather in conditions such as safety, warmth, acceptance, and connection (incidentally, the environment any decent parent would try to create for their child), the very same survival instinct shifts us into a mode of restoration and repair known as the relaxation response. This is, in fact, the original, natural state of the body-mind. Such is the state our being prefers to be in and will return to on its own with enough exposure to conducive conditions. Stress, heartache, and anxiety are additive layers that both obscure our natural state and yet somehow call us back toward it.

That said, ever found yourself *trying* to relax? It doesn't work. One cannot *do* relaxation. Relaxation is an undoing. What we *can* do is let go of the tension, stress, unresolved emotional material, and fatigue that is held in our body. If we were to thoroughly let go of tension and stress, what would be left is a relaxed, open, balanced state of being—a state wherein our resources are utilized for growth. Such a state also includes far more room to receive the vividness of our experience of life. This is both a biological truth and a psychological truth. Some would even say it's a spiritual truth as well. In Buddhism, this points us toward the notion of *basic goodness*: that we possess a fundamentally sane and whole nature at the bottom of it all; a concept that is well aligned with the view of radical nonpathology.

I realize that *let go* has become one of these vague and lovely terms, like *self-love* and *gratitude*. Many of us see such terms on an inspirational social media post and think to ourselves, "Great! But, *how*?" How we learn to let go, specifically so we can make space for our natural propensity to heal, will inform our focus here to a great extent. It begins by working directly with the contractions, tension, and fatigue held in the body.

The Body Holds the Key

Meditation is often referred to as a mind-science and a mind-training. In our culture, we think of the mind as being located in the head, and then meditation also becomes something we do in our heads. If we practice meditation in a way that merely pays lip service to the body and then moves on to, for example, focusing on the breath at the tip of the nose (i.e., on the head), we're only deepening our sense of the body's irrelevance, and our meditation is necessarily going to be limited.

The cultural assumption that the mind correlates with the head is due to another outdated assumption: that the brain is only in the head. Rather, the brain is spread throughout the body. You have neurons and neurotransmitters firing in your throat, heart, gut, and various other nervous systems that extend all the way out to the tips of your fingers and toes.

Reconnecting to the body is the first order of business in meditation for many reasons. First of all, the body is the mind's home. The work of somatic psychologists Bessel van der Kolk and Peter Levine has gone a long way to demonstrate that the body is the storehouse of all mental processes, emotions, experiences, intuitions, and memories.[1] Furthermore, meditation is synonymous with the notion of "going within." Well, within where? Where else is there to go within, other than the space of the body? More important, it's illogical to expect peace and clarity to arise in our practice if the most immediate aspect of our being is anything less than front and center in our experience.

How I Came Home to the Body

Five years ago, I hit a moment when my meditation practice was no longer supporting me or nourishing my life. I was fresh out of social work school and working in clinical foster care, one of the most intense jobs in the field. Bearing witness to the lives of impoverished children and families in the midst of institution-alized racism, working incredibly long hours, being constantly stymied by red tape and paperwork, and observing the terrible decisions made in family court that incur traumatic ripple effects in people's lives . . . I began to snap.

I felt like I was doing all the things, ticking off all the self-care boxes: therapy, exercise, regular meditation, clean diet. And yet my nerves were going haywire. Most of my days off were spent in bed. Then there came a fateful verbal altercation with a foster parent that ended with me throwing my office phone against a wall. As I turned to storm out of the office I found my boss standing right behind me. There was no argument when I announced I'd be taking some vacation days.

I sat by the ocean for a week wondering what was missing. Over the course of some days, as I recovered my ability to relax, I began to feel a visceral connection to the earth below and the environment all around me. With this, my body relaxed and unfurled further.

I began to recall time I'd spent studying with some folks in the *Theravadin* ("old school") tradition of Buddhism who place great emphasis on feeling into the body. Working with the body in meditation is so crucial to them that "body scanning" often took up half of our practice time. Then another memory: That time when I was trying to impress my hippie girlfriend by attending a Reiki attunement. We were guided in meditation to visualize our spines as the roots of a tree growing downward into the earth. We were instructed to imagine the earth nourishing our bodies in the same manner that actual roots of a tree are nourished by the soil. I hadn't really thought about that since then, but here I was two decades later, sitting by the South Jersey shore, imagining my spine growing down into the earth. I felt ridiculous. And I also started feeling better. Connecting to the earth through the vehicle of my body was doing something for me that I couldn't place my finger on. Not just that, but when I reengaged my usual mindfulness practices in tandem with this sense of connection, the practice felt alive in a way I had never experienced before.

Righting the Brain

Unbeknownst to me at the time, there is an entire canon of Buddhist teachings centered on embodiment and recovering the soma's visceral sense of connection to the earth. Turns out, I was not alone in feeling stuck in my practice and sensing that something had to be missing. These matters had already been thoroughly unpacked by renowned Indo-Tibetan scholar and veteran meditator Reggie Ray. Ray has produced a stunning amount of material elucidating how the body is not only our most powerful ally in the process of meditation, but it also holds the essence of everything the meditative journey is about.

Ray often refers to the common knowledge that there are two hemispheres of the brain, which have different qualities and functions. The left hemisphere is responsible for our so-called rational and linear processes such as computing, planning, and strategizing. It's also the linguistic side of the brain, the side responsible for the mental chatter and inner dialogue, the monkey mind. It's the side of our brain that is constantly describing our experience to us one nanosecond after we've had the actual experience—what Alan Watts calls "eating the menu," as opposed to enjoying the meal.

The right hemisphere of the brain houses functions that are more abstract, creative, intuitive, and *prelanguage* in nature. The right hemisphere also happens to be more deeply connected to the neurons and neurotransmitters that are spread throughout the body. Thus, it logically follows that, when we invest the mind's attention in the body, we are activating the side of the brain that is not engaged in mental chatter. Ray often cites renowned psychiatrist Dr. Dan Siegel as saying we shouldn't even call it the "right hemisphere" anymore. We should call it "the body."[2]

If we factor in the theory of experience-dependent neuroplasticity—that our brains are constantly being rewired and strengthened according to where our attention goes—we must conclude something very promising is happening in these forms of meditation. Inhabiting our bodies with our attention in meditation, we are wiring ourselves to strengthen the right brain and develop an unconscious and automatic habit of abiding there. Over time, this bolsters our capacity for embodiment, and by extension, mental quietude.[3]

Kalila B. Homann, an expert in Expressive Arts Therapy, writes, "The right hippocampus seems to be more linked into 'right brained' ways of perceiving experience and processing information—body based, emotionally engaged, and symbolic. It informs our perception of events in a way that is not literally languaged; yet it is felt and sensed and underlies all of our experience."[4]

THE OBSERVING SELF AND THE EXPERIENCING SELF

Psychodynamic theory has long posited that we have both an observing self and an experiencing self—a theory that loosely correlates with this discussion about the brain's hemispheres.[5] The experiencing self is the aspect of our psyche that is directly in touch with our present-time experience. It is engaged by what comes in through the portals of the five senses. The fact that sensations can only occur in the present moment is one of the reasons why the esoteric schools (*Vajrayana*) of Buddhism embrace the five outer senses as inherent gifts. Our sense fields offer us a fantastic lifeline back to the present any time we find ourselves lost in thought, be it in meditation or otherwise.

The observing ego, on the other hand, is the aspect of psyche that actively overlays our experience with narrative. It constantly describes back to us what's happening, anxious to confirm that our experience is what we think it is or want it to be. The observing ego is the part of the psyche that remembers, that fantasizes, that plans and worries for the future—and therefore the part of us responsible for the emotional cost of mind wandering.

It's not that the observing ego is bad. We need the rational, reflective, and strategic aspect of our minds in order to discern and navigate what's being taken in by our experiencing self. The problem is, we tend to overprivilege the observing mind at the expense of our raw, naked experience—what Mary Oliver calls "our one wild and precious life."[6] The observing mind is always devouring menu after menu, it is incapable of tasting Alan Watts's proverbial meal. Meditation is our opportunity to rebalance these aspects of our mind. Meditation gives us a direct inroad to experiencing the vibrancy of our actual lives as opposed to living in a mental story.

The body and mind are forever working in tandem with one another. One is impacting the other and vice versa, simultaneously. It's a transactional relationship. We don't have a mind or a body so much as we have a "body-mind." In the guided meditation that accompanies this chapter, we will explore a body scanning practice in which, when we invest our attention in various regions of the body, we can then encourage those regions to relax and release long-held tension. You will most likely notice that, as the body relaxes and opens, the psyche naturally follows suit.

The body has a natural intelligence; it knows that holding stress is toxic. The body itself desires to surrender unnecessarily held tightness and clinging, and we can directly experience a natural untangling of the body simply by attending to it. As we move toward a mental union with our somatic (bodily) self, the body organically shifts toward ease, taking the mind along with it.[7] Allow me to break down two important concepts regarding the body and then we will dive into an experience informed by just this.

TOUCHING THE EARTH

There is a moment in the mythos of Sakyamuni's (who later would become the Buddha) awakening that relates directly to the body's contact with the ground in meditation—what I'll refer to as "touching the earth" from here on out.

Sakyamuni followed the classical trajectory: He became frustrated with status quo life as he encountered repeat disappointments and endeavored for a spiritual quest as a result. Like our monkey minds, he went from place to place, from teacher to teacher, and tried practice after practice in hopes of experiencing a lasting satisfaction and peace. He studied with the luminaries of his day (the Deepak Chopras and Tony Robbinses of ancient India, if you will), who all taught practices that were centered on bodily mortification. The conventional wisdom at the time was that, if you wanted to get to spirit, you had to go beyond the body. Thus, practitioners would put their bodies in untenable situations in an attempt to transcend fleshly existence. The Buddha later spoke of performing austerities such as extreme fasting to the point of emaciation, staring into the sun from dawn till dusk, sitting on beds of nails, and listening to early Madonna hits on repeat (OK, maybe not that last one). Such practices induced high states of consciousness, and yet Sakyamuni found that what went up always came down; he always returned to the same neurotic and contracted self. It was still samsara, just a spiritualized version of it. Disillusioned by the recurring experience of attaining only temporary relief from each practice he mastered, he stopped following various teachers around and started wandering alone instead. Eventually he found himself possessed of a great resolve: he would sit down with his back against a tree and not get up until he had found, within himself, the awakening he had spent years searching for.

As they do with all worthwhile endeavors, a slew of obstacles came young Sakyamuni's way. The myth continues that the demon-god of delusion, Mara (quite similar to the Maya of Hindu lore), came to the meditating Sakyamuni in three attempts to shake the soon-to-be-Buddha's resolve and get him to give up his meditation.

Mara's first attempt was to conjure lust. He brought out his three daughters—Desire, Fulfillment, and Regret—and offered them up to Sakyamuni for his pleasure, yet the meditator remained unmoved. Mara then upped the ante and tried to evoke mortal fear. An army of demon warriors appeared and shot flaming arrows at Sakyamuni. Yet the kindness of Sakyamuni's presence ran so deep that his force field of emotional warmth turned the arrows to flower petals that then dropped at his feet. Finally, Mara, desperate, went medieval on the young aspirant: he got personal. Mara attempted to hit Sakyamuni in a place that's a red-hot sore spot for so many of us: he tried to make him feel worthless. He said, "Just who do you think you are? What makes you think you're so special? You're not good enough, not worthy of this, and we both know it. Oh *sure*, no one else has managed to figure out this whole ultimate liberation thing, but *you're* going to. You're just another imposter. A total fake. A loser. I can't *wait* to watch you fall flat on your face in front of everyone. You don't have what it takes."

What Sakyamuni did next is very telling. When the pressure was turned up on him as far as it could go (in this story at least), he placed his left hand on the ground. With this, the soon-to-be-Buddha acknowledged the earth as his ally and proclaimed, "With the earth as my witness, liberation is my birthright. I deserve to be free from suffering and confusion. I am worthy of walking in perfect clarity by virtue of being alive." And with that, Mara was vanquished and Sakyamuni was free, awake.

This moment is rich with clues. When we are stressed, when

we feel persecuted by the world or, worse, by our own minds (which often play Mara's last card by telling us that we're not good enough in some way), at these times we can claim the earth as an ally. We, like Sakyamuni, can touch the earth; we can literally lie our bodies down on the ground, feeling and breathing into the vast and complex universe of sensations alive within us. We can allow the gentle tug of gravity to untangle the tension held in our bodies. We can rely on the support of the floor to restore us slowly, slowly to a sense of wholeness.

As the Chinese proverb goes, "Relaxation is who you are. Tension is who you think you should be." That is, relaxation and living from our deeper nature seem to be one and the same thing, and neither state is attained or acquired. Rather, they are what's left when we release the grip of our fixations. The Buddha's story tells us that an embodied relationship to the earth has something to do with the end of neurosis and the reclamation of connection. As we learn to allow the natural calm of the body-mind to emerge, the limiting beliefs we might have about what we're worth, what we deserve, and what our lives is meant for begin to dissolve on their own as well.

The Holding Environment

The "holding environment" is an experiential concept given to us by psychoanalyst and child development theorist Donald Winnicott. It's defined as a metaphorical space that is infused with caring so that hurts, frustrations, and confusions can emerge, be related to, and eventually dissolve. It is an atmosphere that bolsters our resilience: our ability to be challenged and distressed for some time and then return to relative balance. The metaphorical space Winnicott refers to is developed within the therapist-client relationship. For Winnicott, it's part of the therapist's role to create a "container" wherein the client feels "held," cared for, received, validated, respected, and understood. A good therapist wants the client to feel they are in the presence of someone who is competent, of sound character, and empathically attuned like a good parent would be. Such are the conditions in which our natural propensity to heal and restore is elicited.

Beyond the interpersonal aspect of the therapist-client relationship, there are structural factors that help create the holding environment. Often called the "therapeutic frame," these factors include the fact that sessions have definite start and end times, that sessions are held at the same time each week, that therapists are composed and consistent in how they comport themselves, and that therapists don't discuss their own hang-ups in a session.

I like to think of the "holding environment" in relation to a concept borrowed from the *Tao Te Ching*. Each morning when I reach for a coffee cup in the cupboard, although I think that I want the cup, what I really want is the space inside the cup so I can fill it with coffee. That empty space is created by the boundaries, the form of the cup itself, but it is the space inside the cup that makes it useful.

Like the walls of that coffee cup, the boundaries of therapeutic work are only important in that they create space. The space is what is useful. With that in place, a skillful therapist can imbue the container of a session with a sense of safety, warmth, positive regard, acceptance, and competence. (Why else would therapists have their degrees on the wall?) In that, the space of a session becomes a holding environment, analogous to an actual embrace, a cradle where a fearful heart can come to rest.

We will get much deeper into how this all works at the neurobiological level in chapter 4. For now, suffice it to say, it is when we sense ourselves in a "holding environment" that our restorative relaxation response kicks in. It is in this sort of atmosphere that a client can become trusting enough to get truly open and start to heal their body-mind's armoring and hurts.

Other places in our life can become holding environments

as well: the space of a workshop or a class, the intimacy between lovers that dwells within the boundaries of mutual consent and respect, our home. This is also true of our meditation practice. There are forms and boundaries to having a genuine meditation practice: we set a time for it, it's at a similar time each day, we do it in a similar place each day, we have a certain respect for it, and we do our best not to skip days. Within such a container, we can imbue the qualities of an embrace: our *trust* in the instructions (as, hopefully, we've received the instructions from a reputable source), our *trust* that it's a worthwhile endeavor (especially as we continue and begin to taste the relief that comes with consistent engagement), our *positive regard* for ourselves, our *acceptance* of the neuroses and scatteredness that invariably emerge in this space (after all, that's exactly what holding environments are meant for), our acknowledgment that we *belong* here, our *connection* to the earth and our bodies, and the *gratification* of relief.

Paying attention is itself a form of holding. There are boundaries to paying attention; that is, there is a place where our attention is and a place where it is not. And we can hold with our attention in any number of ways. We can hold something in our attention with animosity, rigidity, ambivalence, or warmth. This is as true of our inner world as it is of objects in the outer world. We can hold our inner world with care in order that we might become unburdened, so that we can train ourselves to become available for the richness of life—perhaps even the pleasure of our own warm presence. Interestingly enough, the Sanskrit word for happiness and ease is *sukha*, which translates literally to "good space," and is synonymous with "holding environment." Sukha also sounds a bit like the English word *sugar*, which comes in part from the Arabic, *sukkar*. Thus, when we amplify the empathy in our lives, not only do our burdens begin to dissolve, it allows us to taste the sweetness of our lives, that which our burdens tend to inhibit.

Making Practice Trauma Sensitive

Many of us have extraordinary trouble relating to our bodies and "going within" for any number of reasons. Some of us have bodies that have been through a lot (and for some, that's a gross understatement). Some of us have been conditioned to feel ashamed of our bodies—their shape, their color. Some of us get incredibly antsy or emotional when we place our attention in our bodies or attempt to be still and don't even understand why. Some of us get bombarded by intrusive thoughts and images when we try to slow down. While meditation is a practice centered on relaxation and healing, such concepts can feel out of reach, especially for those of us who have struggled mightily in this life. If this is you, first of all: This is not your fault. You didn't sign up for this experience. Second, it's fantastic that you have an awareness of your own limits. Please continue to respect them. Finally, there are options. You belong here as much as anyone else, and working with your limits in this practice can be a catalyst for transformation as much as the practice itself.

Meditation, as presented in this book, is not a practice of protecting ourselves from becoming triggered. Rather, this is a practice where all of us, regardless of history or demographic, will inevitably meet with our limits in some way. *This is an opportunity.* An opportunity to develop some choices around what to do when we feel cornered by our own minds, which is how we ultimately dissolve the neuroses involved in that. Meditation is ultimately a healing practice, and the tough truth is—emotional healing can only take place in moments of emotional activation. There are no shortcuts. Believe me, I worked my ass off looking for one. That said, we never want to do this work in a reckless or ambitious fashion. We want to be courageous and consistent, but ambition will prove to be counterproductive. At times, it will be appropriate to back up or take a break. At other times, we might want to take a break, but the best thing for us would be to find an alternative that allows us to stay in the game, such as what I will be offering here.

I recently spoke to a woman, a soldier who had developed PTSD due to her experiences in active combat. Her therapist started her on one minute of meditation per day, every day. The next week she practiced for two minutes. The next, three minutes. She worked respectfully, incrementally, and consistently with her boundaries. Over the course of six months, she got up to a full twenty minutes a day. Her gratitude for the practice was tremendous, and she spoke about how much daily meditation enhanced her ability to heal her trauma.

The objective is to expand your comfort zone incrementally. Engage the practices as best as you can, and when you find the edge of manageable discomfort, learn to work with that edge in some way without crossing the boundary into full-blown emotional activation. What follows are options for doing just that. This will allow you to grow into the full expression of the practice here, and, by the grace of neuroplasticity, it will impact your experience of these repetitive activations over all. If you would like more on the "how and why" of this or a visual aid, you can turn to page 199, "Working at Growth's Edge."

Turn the Volume Up on the Holding Environment

Turn it all the way up to 11. Emphasize to yourself, to your body that you are in a safe space. Notice that you can breathe just fine, you're not hungry, there's plenty of water around, and there's no threat in the environment whatsoever (if there is, it's obviously not the time to practice). Affirm these things to yourself. Remind yourself that you're doing this practice because you care about yourself and your well-being. Pat yourself on the back for sitting down in the first place. Just that much is huge. As runners sometimes say, "the hardest part is getting your shoes on."

Catch the Activation Early

Emotions have three general phases: (1) the revving phase, (2) full-blown activation, and (3) the reconstituting or regulating phase wherein we begin to recover our baseline or homeostasis. The revving phase, the moment(s) when we first feel a strong emotion coming on, is the phase where we have the most power to influence our body-mind state. Ideally, it is in this moment that we will want to apply one of the below techniques (or something else you know to work for you) in order to intervene. The ability to notice the shift in body-mind state as early as possible will strengthen and refine over time. This skill alone will serve us well in everyday life. If you'd like more on this or a visual aid, please turn to page 125, "The Life Cycle of an Emotion."

Externalize Mindfulness

If going within is too much to begin with, go without. That is, practice mindfulness with the sensations of the world around you. Let your eyes trace the shapes and contours of various objects in front of you. Notice the colors and textures of those objects. Feel the temperature of the air touching your skin. Listen to the subtle symphony of sounds both large and small that are happening around you. What matters is that you work on being present with the sensations in the moment and that you return from distraction again and again. This is also an excellent practice to engage should you feel a panic attack coming when you're not meditating.

When you are ready to go deeper with this, you can begin to notice something I find quite fascinating: the sensations are closer to you than they seem. For example, what we call a *sound* is actually a particular type of wave of molecules that are vibrating in such a way that they are picked up by the ear. There is a veritable symphony of refined receptors in our ears called *cochlea* that then translate the vibrations of the molecules into signals sent to the brain. The brain then generates a representation of those signals, and this is what we've been taught to call "sound." The brain's spatial awareness capacities also kick in to create the perception of where "sound" is coming from—but the experience itself isn't actually coming from "over there," it's coming from the cochlea in the ear. Thus, when we are ready to move closer to the body, we can begin to sense the sounds in the room as actually happening in the ear and sights as happening in the eyes. Eventually, your system will get the message that it is safe to begin entering the body.

Take a Break, but Don't Drop Out

This one is self-explanatory, but there's a couple caveats. Yes, give yourself permission to take a break: open your eyes, take a breath, mentally slough it off, maybe switch the crossing of your legs . . . and then return as quickly as is reasonable for you. But be wary of giving yourself excuses to drop out just because it's challenging. Go easy on yourself, but stay sincere.

Apply Breathwork

There are four styles of breathwork for regulating the nervous system described in this book. I would recommend becoming very familiar with the "4-8-12 Breathing" on page 103 (there are further tips on working with panic attacks in this section as well) and "Setting the Breath in Its Natural Rhythm" on page 74. These can be used in the beginning, middle, or end of your practice. Use them as much as you want or need.

Weighted Blankets

Originally developed for children with ADHD and sensory issues, weighted blankets have become quite popular for a reason. They work wonders when it comes to regulating the nervous system and creating a sense of containment within the body. They've been known to ease people out of panic attacks and highly aroused emotional states, and they're a tremendous help with insomnia.

Many people find it useful to practice meditation with a weighted blanket on their laps for extra groundedness as well. Unfortunately, they're not cheap, but they're well worth the investment if you can swing it.

Practice with Your Back against the Wall

This will help put your primitive survival system at ease by reminding your body that you are safe.

On Good Days, Go Surfing

"Urge surfing" is a common mindfulness practice within recovery communities taught to help addicts relate to intense cravings without giving in. The practice is simple: when an intense feeling arises, one simply stops, mentally turns toward it knowing that it is going to intensify for a while and then die down, eventually disappearing *as all feelings do.* The practitioner simply "surfs the wave" of feeling and "rides" it to its natural end. If it's a day where you feel strong and up for a challenge and you find discomfort arising in the practice, surf the emotions as they peak and then dissolve. This is a most powerful and transformative option. When we ride an intense feeling all the way out, we see that the feeling isn't going to annihilate us and that we are stronger than we previously thought. We come to fear our emotions less and we are actively shifting our relationship to all emotions. While all emotions are valid and important, the strange thing is, they're a lot like thoughts—once we get to know them, we start to see that they're not very substantial. They are, as the Tibetans say, "more like wind and less like rock." Coming to see this for yourself is a huge step toward liberation.

Treat Yourself

A yoga teacher once told me about a student who would consistently walk out in the middle of class and return some time later to finish the practice. The teacher thought the student had digestive troubles. But then one day the teacher looked in the studio lobby while the student was absent and no one was in the bathroom. It turned out the student had a ritual of getting through the hardest parts of class and then going to a café next door and buying herself a croissant. Then she'd return in time for corpse pose at the end of class. One part of her was so resistant to going to yoga even though another part of her knew it would be really good for her. So, she cut a deal with herself. And it worked.

In the beginning of your practice, do what it takes to get yourself there consistently. Incentivize it. It would be much more conducive if you could wait until *after* the practice, but if you're a trauma survivor and you need a crutch to help you show up, so be it. You can remove the crutch later once the practice is embedded in your life.

MINDFULNESS OF THE BODY: TWO PRELIMINARY PRACTICES

We have just begun to scratch the surface in our discussion of the nature of the thinking mind, how mindful embodiment can help us address its problematic aspects, and how that process has deeper implications regarding our emotional and even spiritual lives. There's a lot more to unpack, and we will get to that, but these ideas mean very little if they aren't translated into actual experiences. Without further ado, I'd like to introduce two preliminary meditation practices centered on embodiment. You can either read these and practice them on your own, or you can utilize the guided recordings. Either way, I'll say just a few things about them and then we'll get to it.

The first practice is done lying down. The formal posture is lying down on the ground (not in bed, but perhaps on a yoga mat or a carpet) with your feet flat on the floor and your knees bent.

This will feel best either with your feet spread apart and your knees falling in toward one another or with your legs parallel to one another and your feet right in line with your sitz bones, or sitting bones. If it feels best to have your knees falling inward, you may want to grab a tie, scarf, or yoga strap to tie around your legs just above the knees so that your thigh muscles can relax.

There are several versions of this practice we can point to. Reggie Ray refers to his version as "10 Points Practice," because there are ten points of your body connecting to the earth in this posture (two feet, two sides of your pelvis, two elbows, one point in the mid back opposite the sternum, two shoulder blades, and the back of the head). Another Buddhist teacher, B. Alan Wallace, calls his version of this practice "The Infirmary," because an infirmary is where one goes for healing. When we lie down, our bodies touching the earth, we begin to induce the relaxation response, putting our bodies in a mode of restoration and repair. This practice falls within what the Buddha referred to as "Mindfulness of the Body," and he too advocated for sometimes practicing while lying down.

This practice entails placing our attention in various regions of the body; feeling directly the raw, living sensations that are present there; and allowing those regions to relax and let go. Three things will help us in this endeavor. One of them is our breath. In this practice, I will ask you to notice and feel whatever region of the body we're focusing on as you breathe in, and then to allow relaxation to unfold as you breathe out. These two sides of our breath have natural qualities to them: the inhale has an energy of coming alive, coming to presence; the exhale has an energy of release, softening, and letting go. In fact, the literal translation of the Sanskrit word used to describe the state of final enlightenment, *nirvana*, is "to blow out."

The second bit of assistance we get in this practice comes from the earth: gravity. As you lie down, you might notice gravity as a force that is constantly acting on the body, pulling us down. You can viscerally feel how gravity pulls you toward the earth and how, in a way, the earth rises up to meet you there, to hold you. You will notice that as the body relaxes tensions and stresses are released *downward*, into the flow of gravity. We simply pay attention on the inhale and release bodily contraction, tension, and fatigue along with the exhale, and gravity does the rest. In this way, Mindfulness of the Body practice teaches us how to do that mysterious thing called "letting go."

The third thing that can help us here is our imagination. It's been well established that our brains don't discern so well the difference between imagination and reality; for example, we know that mentally rehearsing things like the piano or sports can lead to physical results. So, even if you don't feel your body relaxing in this practice, you can imagine that it's happening and your brain will eventually catch on.

Finally, no special breathing or deep breathing is required in this practice. Just natural breath and natural awareness. Nothing extra is needed.

The second practice is, to borrow a phrase from Pema Chödrön, an "on the spot" practice, a brief practice that helps us maintain a healthy relationship to our experience throughout the day. "Sun Meditation" is a practice I received from my friend and hypnotherapist Morgan Yakus. I recommend that you utilize this practice a few times during the day, perhaps when you are on the train, about to enjoy a meal, or need a moment to ground yourself at work. (I'm a huge advocate of disappearing into the bathroom at work for one-minute meditations.) Like all on-the-spot practices, Sun Meditation is much more likely to impact your life meaningfully when it is used as a supplement to more formal practices, such as Mindfulness of the Body.

PRACTICE: *Mindfulness of the Body*

Lying comfortably, spend a few moments noticing the points of contact between your body and the floor. Notice the force of gravity very subtly pulling on you. You might sense almost immediately that the body begins to unwind just from lying in this position.

Start by feeling your feet and the many different types of sensations present in them. You might notice tingling, electricity, the pressure of the floor, the temperature of the room. Go ahead and let your mind's eye wander through your feet, feeling sensation as you go. You might notice that the sensation in your toes contrasts from that of the arches, which contrasts from the sensations present in your heels, ankles, and so on.

Then, begin to notice that your feet have tension stored in them. You can feel where there's tightness, discomfort, and even fatigue present in the feet. In fact, you'll begin to notice more and more of these types of sensations as you go looking for them. Though it's uncomfortable, the fact that you're beginning to notice means that you're beginning to untangle the tension. Start using your breath: breathing in to be with the tension, breathing out to allow its release into the flow of gravity. At the very least you can imagine this is happening.

Then move to the calves, shins, and knees. Feel all around: muscle, skin, and bone, all the aliveness, all the sensations, and all the tension. Breathe in to let your mind be in this region, breath out to imagine and sense release.

Then move to the thighs, feeling with as much detail the contours of the thigh muscles, the inner groin on both sides, the outer hips. Breathing in to notice tension, breathing out to relax and soften.

Next feel your way into the complexities of the pelvis. How much space is present from the back of the pelvis where it's contacting the floor to the front of the low abdomen? If you filled this part of yourself with water, how much would pour in there? Breathing in and out, feeling and releasing.

Continue on into the belly, the low back, and the organs. Then feel into the arms, joints, hands, and fingers. Then into the head, the face, the eyes, the cheeks, the jaw. Be as thorough as you can be, feeling as much detail as is possible for you, becoming more and more relaxed and more and more present with each breath. Notice as you go that, as the body begins to soften and open, the quality of your awareness follows suit. As the body becomes more spacious and quiet, the mind inches its way toward serenity in tandem. You may still have to redirect your mind from distraction, but notice how different it is when the mind is placed in the body as you allow gravity to pull you toward the earth.

Finally, feel the whole body at once. These are the Buddha's literal instructions: "Breathing in, I feel the whole body breathe. Breathing out, I feel the whole body shift toward ease and tranquility."

Stay here as long as you like, feeling the relaxation that's emerged. Let it soak into you.

On-the-Spot Practice: *Sun Meditation*

Close your eyes and imagine the sun shining on your face. It's a clear, perfectly temperate day, not a cloud in the sky, and the sun is shining magnificently. You feel its light and warmth on your brow, on the bridge of your nose, on your cheeks, on your lips, all over your face. It feels good. It's nourishing, wholesome, welcome. It's so bright that the black and purple colors dancing on the backs of your eyelids begin to brighten to lighter hues. You may even sense an inclination to tilt your chin upward to receive more of that light. Notice that the muscles in your face are beginning to relax and soften as you bask here.

Then the light and warmth and relaxation of the sun begins to sink down, past the skin layer, and into your head. You feel it seeping into your brain, into the skull, down the neck. You feel it washing over your shoulder tops, down the arms, through the wrists and into the hands and fingers. You feel it shining in your chest, touching your ribs, lungs, heart, and shoulder blades. You feel it shining down the articulation of your spine. You feel the sunlight reaching down into the belly and organs and low back. You feel it shining down into your pelvis, hips, and glutes; down into your legs. Down, down, down into your feet, toes, and down into the earth. You now feel the sun shining from the sky, all the way through you, and into the earth, creating a sense of connection, of completeness.

4

Evolving the Monkey's Motivations

Guard within yourself that treasure, kindness. Know how to give without
hesitation, how to lose without regret, how to acquire without meanness;
know how to replace in your heart, by the happiness of those you
love, the happiness you may be wanting for yourself.
—George Sand

ONE HEAD, THREE BRAINS, TWO EMOTIONAL RESPONSES

To paraphrase Joseph Campbell, just as the basic physical structure of all human bodies is almost identical regardless of culture
or place in history, the same is true of the human psyche. Exceptions notwithstanding, the human body is composed of two arms,
one head, two eyes, ten fingers, bones, muscles, blood, the same
vital organs, and so on. Similarly, although the inner life of each
person is incredibly unique and complex, each of us seems to
be working with a common basic setup. Memory banks, inner
dialogue, the propensity to construe meaning out of experience,
spatial awareness, emotional intelligence, and motor functions
are all examples of this. Our fundamental motivations also seem
to be universal. Understanding them will help us get clear on why
we are the way we are so that we can do something about it.

Although there are varying plausible theories as to which of
those motivations are most primary to us, I will refer here to neuropsychologist Dr. Rick Hanson's delineation of our drives according to the root needs of the three main regions of the brain.[1]

The human brain is very much like a three-layered cake. The
brain stem forms the bottom layer—often referred to as "the

reptilian brain"—and is responsible for our most basic functions such as alertness, breathing, and keeping our heart beating. Evolutionarily, this is the oldest region of our brain, and it is primarily concerned with our survival, the unifying motivation of all life forms. Put another way—we are universally driven to feel safe, to avoid disaster and pain, to have enough resources, to not feel threatened, and to be healthy. The midbrain, or "mammalian brain," is primarily concerned with feeling. It seeks gratification, rewards, and feeling good. It's the region of the brain that can be gratified by quick fixes, such as hedonic pleasure, but can also be satisfied by the slow burn of growth, learning, and accomplishment. These first two tiers of the brain are considered to be the domain of the limbic system, which is responsible for the fight-or-flight stress response. (We also have as part of our defensive structures the "freeze" response, however this response is born of a different type of activation in our bodies altogether. In the freeze response, our bodies engage what's called our parasympathetic nervous system, which is ordinarily involved in calming us down and keeping us regulated. Some of us have a natural predilection toward this response, wherein a perceived threat will send the parasympathetic nervous system into overdrive in an attempt to "play possum," in hopes that the danger may just pass us by.)

These regions of our brain have existed for eons (250 million and 150 million years, respectively), so they have had countless generations to hone their efficiency. The limbic system, then, eats up relatively little glucose, works lightning fast, and is a dual processor: it can process a vast amount of data coming at us from multiple sources at once with minimal cost to the body.

In other words, our bodies are often duped into believing we should act from the stress response simply because it's so efficient and familiar to do so. Our biology is often erroneously convinced that the stress response gets the job done best. It's true that we sometimes need our fight-or-flight reaction, and it does save people's lives all the time. However, the biochemicals associated with stress, such as adrenaline and cortisol, are among the most toxic substances we can have continually circulating in our systems.

But what about that third part of our brain? The neocortex, or forebrain, is the most social, moral, skillful part of our brain. It houses the prefrontal cortex and is involved in what is sometimes called our *higher order emotional functions.* This region of the brain is involved in our sense of self and a sense of connection to others; a sense of values, gratitude, compassion, empathy, love, willpower, and tenacity—the places we all prefer to be coming from. The fundamental drive of this region of the brain is to connect with others: to love, to be loved, to feel seen, to belong within families and close relationships, and to have community.

Humans aren't the only animals who have this region of the brain, but we are the only ones who have developed it to the extent that we do. With regard to evolutionary age, the human neocortex is an infant, however: the fully developed human neocortex is 200,000 years old (a generous estimate), which means our overreactive stress response is 1,200 times older than our most evolved human emotional responses. Thus, the neocortex is still a much more crude system: it eats up far more glucose, moves slower, and can only handle a little bit of information about our experience at a time. This is why things like generosity come less easily to us than—oh, say—anxiety. I am reminded of a Morrissey lyric: *"It's so easy to laugh, it's so easy to hate. It takes guts to be gentle and kind."*

THE TERROR EMBEDDED IN LOW SELF-ESTEEM

The respective needs of the mammalian brain and the neocortex—to get rewards and to belong—are arguably just sophisticated extensions of the oldest, reptilian need: the need for safety. That is, as we chase rewards (the more mature the type of reward, the better), it logically follows that we will become progressively more skilled in life and thus increasingly able to fend for and provide for ourselves and our families. Enjoying rewards also increases our chances of being liked and admired by others, in the same way a person who wins the lottery might find they suddenly have an infinitude of friends. It similarly follows that, if we are connected to others and have a sense of belonging within a broad range of relationships, that also bolsters our safety. If others identify with us, if we are loved and/ or respected, if we belong and participate in community, others will naturally feel inclined to share their resources. We will have places to go when disaster strikes—or when our mission in life seems to be failing—to gain moral support or resources such as a place to stay or a meal.

Also playing a factor here is the reality that our bodies and their processes are much more primitive than our societies and families are. After all, in hunter-gatherer times, if we were insufficient to the effect that we could not pull our own weight, we might be considered a liability. We could be perceived as compromising the sustainability of the entire group. It's possible that we would be kicked out of the tribe and left to fend for ourselves in the name of the greater good. I saw this primitive tendency in action myself when I was growing up, with our family cat, Milkbone. One day Milkbone gave birth to a litter of kittens, one of whom was a runt we named Sky. We thought Sky was adorable. Milkbone saw things differently, which we discovered when we found her sitting on Sky, attempting to smother her own kitten to death (don't worry, we saved little Sky and bottle-fed her until she was grown). Milkbone had a half-dozen other kittens to look after and couldn't afford to be weighed down by this extra burden. From this we can see that when we feel insufficient in some way, there is an instinctual intensity underneath the feeling that is simply mismatched with regard to our actual situation.

We've touched on the experience of feeling not good enough,

unworthy, unlovable, or like a failure as a common concern that informs anxiety, panic, perfectionism, and depression on a mass scale (though we are yet to discuss where these experiences actually come from). If we accept that our fundamental needs for belonging and rewards are actually rooted in survival, then it logically follows that feeling unworthy in some way is, subconsciously, a matter of life and death. I believe that this is a big part of why these feelings are of epidemic proportions in society, and why such feelings drive so many of our motivations, behaviors, and life choices. If our worthiness implicitly carries such intense gravity, this explains why we often find ourselves compelled to fight at all costs not to expose such a shortcoming. We must feel dominant, we must compete, we must prove others wrong, we must win the argument. When we fail at these, either we become driven to do better or we become depressed and feel there's no point. Our bodies either contract with tension or become heavy with indolence.

This can be especially pronounced in adult life for many of us who did not feel loved, loveable, or unconditionally accepted as children. Because our child psyche also associated rewards and a sense of belonging with survival *and* all our basic needs had to be met by caregivers, if we experienced failure, felt not good enough, or sensed our "otherness," this probably translated into what psychologist Richard Schwartz calls "survival terror." This, in part, gives rise in adulthood to mindsets like the inner critic and imposter syndrome as well as panic attacks and endless cycles of stuckness in relationships and modes of livelihood. We'll work more thoroughly with each of those in the chapters to come, but the good news is, we've already broached the most fundamental way to walk back these chains of compulsive behavior, of feeling unworthy, and of fearing for our safety and survival.

Mindfulness and meditation practice speak directly and

eloquently to the evolutionary imbalance in our brains. Mindfulness-based meditation training, with its emphasis on intentional warmth and altruism coupled with discipline and rigor, offers an ideal recalibration. Notice that the empathetic elements present in Winnicott's "holding environment" meet the fundamental needs of the brain. By inviting in a sense of safety, growth, and connection to ourselves in meditation, we are already inviting settledness and ease, sukha.

The good news is, our limbic and neocortical systems operate on different synaptic networks. That is, they are not mutually exclusive—it's not one or the other. We can train them to work together. We can train ourselves to keep generosity and empathy in the mix when faced with pressure and threat. We don't have to be either/or; we can learn to be both/and. In fact, this may be exactly the right kind of response to the global crises we currently face: to realize that we are in an urgent situation and that compassion, connection, and cooperation are actually our best options for survival.

As we establish a sense of safety, gratification, and belonging within the space of our practice, confidence and resilience tends to arise in our daily lives. With confidence and resilience comes a meaningful opportunity: to use our practice to heal at deeper levels. Over time (and over the course of this book) the practice becomes an arena for resolving the heartbreaking and traumatic experiences we've had in our past— the very psychological material that gives rise to negative beliefs about ourselves and overreliance on the stress response.[2] In subsequent chapters, we'll look more closely at how to heal trauma in the holding environment of meditation. But first we have to deal with a prerequisite to that kind of work: none of the benefits happen if you don't practice regularly. Having surveyed the universal needs or drives coming from our brain's evolutionary inheritance, it's time to look at how we can channel those motivations to do what we know is going to help: establishing a regular meditation practice.

Cultivate No-Matter-Whatness

Thus far in this chapter, I've discussed some of the evolutionary bases of our brain systems as a way of explaining our tendency to employ ancient and universal drives in ways that often lead to more suffering in our contemporary circumstances. But of course, the motivations of the reptilian or mammalian brain aren't the whole story. We are possessed of conscious motivations as well. Our attitude, attention, and will are the vehicles of our conscious motivations (and are perhaps the only things we are actually in control of in this life). When we train them via meditation, meditation will pay us back, with interest, in terms of their growing power and availability.

Cultivating a daily meditation habit is a practice unto itself, one that many of us find challenging. Here, our attention, attitude, and will—that is, our sense of motivation—are of special importance. *Daily* and *practice* are perhaps the two most important words in my meditative life. At the risk of sounding hard-line, without our establishing and maintaining consistency in meditation, all our other efforts tend to come undone.

A common practice among secular meditation teachers is to give beginners exceedingly rudimentary instructions. If the practice gets too complex or if it takes more than ten minutes, people are less likely to practice. That's the logic, at least. I agree that this can be a skillful approach, and am sometimes a proponent of it myself. What matters most is that you practice and that you keep going once you've begun. So, if you must, you have full license to abbreviate any of the practices in this book to suit your needs. However, it's important that you keep things as consistent as possible. That is, for example, if you commit to ten minutes a day, do ten minutes a day, and do your best to not waiver from that. That said, I would be doing you a disservice if I let you settle for *just* ten minutes a day without at least the intention to grow your practice.

Most of the amazing and groundbreaking studies on mindfulness meditation that you may have seen in any number of major publications have entailed meditators practicing for twenty to thirty minutes a day, seven days a week, for six weeks or longer. It is within these parameters that we start seeing meaningful and lasting changes happen for people at both physiological and psychological levels. Moreover, researchers consistently find that, when they follow up with participants six months or even a year after these studies, a significant number of participants are still practicing, even though they're no longer being paid to do so, because they find it so beneficial.

Consciously evolving your life takes commitment. We need to cultivate what Father Greg Boyle calls, "no-matter-whatness."[3] We need to become both gentle and tough.

On Distress Tolerance and Living Your Best Life

Shamatha translates literally to "calm abiding" or "making peaceful," and it is the most popular form of meditation being practiced on the planet right now due to the mountain of research that validates it. It is the practice we'll be moving into in the section to come, as it grows seamlessly out of Mindfulness of the Body. This practice is also often called *vipassana, ch'an,* or *zazen,* depending on whom you talk to and on the specific technique. Fundamentally, it's the famous practice of "following the breath," except I'm not so sure *just* following the breath ever did anyone much good. There's more to it than that—and frankly, there's more to it than is commonly taught these days.

When we apply a growth mindset to the monkey mind, we see that the purpose it serves in the realm of shamatha meditation is that of sparring partner—and in the words of Mike Tyson, "Everyone has a plan until they get punched in the face." Ahem. That is, if you want to get good at playing chess, a great way to do so would be to find someone who's way better than you and then play them (and lose) and play them (and lose) and play them (and lose) until the day comes when you've learned so much by watching them play, you win. The monkey is that chess opponent, and it's damn good at playing this game called "Distraction." Playing Distraction against the monkey is a great idea, because in doing so there are countless desirable benefits. Traditionally speaking, they are described as developing a mind that is strong, clear, and agile. If we were to turn to what neuroscience and psychology have unearthed through research, I could fill this entire book with the benefits of this practice. Furthermore, each of the benefits associated with this practice—from stress reduction to cognitive flexibility to better sleep to increased empathy—balance out the evolutionary mismatch we've been discussing.

Admittedly, becoming distracted in meditation can feel a bit like a punch in the face. When we find we've lost the moment, our habitual response generally ranges from deflation all the way up to self-loathing. This is actually deeply psychological. Our reactions in such moments reflect how we treat ourselves in other situations in which we perceive we're some sort of failure. After all, we've come to define the word *mindfulness* as "paying attention," when its true definition is slightly different. We get the word *mindfulness* from the Sanksrit *smrti* (or the Pali *sati*), which translates as "to remember." To remember is to return from forgetting. That is, the actual definition of mindfulness is "to return from distraction." Thus, becoming distracted in meditation doesn't represent a failure in our mindfulness—it is what creates the opportunity to practice mindfulness in the first place. In seeing this, we can also begin to notice our neurotic patterns when we drop the ball in meditation and train ourselves to have a better relationship with the experience. In doing so, we are actually rewiring how we handle ourselves in other, more significant moments of so-called failure and forgetting.

Returning from distraction, what is often called the "mindfulness push-up," strengthens our minds so that we evolve toward a state of constant remembrance. It also impacts our neurobiology and creates massive ripple effects in our lives. Beyond strengthening our attention, mindfulness push-ups have been shown to strengthen the prefrontal cortex, arguably the epicenter of our well-being and capacity for stable happiness. Interesting enough, the prefrontal cortex itself works like a muscle: if you work it out, it gets stronger (though if you work it too hard, it will tire out on you). It is for this reason that neuropsychologist Dr. Kelly McGonigal says, the worse you are at meditation, the better it is for you. The more you drift off, the more opportunities you're given to do mindfulness push-ups and the higher your *distress tolerance*[4] (we'll come back to this in a moment).

The positive effects of strengthening the prefrontal cortex are some of the major benefits of meditation, and specifically relate to the rebalancing of our evolutionary mismatch.[5] If you've ever had a moment when someone you love has said something that pissed you off, and you were able to catch hold of yourself, pause, and respond rationally instead of biting back, your prefrontal cortex was involved in that. If you've ever been halfway to a full-blown anxiety or panic attack but you were able to remember some breathing exercises, your prefrontal cortex was involved in that. If you've ever been upset about something but were able to reframe the situation or see the bigger picture, your prefrontal cortex was helping you out. If you've ever been able to choose something that would lead to long-term happiness over a short-term pleasure, thank your prefrontal cortex. If you've ever been challenged by a task or project, so much so that the very end of it felt like it was impossible to get through, but you were able to summon the tenacity to complete it, the prefrontal cortex was working with you. And if you've ever done the right and kind thing even though no one was watching (a little thing we call having values and respect), guess what: your prefrontal cortex again.

Not that it's easy. On the other side of making these kinds of choices, usually there are options that seem easier, juicier, or more fun. There can be a burning quality to holding our center in the face of such temptations, not unlike "feeling the burn" at the gym.

The prefrontal cortex is the region of your brain that gives you the ability to tolerate the distress that often naturally accompanies our best decision-making and our healthiest behaviors. These choices so very often move in a direction other than the loud pull of our habits and fears, and so very often they entail listening to the subtler signals and whispers of our deeper wisdom (also known as intuition) that I spoke of earlier. Increased distress tolerance could make the difference between a thriving relationship versus a failing one, between making it through another finals season versus giving up on school altogether, between going further in your career versus idling, or between waking up respecting yourself in the morning versus waking with a heart full of regret. In general, the capacity for distress tolerance is the key to having a high quality of life as opposed to a life where you're dragged around by fleeting pleasures, disconnection, and the fear of difficulty.

Indeed, a well-trained mind is an ally worth sparring for.

POISON IN THE BEGINNING, NECTAR IN THE END

Here's a question: *Why settle for bronze when gold is on the table?* How many times a day do you waste an extra ten minutes on something utterly useless? At what point do we ask ourselves why an extra ten minutes of meditation seems *so* intimidating. Is it really that excruciating, or is that just a story we're telling ourselves? Doesn't the fact that we are so averse to being with ourselves make you curious? Why are we? And are you actually comfortable with going through your entire life that way? Might it be a good idea to start investigating this now?

There's a saying in Vedic religion: "Things of a material nature are nectar in the beginning, poison in the end." Think about it: everything that provides quick fixes and easy pleasure starts out good but then doesn't end so well. Perhaps the easiest example we could point to is a night of indulging in drinks with friends. Starts out great, ends with a hangover. The same goes for every computer, cell phone, or car—at least the ones I've owned. They start out working wonderfully, but as time goes on things get more complicated and expensive until the thing dies and we're left stranded, in one way or another. Another example is the "honeymoon period" in love relationships.

There's a second part of that Vedic proverb: "Things of a spiritual nature are poison in the beginning, nectar in the end." Now think about everything meaningful and worthwhile in your life: it started out tough, and then it got satisfying. Whether it was your education, saving money, going to therapy, starting a workout regimen, changing your eating habits, quitting an addiction, or having kids—all of these felt like poison in the beginning. But if we stay with such things long enough, the nectar, the enjoyment, the satisfaction starts flowing. We end up happy that we stuck it out, just about every time.

You can meditate for stress relief, or you can meditate to move toward self-actualization. Lower your blood pressure, or move in the direction of becoming a total badass in your world: choose your own adventure. The thing is, if you go after a life with maxed-out depth, the stress relief and blood pressure will happen along the way as perks. If you go after the gold, you pick up bronze and silver along the way.

CUTTING THROUGH

There is an urban legend that David Bowie almost ordained as a Tibetan Buddhist monk at Samye Ling monastery in Scotland when Chögyam Trungpa Rinpoche was still the guiding teacher there.[6] The story goes that Trungpa told him that the world needed his music too much instead. It's also been said that Bowie got his stage name from Trungpa. David Bowie, born David Jones, knew he needed to distinguish himself from Davy Jones of the Monkees. Reportedly, he went to Trungpa with this concern, who told him, "You need something that will *cut through*, like a bowie knife."

If you've ever seen images of wrathful bodhisattvas or Vedic deities such as Kali Ma, you may have noticed they're almost always holding swords. The sword symbolizes the power of wisdom to cut through our delusions. No negotiation, no bargaining, no hesitation. It's very much like when we have one of those moments of clarity that a lover is the wrong person for us, or when we *must* leave a job we're stuck in. There's simply the dropping of the blade and the deal is done. There's no going back. This is the piercing, direct nature of awakening.

This is the very kind of energy we so often need to bring to our practice and our life in the name of no-matter-whatness. Just cut through the excuses. Just stop mentally fidgeting around; stop negotiating. Very, very gently we can drop a sharp, heavy blade right through the resistance. We can even come to enjoy the mild sting involved in doing so, develop a taste for it. We can cut through the sting, too. Cut through everything. Sit down. Practice. Don't try, just do.

STAY CLOSE TO THE "WHY"

Think about the last time someone started telling you what you should do about something without your asking for their advice. We've all had this happen to us. We're talking or venting about some issue in our life, and without invitation someone says, "You know what you really should do is . . . ," or they start posting links to related articles and videos on our Facebook page. We might pay lip service to that person, but if we're to be honest, what's our most likely internal response? *Eye roll.* (Does anyone ever do more than skim those long articles and videos, really?)

How many times has someone's telling you what to do, even if it was validly life changing for them, led you to adopt that practice? Close to never, I'm willing to bet. Yet for some crazy reason we think we can do this same thing to ourselves regarding our meditation practice and get results. We tell ourselves over and over again, "Oh, I really should meditate," and that intention instantly joins the heap of things in the back of our mind where great intentions have gone to die (right next to "try a raw food cleanse" and "get really into kickboxing" and across from "spend three months backpacking through Asia"). Nobody likes being told what they should do. And yet we tell ourselves what we should do and expect a different result?

I call the remedy to this resistance *staying close to the why.* Contemplate for one minute each day why you want to meditate. This is infinitely more effective than a thousand obligation-laden shoulds. What's going on that's been kicking your ass hard enough to make you interested in evolving your mind and life? What do you imagine meditation will do for you? What are some cool things you've read about it recently? Who do you know who's doing it, and how has it changed them? Spend one minute each day thinking about things of this nature, and you'll find yourself on the cushion soon enough. Find your why. Stay close to it.

There's wanting to do something, and then there's *wanting to want* to do something. Sometimes we are convinced that we want to do something, but we actually only *want to* want to do it. The truth is, we do what we *actually* want to do—that is, whatever our midbrain deems is gratifying in some way. Nothing about thinking we *should* do something feels savory to us. So, the trick to moving out of *wanting to want* to actually *wanting* is to stop thinking about the should and start thinking about the why.

A Note on Obstacles

After we overcome our motivation problem by staying close to the why, we're likely to meet with obstacles to practice. Obstacles can look like sleeping through your alarm, important obligations coming up "out of nowhere," being "too busy," or just garden-variety, flat-out resistance to the practice. As my friend and fellow author Adreanna Limbach says, "Right when it's time to meditate, I somehow find myself reorganizing the sock drawer." There are mornings when I find myself standing over my meditation cushion, exactly thirty minutes left before I must leave for work, scanning my mind for something I may have forgotten to take care of. I'm not admitting it consciously, but I'm actually looking for a reason to flake out on myself. The answer in these moments is to simply cut through. Just sit down already, and never mind everything else.

There is an ancient teaching that, just before something auspicious is about to take place, all the dark and negative forces in the universe begin to rise up to prevent it. This isn't considered to be unjust or unfair; it's simply the natural balance of the universe. In the Buddhist teachings, such obstacles are referred to in Tibetan as *döns*, unseen beings who personify obstacles. Before any important day, such as Tibetan New Year, we plan on a week we call "dön season." We simply assume that, because something beneficial and enjoyable is afoot, obstacles will precede it, and thus we prepare to embrace and work with the situation.

I'll never forget the time I called my friend and teacher Ethan Nichtern the week before Tibetan New Year and told him about all the things that were falling apart for me. There was no real tragedy afoot, but I was definitely feeling and acting like there was. Ethan's response: "Well, it's dön season, so expect nothing to go right, but do maintain a cheerful attitude." It took me about three years, but I've come to appreciate his response.

Some of us are superstitious without even admitting it to

ourselves. How many of us refrain from telling people about something exciting on the horizon for fear of "jinxing it"? Similarly, how likely are we to start thinking something is "simply not meant to be" when too many things go wrong before it's expected to happen? (Remember the "roadblock" I hit when I first sat down to write this book.) The gift of this teaching about dön season is that it tells us the exact opposite. If the going gets tough right when we're about to do something meaningful, it is simply the balancing act of nature doing its thing. In fact, it could very well mean that something more tremendous than anticipated is afoot.

Superstitions aside, I have come to enjoy the moments when nonsensical resistance to practice arises and I sit right down anyhow. It might burn for a moment, but I know that what's burning isn't the real me anyhow.

Part Two: Mind

A Monkey Molded by Model Scenes

THE MONKEY'S MESSAGE to us in part one of this book is to wake up from autopilot, to offer ourselves the holding environment—the safety, rewards, and belonging that we crave and deserve. The monkey's function in this realm of our ecosystem is that of a sparring partner or expert chess opponent. Acting as both an agitator and an ally, the monkey mind calls us into the ring and gives us excellent conditions for expanding our distress tolerance. We also explored the surface layer of why the monkey mind exists and the benefits of stepping into a kinder relationship with it. We saw that taking responsibility for our own happiness requires facing up to the magnificent mismatch between our physical and social evolution as human beings. Meditation, again, offers us an elegant means for addressing this mismatch. As we saw in chapter 3, for meditation to be transformative toward these ends, we first need to learn how to befriend our bodies through the vehicle of our attention.

In the next part of this book, we'll momentarily press pause on this discussion so we can develop some skill and resources in our amicable tête à tête with the monkey. Here, we'll truly begin to explore *shamatha,* calm-abiding meditation: the prescribed practice for regulating our nervous systems and clarifying the mind, ultimately allowing us to glimpse the natural state. Most mindfulness instructions are teaching some version of this practice, and for good reason: it's well supported by scientific studies. But in this book, we'll use it to go a little deeper.

While writing this book, it occurred to me that I could produce a nice, accessible book about understanding the nature of thoughts and developing a mindfulness practice. I questioned how far I'd allow myself to go in terms of exposing the far-reaching implications of matters such as empathy and presence—not just within our lives but in society at large. Ultimately, I decided not to underestimate my audience. We've got to go all the way down to the bedrock of things if we are to gain a meaningful understanding that can translate into clarifying experiences.

Thus, toward the end of part two, we will move from what's universal about us into what makes us unique: our individual developmental experiences, how they come to form the tendrils of our mental-emotional infrastructure. I'll elucidate what kinds of experiences embed themselves most deeply in us, how they manifest in very specific ways in our day-to-day lives and also ripple out into the world. This dovetails into the monkey's ultimate message: the call to heal the traumas that literally run our lives.

5

The Body of Breath

The Church says: the body is a sin.
Science says: the body is a machine.
Advertising says: the body is a business.
The body says: I am a *fiesta.*
—EDUARDO GALEANO

MINDFULNESS OF BREATH is just one aspect of the holistic, foundational practice of shamatha. Over the next few chapters, we'll unpack the most crucial aspects of shamatha practice to allow us to engage it with greater precision and depth. For now, we will begin with a simple form of shamatha. Our focus here will be four things: setting the attitude that practice is a holding environment, deepening our embodiment, returning from distraction over and over again, and *setting the breath in its natural rhythm.* I've created a mnemonic, **HERE,** to help you remember these four elements:

Holding environment
Embodiment
Return from distraction
Easy breath

To add to your repertoire of On-the-Spot Practices for emotional self-regulation, on page 79 I also offer "The 5-3-1-1," a practice you can do first thing after you wake up. Finally, a meditation you can do without getting out of bed in the morning.

SETTING THE BREATH IN ITS NATURAL RHYTHM

Like the body, the breath has its own natural intelligence. It has a natural mode that reflects well-being and restoration. However, over a lifetime, we've built some unconscious habits around breathing that reflect our neurotic tendencies. In general, we either pay the breath no mind whatsoever, or when we finally do pay attention, we start pushing and pulling on it, thinking it needs to be fixed. It's common for us to force ourselves to breathe especially deeply during meditation because we have some idea that it's a more "spiritual" way to breathe. This is one of many subtle forms of self-abuse commonly enacted in meditation practice. We either neglect the breath entirely or we push it around. We would never do this with a child (I hope), so why would we do it to the living force of our breath? Our relationship to our breath is actually reflected in other arenas of our life, and it's one of the easiest relationships to smooth out.

We can learn to trust the natural intelligence of the breath by learning to listen to its signals and whispers. The breath will sort itself out if we surrender the tension we place on it, and as the breath sorts itself out, our nervous system and emotions will follow suit. Finding the middle path between ignoring it and manhandling it pays dividends in serenity.

The natural breath has four parts:

1. exhale
2. the space between exhale and inhale
3. inhale
4. the shorter space between inhale and exhale

The key to settling the mind lies within the spaces between breaths. It is in these gaps, and especially in the gap between exhale and inhale, that we can let go of the breath and allow breathing itself to take the driver's seat. I include this instruction in the guided meditation, but even as you read this you can begin to practice: simply let go of your exhales. Whether they are long or short doesn't matter, just let them exit the body with as little effort as possible. Allow for a sense of them dissolving into space, and don't breathe in right away. Linger in the space after the exhale. Wait for the subtle signal from the body (usually felt in the abdomen) that the inhale wants to come. The space will range anywhere from a couple seconds to much longer. Don't hold or force the breath out. Let it simply be a moment of suspension. If you're truly letting go of the breath in this gap you will feel your belly and other regions of the body soften, and you will experience a palpable downshifting of your mental state.

Next, you'll feel the inhale tug at you. Shepherd the inhale in. Assist it, guide it in, don't pull it. We want a light effort. If you are tuned in, you will feel where the inhale itself wants to stop (which may not be the full breath you think you should be taking). Then allow the natural, shorter pause at the top of the breath before the next exhale begins again all by itself. Not by accident, you'll have to be present with the breath in order to feel its cues. Allow the spaces between breaths to take precedence in the mind. If you make a point of being fully present in the gaps, the attention on inhale and exhale will come much more naturally. Breathe as you review: exhale is released . . . space . . . impulse to inhale is felt . . . gently guide in the breath . . . inhale stops on its own . . . short pause . . . exhale initiates itself . . .

PRACTICE: *Foundational Shamatha**

Sit cross-legged on a cushion on the floor, or sit in a chair. If you are sitting on a cushion, make sure it is tall enough that your knees are at or below the level of your hips. If you are in a chair,

---

*This version of shamatha practice corresponds with guided audio track of the same title. If you would like a more detailed description of meditation posture first, skip forward to "Posture as Aligning with the Earth" in chapter 6.

place your feet flat on the ground. Your knees should be bent at 90 degrees. You can place a pillow underneath your feet if they don't touch the ground. Place your hands on either side of your lap at mid-thigh, facing down. Take a moment to make sure you are sitting upright with the crown of your head over your tailbone.

Set the attitude that your practice is a holding environment: Notice the body touching the earth. Feel the visceral sensations involved. Know that the earth is supporting you in this practice, and is your ally. You are safe here. You belong here. You are engaged in a practice that is aligned with your desire for growth and well-being, and you are here to connect with yourself in a meaningful way. You sat down today because you care for yourself, whether you were cognizant of that or not. Give yourself permission to feel good about this.

We'll utilize a variation on the Sun Meditation to drop into and relax the body: Imagine the sun shining on your face. It's a gorgeous day out, and the bright, warm sun is shining on your face. You're basking in it. You can feel it on your brow, your eyelids, the muscles around your eyes, your cheeks, and your entire lower jaw. Take a breath here, and as you exhale, let your face melt in the sunlight. Your face loses its shape.

Feel the sun drifting down your shoulder tops and into the arms, into the hands. Feel it in your muscles, skin, and bones. Feel the especially bright, tingling sensations of the palms. Take a breath here, and as you exhale, the shoulders, arms, and hands all relax. It's like a wave of sunlight washes over them and carries away any tension held here.

Feel the sun shining in the chest. You feel it in the ribs, the heart, the lungs, the back of the heart, tracing the ridges of the shoulder blades, and the muscles around the shoulder blades. With each breath, you feel the sunlight in your chest, and the wave of each exhale washes away any unnecessary holding.

Feel the sun shining down, down, down into the solar plexus and mid-back. Feel it shining down the sides of the body. Feel it shining down into the belly, the organs, and the inward articulation of the lumbar spine. Breathing in, you feel the lower torso; breathing out, you feel a wave washing away tension.

Feel the sun shining in your pelvis. It's there in your hip points, in your tailbone, your sitz bones. You feel the sun shining in your hips, in the pubic bone, and in the groin. Feeling, releasing. Breathing in, breathing out. Waves of exhale washing it all down and away.

Feel the sun shining down the thighs, knees, calves, shins, feet, and toes. Feel as much detail as you possibly can as your attention follows the sunlight down the body. With these final exhales, the lower body shifts toward relaxation.

Finally, you feel the sun shining all the way through you, from the sky above and into the ground below. Appreciate anything that's shifted since you began.

Stay with your sense of the body breathing. Feel the rise of the torso on the inhale, the fall of the torso on the exhale. The embodied breath is like the waves of the ocean. On the inhale, a wave rises and reaches shore. On the exhale, that wave recedes out, back into the totality from whence it came.

After a minute or two of settling into working with the breath, set the breath in its natural rhythm. Start by letting the exhale go out—no effort, no pushing. Let it go completely, without assuming an inhale is coming. Stay in that space where the breath goes out and out and out. When you feel the impulse to inhale, shepherd the inhale very gently. You'll feel the place where the inhale itself is finished, you'll feel the brief space at the top, and you'll feel how the next exhale initiates itself with no effort from you whatsoever. All that's truly required from you is your attention. Again, the trick is to pay more attention to the space in between breaths and to feel what happens there. You'll know you're really letting go of the breath when you feel the belly release at the end of the exhale. With every breath like this, there is a downshifting, a softening of body-mind.

Once the natural breath has brought about some settling of the mind's activities, refine your attention within the torso to just the belly or the chest. The belly is an excellent option because it is deep in the body and far away from the head. It's also harder to feel the breath there. The center of the chest—that is, the space of the heart—might be easier. If you go with the heart (sound advice for just about any situation, really), please find the lower part of your sternum and trace back into the body a few inches so your attention is a bit closer to the spine. In either case, the body is continuing to rise and fall in response to the waves, and the breath remains spacious and gentle.

After some time, your attention will get pulled away from the body or breath. Simply return to the body and feel the next exhale drop. Do this every time you notice you've become distracted. Each time you notice, that's good news, a success. As the session progresses, you might begin to tire of this. Just like at the gym, you're feeling the burn. Simply cut through and return to the body. You may want to remind yourself from time to time of your holding environment attitude.

We'll conclude this practice with an advanced (though very simple) technique: Take the two corners of your mouth and let them grow apart from one another. This literally opens up the energetic body and elicits serotonin from the brain. Maintain this for a good 15 seconds or longer, and notice the shift in your awareness.

Transition very gently from your practice.

On-the-Spot Practice: *The 5-3-1-1*

There's a reason why they say breakfast is the most important meal of the day: we can feel the residue of our first meal well into the day. If I have a stack of chocolate chip pancakes drowned in syrup for breakfast, it's going to be a different day than if I had chosen the veggie omelet. Same thing with the mental impressions we take in. Mental impressions are a form of nutrition as well, and they matter. What you mentally consume first thing in the morning can alter the rest of your day, and the 5-3-1-1 practice is my favorite way of meeting that truth with intention.

Stay in bed for an extra five minutes. Or, if you know you'll pass out again if you stay there, endure the nanosecond of pain it takes to swing your legs out of the bed and sit up for this. You'll thank me later. Either way:

> 5—Take **five** big, deep breaths.
> 3—Think of **three** things you're grateful for. Feel them. Linger in the feeling.
> 1—Invoke **one** very fake smile. Just pretend you're Jim Carrey. No one will know.
> 1—Set **one** intention for how you want to live today.

That's it: a few minutes out of your day to thoroughly set the tone. Science estimates that this practice is about one million times better than checking your phone first thing in the morning. ☺

6

Our Monkeys, Ourselves

As long as you keep secrets and suppress information, you are
fundamentally at war with yourself. . . . The critical issue is
allowing yourself to know what you know. That takes
an enormous amount of courage.

—BESSEL VAN DER KOLK

THE TITLE of Cheri Huber's book *How You Do Anything Is How You Do Everything* highlights the fundamental interconnectedness of the various facets of our life. It also underlines the truth that the way we treat ourselves has everything to do with the way we treat everything and everyone else we encounter. In meditation, it is not just the fact of paying attention that matters; the quality of the attention is also crucial. The theory of neuroplasticity (that every experience we have, either generated by us or taken in from the world, leaves behind traces of neural structure in our bodies) bolsters this point all the more.

Similar to the body, the mind is a living process and not an object. Similar to the body, the mind deserves more compassionate consideration than it often gets from us. Even though the mind expresses itself in and through us, it can be helpful to treat it as its own entity. It certainly has a volition that seems to be distinct from our own at times. Acknowledging the mind as a discrete, sovereign living force helps us to regard our mind with an attitude of empathy and kindness, which not only lends itself to mindful presence—genuine empathy is presence itself. They are inextricably intertwined; we simply cannot have one without the other. Seeing through this lens makes it illogical to approach the mind with cruelty, judgment, and a desire to lock it in a closet. Say the mind is having what amounts to a childish tantrum. Within this view, we can begin to think about how we'd best approach a child having a tantrum. We can shift our attitude and approach in a way that might help soothe that child. We can begin to act as a decent parent, with warmth and patience. The busy mind is so often no different from a child (in case you haven't noticed)— and as odd as this may sound, it often responds positively when we treat it as such.

Be the Change You Want to See in Your Mind

In my work with families in the mental health and foster care systems, I have counseled many parents to employ "benevolent ignoring" when a child is negatively and inconsolably acting out in an attention-seeking manner. Eventually the kid realizes they're not getting any more attention from their parents until they chill out, and by staying calm themselves, parents provide an excellent example of what appropriate behavior looks like. It's being the change you want to see in your child, basically. When parents practice this, they are also refraining from adding to the distress of the child, who is hardwired to read and internalize the stress and agitation of their caregivers. Now, this doesn't mean that parents should take their eyes off the child or *actually* ignore them. The trick is to stay present, warm, and calm in the background.

It's utterly possible to work with your busy mind in the exact same way in meditation: in a very kind way, staying present but unattached to its activities, and letting it see that its calmer aspects—in this case the body and breath—are much more important and interesting to you. When the tantrum inevitably pulls you away, revoke your attention once again, but with the same wholesome firmness a tender child needs in order to calm down. Acting without kindness will only exacerbate the situation and wire a lack of kindness into your brain. How we do anything is what we are wiring into our nervous systems.

Obviously, we become distracted by much more than the machinations of thought during meditation practice. Emotions are just as present, if not more so, in meditation. There is an emotional state beneath the content of all thought, whether we notice it or not. We are never not in an emotional state. As obstacles we face in practice, the emotions we primarily deal with are those that are considered to be the most socially acceptable and often the safest to express in families: irritation, cynicism, anxiety, anger, boredom, numbness, restlessness, and fake niceness. As we progress in the practice, the basis for more vulnerable emotions can and will begin to arise. Commonly these include feelings such as hurt, disappointment, vulnerability, rawness, longing, loneliness, disillusionment, and confusion.

Such emotions tend to either be the bosses governing our experience or our enemies that we shove aside with valiant effort. When we shift our relationship to them toward the model of friends or allies, emotions begin to serve a perfect purpose in our personal ecosystem. In shamatha meditation, whether the experience is pleasant or unpleasant, cognitive or emotional, difficult or neutral, we simply stay with it. We breathe with it, feel into it. This not only advances the distress tolerance capacity related to the prefrontal cortex (discussed in chapter 4), but with regard to emotional experiences, staying present to states of emotion also actually begins to *process* the experiences the emotions came from.

The emotions that we all hold—borne of our experiences and often surfacing in our practice—are not unlike food. They must be chewed, swallowed, digested, and metabolized. They need to be integrated into us in order for us to be able to move on from them. When we fail to integrate them, we get stuck. We get bound up, weighed down, burdened by all we've been through. When we metabolize our experience, we get insight and learn from the emotions themselves and the experiences that brought them about. They offer us growth. They add meaning to our lives. As we come to understand our own experiences and emotions, we begin to understand what other people are going through, and in this way feeling into our own experience also lessens interpersonal chaos in our lives. Again, we are not different from one another at the most basic levels.

It's unlikely that anyone told us when we were growing up that the skill of digesting our emotional experience is a necessary aspect of having a healthy life. As a society, we've known for ages that exercising the body is important, and we're starting to figure out that working directly with the mind is a good idea. Processing our emotions is at least as important as both of these, if not more so.

We become so disconnected from our emotions that sometimes something can happen to us and it could be hours, even days, before we realize that we're upset about what went down. We will cover this topic in depth in chapters 8 and 9. For now, know this: although it is true that no one has taught us how to process our emotions, in a sense no one actually can. It works differently for each of us. Our emotions themselves function as our teachers, and we start to learn by simply becoming willing to feel them. Just like working with the breath, we feel them, stay present with them, relate to them, get to know them, find ourselves distracted from or caught by them, then return to presence, over and over. This, too, is why we must set the attitude of practice as a holding environment. Presence and empathy are one and the same thing.

The Experience of Insight

Slow down, take a step back, stay curious, and observe the natural unfolding of the invaluable gem of clarity. When we release the locked-up energies of the body and allow relaxation to reveal itself, we find ourselves open to the subtle whispers, signals, and guidance of the body. Make space for this somatic intuition. Open the aperture of awareness, and experience the seething, pulsating, humming, disruptive, sweet, living symphony of present-time being. We will find endless variety; no moment ever repeats itself. In this space of receptive presence, a special kind of learning begins to take place.

We begin to see things about ourselves and our habits and about the nature of reality. We get useful and new information that we couldn't have gotten otherwise. We get insight. We get wake-ups. Lightbulb moments. Memos that spontaneously slip out of the dark recesses of the unconscious body-mind. Or sometimes insights come from the realities around us that we simply hadn't noticed. In meditation, these tend to be the kind of realizations and understandings that change the way we see and approach things, that bring us back to a deeper sense of who we are, that help us to see how asleep we've been. And quite often we see these truths in such a way that they change us forever. This is simply the nature of gaining perspective.

If I were to bring the keyboard of the computer I'm typing on now right up to my face so that it touches my nose, all I would see is the gray color of my computer's casing, or maybe the black of the keys. If I were then to slowly pull the computer away from my face, little by little I would begin to discern shapes that would eventually begin to look like letters. Those letters would grow in number as the distance between my eyes and the keyboard increased. Eventually, I would be able to see the entire alphabet arranged in QWERTY formation as well as the screen, the edges of the keyboard, my own hands, and the objects surrounding the keyboard.

Similarly, we tend to spend most, if not all, of our life without any distance between us and our experience. Instead of learning how to gain perspective, we tend to live in what Buddhist author and psychologist Tara Brach calls "mind movies," the multiverse of our spinning projections, recollections, and fantasies about things. The formal psychological term for this is *cognitive fusion*: a quiet, unconscious sense of identification with whatever it is we're perceiving in any given moment. Cognitive fusion means there's no sense of space between our self and whatever's happening; we're *in it* as opposed to *with it*. In shamatha meditation we begin to slow down. We begin to break our identification with our mind movie. We take a step back from our narratives into a more intimate interaction with our immediate experience via somatic presence. We literally come to our senses.

Sound impossible? Don't worry: if the experience of just about every other person who has ever tried it (with some earnestness and persistence) is any guide, you can safely assume that you can have this experience in meditation, too. Clear seeing (*vipashyana*) is the natural by-product of calming down (*shamatha*). It's one of the many reasons why the recommended practice period starts at around twenty or thirty minutes. It takes time to simmer down and step back. Once we do, we become increasingly available for clarity and insights to emerge as we sit. We make space for intuitions to percolate up from the depths of our bodies, from our bones. Just like the breath set in its natural rhythm, grace tends to reside in the spaces between things.

While practicing we might suddenly connect the dots between any number of goings-on in our life that we previously thought were unrelated. Or the realization might be about a concept or a passage we've thought about a million times but now suddenly see and feel in a different way. It might relate to a psycho-philosophical teaching we've heard. It could be about something we've been resisting. We might realize we're tensing or holding on in some part of our body. We might suddenly realize we've been living in an emotion, such as fear or worry, for so long we don't even notice it anymore. We might even be able to simply release it and shift toward ease. Insights can show up as small, seeming almost negligible at first, but turn out to be quite significant. Insights can betray everything we previously thought we knew about who we are or about life itself. It could be ecstatic. It could be painful. It could come as a relief. It could present an all-new and formidable challenge. It might come as a whisper. It might come as a shout. It might come as a nameless, nebulous feeling, a "knowing." We might gain perspective on the nature of living in our very limited mind movie. We might discover a great curiosity about the vast, expansive reality that lies beyond that movie.

It can be very much like an autostereogram, one of those abstract pictures that seem to be just patterns, colors, and shapes until you stare long enough for your eyes to adjust and you realize there's a three-dimensional scene hidden within the once-flat picture. This is the result of consistent daily practice coupled with another quality synonymous with mindfulness: curiosity. With repetition we begin to see our habits, and with enough curiosity those habits will reveal the tapestry of experience that set them in motion. This in turn empowers us to have and make new choices. Insight invites revolution. It might even feel as if a certain truth has come alive inside you.

I am attempting to describe the indescribable here, to capture the ineffable in a crude net so I can show it to you. Words can neither do this matter justice nor instruct you how to have an experience like this. We cannot create or cajole liberating insight. We can merely create the conditions for it. What I can tell you is that, when it comes, it'll be unmistakable and beyond value.

POSTURE AS ALIGNING WITH THE EARTH

Through consistent practice, we discover ease organically unfolds when we connect to the body and its relationship to the earth. We connect through the vehicle of an empathic, warm attention, and the rest unfolds on its own. Finding the upright, dignified posture of seated meditation is a practice unto itself, not at all something rote, and it employs these same themes. An appropriately aligned posture naturally stimulates the body's parasympathetic relaxation response, which is synonymous with calming the stormy seas of the mind.[1]

Not coincidentally, we align the body for meditation from the ground up. Here are what I've taken to be the major points of correct posture. These may differ slightly from the traditional points of posture you've come across before, but the intention is the same.

Knees and Feet

If you are sitting in a chair (I think this is ideal if you're new to the practice or have any sort of injury or chronic issue that might make sitting on the floor unsustainable for you, or if you simply want a break from sitting cross-legged): Sit in a chair in which your knees will be at or below hip level and bent at about 90 degrees, and place your feet flat on the floor. If your feet don't quite reach the floor, you can place a pillow or another object underneath them so you are grounded.

If you are sitting on a cushion on the floor: Ensure you are sitting on a cushion that allows your knees to fall at or below hip level when your legs are loosely crossed. You can play with the placement of your feet in cross-legged position, such as placing your ankles directly beneath your knees or perhaps bringing your knees to the ground so that the ankles cross one another closer to the center of your seat.

Pelvis

Ensure your pelvis is centered on the cushion or chair, and you want to be resting on the center of the sitz bones. As you sit, simply feel for these two oval-shaped bones in your butt, and see if you can land right at their apex. For some people, their posture feels more properly aligned when they lean very slightly forward so that the weight of their body lands just forward of center on the sitz bones.

It bears mentioning that, traditionally, the perineum, which is the opening of the main vital energy channel in Chinese medicine and other Eastern traditions, should be in contact with the cushion or chair. (But don't worry about that part too much.)

Lower Back

There is a natural inward curve to the lumbar spine in your low back. Let your tailbone move down toward your seat slightly, which will straighten this out a little. Do retain some of the inward curve, however. If the low back bows backward, you've gone too far. This action should engender a slight muscular engagement in the lower abdominals beneath the navel. This point beneath the navel, called the *dan tien* in Chinese medicine or the *hara* in Japanese martial arts, is of particular importance in the more esoteric realms of meditation practice. For now, know that the slight activation of the lower abs will help keep the entire spine erect during the practice so that the rest of your muscles don't have to work so hard to hold you up.

Whole Spine

Pretend there's an imaginary string emerging from the crown of your head (where you might place a yarmulke if you're Jewish), and a hand is pulling upward on that string. The crown of your head should be directly above your tailbone, and your shoulders should be right above your hips. This will actually allow the weight of the body to land in the pelvis, causing your two sitz bones to plug into the cushion or chair (an extension of the earth) much like an electrical cord would plug into a light socket.

Hands, Heart, Shoulders

In Chinese medicine, our hands, arms, and heart run along the same energy channels (known as "meridians"). I take this to be one of the reasons why the hands so often express the heart—such as having active hands when we talk. As the Sufi Kahlil Gibran wrote, "Work is love made visible," and all the work we do tends to involve our hands. Thus, we want the hands to be placed in such a way that they support the width of the collarbones and an openness of the heart. I find that almost everyone instinctively places their hands too far forward on their thighs, which creates a sunken-in shape in the chest that has a detrimental psycho-emotional effect. Given that, a way to find where the hands ought to be to support the heart is to simply first place them wherever it is they seem to want to land, and then scoot them back an inch or so.

Back of Neck

We want the back of the neck to be both long and straight. To find the position, ensure that the crown of the head is indeed lifted, the tip-tops of the ears going directly up toward the sky, and then allow the hairline of the forehead to fall forward just one centimeter, and the tip of the chin to tuck down and in just one centimeter. This effectively creates a swivel motion in the head, the center point of which is just behind the spot where the jawline meets the ears. But all that matters is that the neck is long and relaxed.

Tongue and Jaw

The tongue is one of the busiest muscles in the body, and it tends to hold a tremendous amount of tension. The traditional instruction is to allow it to rest in its palate. I sometimes find that placing the tip of the tongue at the roof of the mouth just behind the top row of teeth gives the tongue something to do while allowing it to be still. The mouth is generally kept closed (unless open for a breathwork practice), but the teeth remain parted so that the jaw doesn't clench (as it is wont to do).

COMMON CONCERNS AND ALTERNATIVES

We need to take care of ourselves during practice but simultaneously remain diligent with regard to applying proper effort and discipline. This requires discernment. Almost universally, sooner or later (or all at once) our legs will fall asleep, *we'll* fall asleep, our skin will get itchy, our back will complain, we'll get anxious, and there'll be so many reasons to not stay still. Just remember: as in the body, so in the mind. The more you relax in the posture (yes, even in the face of an itch), the more your mind will settle, period.

From one point of view, if we are properly mindful of our experience during the practice, we'll find that our legs being asleep will hardly bother us at all; that, if we leave the itch alone, it will intensify at first but then disappear on its own (scratch it, and three more will appear); and that, if anxiety or any other strong emotion arises in practice and we sit through it, we will eventually get to the other side of it and be better for the experience.

But then again, if your back is killing you to the point of hijacking your whole experience, it's probably a good idea to place your feet flat on the floor and hug your knees into your chest to alleviate the pressure. Maybe consider sitting in a chair next time (as I did the first year and a half of my practice). If you're falling asleep, well, maybe you really need a nap and should just go with it. Still, make sure your posture is good, and maybe breathe a little deeper. Most important, if your emotional state is extreme and overwhelming, this is not the time to practice formal meditation.

In meditation, we are placing the mind in a situation where the constant stimulation and distraction of ordinary experience has vanished, and without it the mind can get exceedingly desperate. That desperation can show up as thoughts like, "You know what would feel *so good* right now? Some neck rolls. And while we're at it, let's hit that itch on the arm . . . and fix these tingly legs . . . " To a desperate mind, such activity is akin to entertainment. In most cases, if we leave it all alone, everything will sort itself out in due time. Still there will be times when we really should move during practice, and only you will be able to judge whether or not you're doing so as an escape. The most important thing is that you aren't driven to fidgeting. You can avoid that by simply taking a breath and waiting a beat before consciously, *as part of your embodied meditation practice*, moving into a more easeful position.

LITERAL ENVIRONMENT AS HOLDING ENVIRONMENT

The environment that you practice in matters for several reasons. First, meditation can be daunting enough as it is. It's wise to eliminate as many obstacles to practicing as possible. If you have space enough at home to dedicate an area to meditation so you don't have to set up shop every single time, fantastic. If not, still try to meditate in the exact same place every day. Your body and brain love habits, so over time your system will get the message: "Oh, this is the place we sit when we do that thing where we simmer down." Some say that practicing at the exact same time every day will further this tendency. Again, the body loves rhythm and repetition, and this is true of the rhythm of daily practice.

Second, your external environment exerts an influence on your inner environment. Keeping your meditation space clean is a habit that reflects this logic. Having a shrine is not necessary, but make a space that feels good to sit down in, that your mind will naturally be drawn to. Setting up a table with some meaningful and inspiring objects is conducive to this.

The language of the unconscious mind is symbol and metaphor, hence the wildness of your dreams at night. I think of the objects on my shrine as being metaphors that communicate with a deeper part of me. I keep a plant (i.e., something alive, growing, and connected to the earth) on the shrine. There are images of people I admire deeply. Lighting a candle, which is totally optional, can serve as a metaphor for creating light within. Same thing with incense. (Incense was the original meditation timer before we had apps for that. When the incense went out, the session was over.) In the Chinese tradition, however, smoke is representative of spirit and mysticism, and so creating smoke that is pleasing to the senses can follow that logic. Alternatively, there is a modern movement *against* burning incense due to the inherent health risks of inhaling smoke. Some people keep meaningful quotes or written reminders to themselves on their meditation tables. Some people keep their space simple and elegant, others prefer elaborate decorations. No matter what anybody tells you, this is your space and your practice.

Why Dessert Comes Last

Think about the last time you had a great experience, perhaps a vacation or a night out, that ended with something going terribly wrong. When this happens, people commonly say that "it ruined the entire experience." Similarly, think of the last time you had an awful day in which everything seemed to be going wrong, but then toward the end of the day you got some great news. You most likely thought something along the lines of, "I guess today wasn't so bad after all."

Nobel Prize–winning psychologist Daniel Kahneman has scientifically demonstrated that the way an experience concludes will impact our perception of the entire experience more than anything else,[2] and we can certainly apply this to our practice. Even if we've had a mediocre or frustrating experience in meditation, if the practice ends sweetly we will feel better about the whole thing and be more likely to return to it the next day. What follows is three suggestions for doing just that.

Dedicating the Merit

A particularly uplifting closing contemplation in Buddhism is known as "dedicating the merit." It's a moment when we reconnect to our sense of belonging to the global family, a moment when we admit that our practice is not, and could never be, just about ourselves. Our practice impacts the way we show up in all our relationships, from intimate to casual to societal, and is thus an offering to the world.

Dedicating the merit can be practiced in any number of ways. As the unconscious mind relates in metaphors and symbols, so I enjoy thinking of my body as the sun, shining out in every direction from me, in this practice. The sun shines in the sky every single day, delivering nourishing warmth and light to all beings without discrimination. Whether you're a dog or a dictator or a saint, the sun doesn't hold back from shining on you. This is the essence of the dedication of merit: to intend for anything good, warm, or enlivening in our practice to shine out into the hurting world around us for the benefit of all. The traditional approach is to offer some words, either spoken or thought, that reflect this, such as, "May all beings be happy. May all beings be free from suffering. May all beings be free." In classes and workshops, I offer phrases like, "May all beings have what they need to feel safe. May the derivatives of confusion such as fear, ignorance, and oppression be vanquished forever. May sanity prevail in our world. May each of us awaken." Get as poetic or as fierce as you wish.

GRATITUDE

Gratitude is one of the most nourishing mind states we can experience, and it's a fantastic note to end practice on. It's also a concept some of us get stuck on along with "letting go," which I wrote about earlier. Listing things to be grateful for sure is nice, but it won't actually do much for us. The point is to *feel* gratitude. It is always going to come down to feeling. So, if evoking the feeling of gratitude isn't something that comes naturally, try this: Think of a time from the past when you did feel truly grateful for something. It might have been gratitude about something you received or accomplished; it might have been gratitude about some sort of disaster you avoided. Dwell in that memory for a few seconds until you can recall what gratitude felt like. That is, *remember what it felt like in your body.* What are the sensations involved in gratitude? Now that you have a reference for the experience of gratitude, apply that feeling to something in the present moment. Hell, the fact that you're alive and practicing meditation right now is plenty to feel grateful for.

Once you get the feeling going, linger in gratitude for 10 to 15 seconds. According to Dr. Rick Hanson, that's about how long it takes for our *implicit memory* to be rewired by any positive emotion or experience.[3]

The Compassionate Middle Finger . . . *Ahem* Serotonin Brain Hack

Perhaps the most direct method of ending well is this ancient, esoteric, and advanced meditation technique. It's quite simple, though, and you can try it as you read along: You just allow the two corners of the mouth to grow apart from one another. Even if you don't want to. Even if it feels forced. Even if my merely mentioning it causes your most bitter and irritated self to manifest full force. (I'm an old punk rocker, remember?) Actually, I often call this practice, "Giving the compassionate middle finger to my inner jaded teenager." Yes, we commonly know this gesture as a "smile," but I'm not lying when I say this is an advanced and esoteric practice. It opens up the subtle energy channels of the body, which in the yogic traditions begin in the nostrils, so that *prana*, or life force, can flow more freely into the body. It's also a brain hack that's been shown to encourage serotonin release. Hold this for 10 to 15 seconds. It's cheesy, but it works. And no one has to know. (I acknowledge that there is a cultural context here. I acknowledge that women are often inappropriately told to smile by men on the street and elsewhere. I acknowledge that this is an aspect of rape culture. I've done my homework on this one and feel strongly that both the spirit and the letter of this meditation instruction wholly contrasts from the aforementioned harmful and sexist practice. To be honest, I would skip it entirely save for the fact that there is simply no substitute for the simplicity, accessibility, and efficacy of this technique.)

7

How You Breathe Is How You Feel

There is no need to struggle to be free; the absence
of struggle is in itself freedom.
—CHÖGYAM TRUNGPA RINPOCHE

THE BREATH is a most precious resource that we routinely
ignore. Simply put: no breath, no body, no you. Although the
body can go for days without food and water, if you deprive your
body of breath for longer than one minute, you will begin to live
a very different version of reality. It's common knowledge that in
the Eastern traditions the breath is intimately linked with spirit,
prana, the vital force behind our being. In the creation myth of
Genesis, God breathes life into Adam, after forming his body
out of the earth. For us, the breath is the nexus between mind
and body, the place where psyche and soma intertwine. How we
are breathing has everything to do with our physical and mental
states. And yet, how in touch with our breath are we, in the tussle
of our lives?

On the physical plane, breathing stimulates the circulatory
system, which delivers needed oxygen and nutrients (via plasma)
to our cells. Breathing literally nourishes our entire system. We
might spend quite a bit of money putting all the clean foods,
supplements, and green juices imaginable into our bodies, but if
we're not breathing well, they won't do us much good. It's like buying something online and never arranging for it to be shipped.

Oxygen is also both a stimulant and a relaxant: it wakes us up
and puts us at ease at the same time. This is the story of meditation in a nutshell: we are here to do the work of mindfulness and

to relax and let go at the same time. Oxygen is the only known substance that can do either of these things with no adverse side effects.[1]

How you breathe is how you feel. Consider for a moment that crying is a form of breathing. Conversely, laughing is a form of breathing. Shortness of breath is symptomatic of a panic attack. Colloquially, relaxation is synonymous with "breathing easy." These are examples of how our breathing reflects our state of mind. In other words, the stimulus comes before the emotion, which leads to a particular breathing pattern: for example, something absurd happened, you found it funny, and the breathing pattern of laughing began. But we can make it work the other way around, too. We can breathe purposefully to induce states of mind.

In an interesting set of studies, European psychologists Pierre Philippot and Sylvie Blairy confirmed that joy, anger, sadness, and fear each correlate with a specific breathing pattern. They then conducted another study wherein different participants were instructed to follow the breathing patterns identified in the first study to see if they would begin experiencing the same, correlated emotions as the participants from the first. The participants in the second study were indeed able to induce joy, anger, and sadness just by breathing in a particular way (fear was a bit trickier, however). We can think of it this way: whenever we are unaware of our breath, it is reflecting our state of mind *and* our state of mind is being influenced by unconscious breathing patterns, possibly leading us unintentionally to negative mind states. When we are aware of our breath, we gain the power to collaborate with it in order to affect our state of being.[2]

The breath is the most significant bodily function that has the option of being either involuntary or voluntary. Just as the breath is the nexus between mind and body, it is also the bridge between our voluntary and autonomic nervous systems. Given that many diseases of mind and body have been shown to result from underlying distorted patterns in the autonomic nervous system, it is a boon to us that we can rewire our autonomic system with the voluntary one. That is, the more we can introduce healthy and balanced nervous system states through proper breathing, the more likely those temporary states are to become enduring traits.[3]

We need two wings to fly. With regard to the breath's role in meditation, we've already discussed the first wing: allowing the breath to find its natural rhythm. We are about to explore the second wing, which is knowing how to engage the breath with appropriate deliberation. These two can work together to influence the nervous system.

After the next section I'll suggest and elaborate on three breathwork practices so that you can have a repertoire: one for relaxation, one to bring energy, and one for balancing. Forever and always, we want to seek balance in our practice. If we are too heavily on one side of a spectrum, we always want to calibrate toward the other end. Simply put, if we are sleepy, energizing breathwork is best. If we are anxious or jittery, we can employ relaxing breathwork. If we aren't leaning too far on either side of that spectrum, we can employ balancing breathwork. As the saying goes in Ayurvedic medicine, "Opposites are medicine."

How You Breathe Is How You Once Felt

I recently had a direct experience of the psychological nature of the breath. This anecdote will also serve as a primer for our next chapter, where we will discuss *model scenes*: what they are, how they come to be stored in our bodies, and how they show up as repetitive patterns in our lives. What follows is an example of a model scene that showed up in my breathing habits and unlocked a world of insight and healing for me when I was able to stay with it.

I experience burnout, or what's often called "vicarious trauma," in my work more than any other helping professional I know. The nature of my work simply doesn't mix so well with my nervous system, which has been rendered a bit threadbare by years of emotional turmoil and substance abuse. Today, when I push my limits too hard or say "yes" to too many commitments, I invariably pay the price of a certain ache in my bones, a mental fog, irritability, a loss of empathetic connection, and diminished stamina for activity. I resented burnout for being such a frequent visitor after it first started coming around, but thanks to the growth mindset, burnout has become one of my biggest teachers. I am someone with a predilection for intensity and a terrible feel for my own boundaries, but now burnout has stepped in to keep me in check. It's painful and inconvenient, but I doubt my body could get my attention otherwise.

I was in the Bay Area for some teaching gigs when burnout stopped me dead in my tracks. I came to town several days early, hoping to catch up with some old friends, and of course I had worked myself to the bone in the days leading up to my departure from New York. Within a day of arriving in California, my system tanked and I found myself in a pit of exhaustion. I ended up spending the next three days alone, incapable of much more than long periods of supine meditation and breathwork. I had to put myself in what my friend and holistic beauty guru, Britta Plug refers to as "health jail."

On my third day of incarceration, in my third hour of lying on the ground, feeling into the minutia of my breath and body, insight hit. I noticed for the first time that at the onset of each inhale I took, despite my intention to allow it to be natural, there was a nanosecond where I sort of yanked at the breath. A micromoment of rushing, of impatience, of wanting to just get to it already. I started to feel in a new way how I tensed my jaw and my shoulders to pull in breath as opposed to expanding my torso and diaphragm. I could also feel how there was a slight spike of adrenaline that came with this activity. Suddenly I couldn't *not* feel the jagged activation this was causing in my body. My unconscious habits around breathing were putting me on the same mini emotional roller coaster that our phones do when they buzz in our pockets.

I got up and walked into the kitchen where I picked up a plate with that identical sharpness and sense of rushing. *Whoa.* I opened the refrigerator door with the same jolt. *Double whoa.* I reached for a container of leftovers with the same adrenal edge. *Good god. Really?* I put the leftovers in a pan . . . same thing. Then I remembered that my ex-girlfriend Sam had once commented on this odd, dysrhythmic way I have of moving about, saying she found it endearing.

The same habit present in my breathing was also reflected in literally every move I made with my body. No wonder my nervous system was in the gutter. I was asleep to the unnecessary and taxing jagged edge with which I approached just about everything. As my day progressed I became watchful of this. I slowed myself down, trying to ease into my various movements around the apartment. Then the insight deepened in a way I could have never anticipated.

I was in a yoga class later that afternoon, attempting to maintain these slow and steady movements and smooth breathing, when a buried memory emerged. When I was five or six years old, I would spend my summer days at a babysitter's house with a few other kids. I used to eat very slowly as a kid, and this routinely drew comments from adults. But this babysitter wasn't having it. Every day she'd find me still making my way through my lunch while the other kids had finished and were out playing. The babysitter, most likely dying for a break, began making fun of me for this, but to no avail. Eventually she began leaving me in the kitchen and turning off the lights behind her, leaving me alone and eating in the dark. After some days of this, humiliation set in and I began rushing through my lunch like everyone else.

The shame had left an imprint on me. Why else would this seemingly random memory—long forgotten and yet so very connected to my present experience—emerge now? Because I was young when this habit of rushing began, it was like the color of my own eyes: I couldn't see it. Nevertheless, it was there—*right there* in my breath, in my body, in my autonomic nervous system—the whole time. My body was waiting for me to notice, and was delivering to me the gift of an aching exhaustion to point me in its direction.

In fact, the only reason pain and difficulty exists in our lives is to draw our attention to something that needs it.

Once, in the discussion period of a class, an attendee shared his experience of being able to relax his body at first, only to find that almost immediately his body would tense back up involuntarily. His impression was that maybe he just couldn't do the practice, that there was something wrong with him, and he wanted to know if he should try a different form of meditation. I reflected his comment back to him in a more general way. I said something along the lines of, "I heard you that you're able to relax, but maybe it feels a little bit like you're losing control when you do, which is scary, so you tense back up." He agreed that this described his experience. I suggested to him that I might be describing a pattern that plays out in his work and relationships, that I wondered if he felt driven by a need to stay in control and whether he got anxious anytime that grip loosened. The look on his face registered the correlation as he agreed a second time. He also agreed that this was the source of some problems in his life. I invited him to view the practice of embodied meditation as a safe place where he could work on this problem.

This man gained a very personal insight from his experience, but we can also tease out of it another, more universal insight: when we learn how to relax in our bodies, we learn how to open up and allow the natural flow of life to course through us. Maybe that's scary, but I find the only alternative—living a life based on reactive fear and endless bodily tension—to be terrifying.

CALMING BREATHWORK: *4-8-12 Breathing*

The body responds positively to rhythm and repetition. One example of this is the universal inspiration to dance to music. Another example, which is perhaps more germane to our work here, is the way we instinctively rock and sing to babies in order to calm them down. When we introduce rhythm and repetition to the nervous system, it induces the *relaxation response* (discussed in chapter 3).[4]

4-8-12 Breathing can be practiced sitting up or lying down, and it is an excellent method for calming our system. It entails inhaling through the nose for a count of four, holding the breath for a count of eight, and exhaling through the mouth for a count of twelve. You'll probably find that the exhale is finished before the count of twelve is up; simply keep acting as if the breath is still going out, enjoying the space between breaths (just as with the natural breath). It doesn't matter how slow or fast you count, just that you keep as steady a rhythm as possible. In this breathwork, we are holding the breath to allow for maximum oxygen absorption. We are also allowing the exhale to be three times as long as the inhale, which is going to slow the heart rate down and downregulate the nervous system as well. This is an excellent practice to know and use if you suffer from anxiety or panic attacks.

ON USING BREATHWORK TO ADDRESS ANXIETY AND PANIC ATTACKS

If you are intending to use this as a breathing exercise at the onset of a panic attack, please note that a lot of mistakes are commonly made. First of all, in order for any breathing exercise to be useful to us in such a moment, we have to practice it regularly when we're *not* in a state of panic. If you don't practice, and then you try to introduce this technique *during* a panic attack, your mind's going to say, "Oh, really? You think some deep breaths are going to do us any good?" It will feel pointless, and you won't use it long enough for it to have an effect. Also, all breathwork practices have a cumulative effect on our system over time. Again, our nervous system loves familiarity, so the more regularly we practice whatever breathwork it is, the more impact it will have.

Also, start the breathing practice *the moment* you feel anxiety coming on. If you catch the onset of an attack quickly and meet it in a friendly way with skillful breath, you stand a good chance of heading it off at the pass. If you start this breathing after you're in a full-blown attack, probably the best you can hope for is that it will help manage it.

Finally, neuroscience estimates that, for any breathwork to meaningfully downregulate your system, your breath needs to be slower than six cycles per minute (i.e., longer than five seconds per inhale and per exhale). This needs to be maintained for two and a half minutes or longer (a little less than the length of a pop song) in order to take effect.

Energizing Breathwork: *The Twelvefold Belly Breath*

The Twelvefold Belly Breath is excellent for breaking up stagnant energies in the body and creating a sense of energized clarity. It can be practiced sitting up or lying down. I picked this one up through my studies with Dharma Ocean, but reportedly it is a qi gong practice for clearing the lungs. It literally squeezes stale blood out of the organs and allows for fresh blood and resources to be absorbed. It pulls the diaphragm closer to the spine on the outbreath, which is associated with the release of vital energy in yoga, and it encourages full inhalations, which the body loves. Practiced multiple times in succession, it will also break up anything that is stuck in the digestive organs, which has a refreshing effect on mind and body. Energetically speaking, we are clearing out the rust and accumulated debris of past experience and clearing space for fresh vital energy to arise in the subtle body. Another way of saying this is, *it gets you high*.

To do this practice, there'll be some anatomical talk (unfortunately something we shroud in shame in our society). The inhale is a full breath taken into the lowest part of the belly, between the navel and the pubic bone; the exhale is similarly thorough and is where the magic lies. In order to squeeze as much stale air out as possible, we'll pull the navel toward the spine and engage the pelvic floor on the exhale. That is, squeeze in the anal sphincter, pull the perineum (the region about one inch in front of the anus) up and into the body as you pull the belly in. This engagement will take some practice at first to really get, but the payoff is more than worth it. As you breathe in again, the entire system is invited to relax and the breath lands in the low belly, and with the exhale you engage the lower pelvis and the belly again. Do this breath for a total of twelve times. You can repeat this cycle of twelve breaths two or three times if you wish.

Although this practice is fairly vigorous, we want to breathe without creating any strain. This will take some trial and error. Do watch for habitual tensing, especially in the neck, shoulders, and jaw, where we tend to pull the breath from instead of allowing the diaphragm to draw it in. Relax these areas if you notice you are gripping. Full breath does not mean labored breath.

BREATHWORK FOR BALANCE: *The Ninefold Purification*

If you are neither sleepy nor anxious, this is your go-to breathwork. You may know this one as "alternate nostril breathing," or *nadi shodhana* for you yogis out there. There are many variations on this traditional practice—I'll give you the most simplified version I know of. It entails a total of nine deliberate breaths with some short breaks in between. This technique is practiced sitting up.

Take your left index finger and bring it to the outside of the left nostril without closing it off. Take a comfortably full inhale through both nostrils. Close the left nostril with your finger and exhale smoothly through the right nostril. Add a short, staccato push at the tail end of the outbreath by quickly moving your belly inward. Repeat this process three times total.

Let your hand relax on your lap and take a natural breath. You will be able to feel a subtle shift on the right side of your body.

Now we'll switch sides. Bring your right index finger to the outside of your right nostril, inhale through both nostrils, close off the right nostril, exhale out of the left side with a short push at the tail end. Repeat a total of three times.

Let your hand relax after you complete three cycles. Take one easy breath and notice any shift in sensation on your left side.

Next, do three breaths in the exact same manner but with both nostrils unobstructed. Breathe in through both nostrils, then breathe out through both nostrils, adding the slight push at the end. Simply relax when you are done, and allow the benefits to arise in the body.

With all breathwork practices it is helpful to have a sense of stale, stagnant energy leaving the body on the exhale and fresh energy entering on the inhale. You also are welcome to imagine warm light entering your body on the inhale and dark smoke leaving the body on the exhale. That said, I want to remind you that we are not here to make an enemy of anything or anyone in our practice. We are here on a mission of supreme friendliness, not as an angry landlord evicting unwelcome squatters. We are simply assisting any energies that wish to depart in doing so, and filling that space in with something that will support our whole system in the meantime.

PRACTICE: *Embodied Shamatha*

BEGINNING

Take some time to find an aligned posture. Appreciate the body's connection to the earth. Allow your eyes to gently close, or if you would like to keep them open, simply allow your gaze to be diffused so that you see what's in your periphery as much as what's right in front of you.

Take a few breaths and greet yourself. Check in. How does the body, mind, and heart feel right now? Are there aches and pains? Are you feeling energized or sleepy? Is there some emotion you've been trying to keep at bay that wants to be present right now? Just bring some awareness to what your natural starting point is.

Check in with your motivation for practicing. Why are you doing this? What sort of joys and sorrows are informing your sitting today?

Remind yourself of the instructions, and remind yourself that this is about self-love.

MIDDLE

Begin bringing kind attention to the body. Begin in the feet, far away from the head. Begin feeling your toes, the arches, the heel, all over your feet. What's there for you? Tingling, buzzing, electricity, aliveness? Most likely there are places where there doesn't seem to be any sensation at all. Feel into the lack of sensation there as well. It's like your attention is a paintbrush, and you're trying to paint the entirety of the feet: muscles, bones, and skin. Then notice something else: there's tension stored in your feet. Tightness. Gripping. Maybe even fatigue. Despite not wanting to feel those things, I ask that you instead bring your attention more fully into those sensations. Feel those sensations the next time you breathe in. The next time you breathe out, imagine all of that tension relaxing, softening. It's like the exhale is a wave that washes over the feet, taking all the tension with it into the flow of gravity.

Continue to do this, working systematically up and through the entire body. Feel all the sensations present in the body, being willing to feel the discomfort that (oddly enough) we cling to. Breathe in to feel it, breath out to relax it. Travel through the calves and shins, knees, thighs, pelvis, belly and organs, lower back, mid-torso, upper torso, shoulders and arms, neck and throat, and entire head, and conclude with the regions of the face, especially the eyes and jaw.

Following the body scan, its optional to utilize a breathwork practice: 4-8-12 Breathing, the Twelvefold Belly Breath, or the Ninefold Purification. Linger in the effects for some time.

Notice that the whole body is breathing. As you breathe in, the body expands. As you breathe out, the body dissolves and collapses. Inhale, exhale. Rising, falling. Like waves in the ocean. We're starting out with a nice, open target here for you to pay attention to. Allow your awareness to be free in the body, and simply ride the waves. When thoughts come in and take over, simply return to the body breathing.

Set the breath in its natural rhythm. Let your exhales dissolve. Really let them go. Abide in the space before the inhale. Little by little, tune in more and more to the breath's natural cues and move toward less and less effort with the breath (zero effort won't be possible).

Begin to notice where in the body the breath feels best, the clearest: the low belly (beneath the navel), the center of the chest (space of the heart), or the tip of the nose (which includes the openings of the nostrils and the skin above the upper lip)? Home in on the place that calls you today. Go from the whole body breathing to just this one place. This is now your anchor into the present moment for the rest of today's practice.

Notice how you relate to the breath inside you. Hold it just like you would hold a lover. With passion, with tenderness. Don't be clingy, but don't be lazy either. Be faithful. If you stray off into thoughts, simply return. Gladly do the mindfulness push-up and return to your love affair with the breath.

Naturally, there are other things going on: sounds in the room, sensations in the body, temperature and tactile sensations on the skin, thoughts circulating. There's no need to change these. Rather, breathe with your experience. Let the breath be at center stage, and everything else be backstage. The breath is primary, the rest is periphery. There's no problem here. There is only the way it is now. And then the way it is now. And then the way it is now.

Be merciful. If it is a mess, let it be a mess. If it feels like you can't do this today, stay put and explore that feeling. Let your mindfulness co-opt everything in your experience. Unless you are in significant emotional or physical pain, stay put with no-matter-whatness. Keep realigning with the intentions of your practice: kindness, diligence, presence, attention, relaxation. Be a work in progress while holding this blueprint. The feeling of its being difficult is actually the sensation of your brain being re-wired. It is literally the sensation of your life evolving. Embrace it.

End

You have some options here. Maybe you're struggling hard in your life right now, and gratitude practice will help you to keep perspective. Maybe you feel somewhere in the vicinity of relatively good or all the way up to full of joy, and dedicating the merits of your practice to all beings feels appropriate. Maybe you're exhausted or out of patience, and that big, fake smile is all you can muster. Make sure to conclude your practice with good feelings. What you have just done is actually more profound than you or I can fathom.

Interlude

The Stories We Tell Ourselves

FANTASY. REALITY. Fiction. Fact. Subjective perception. Actual events. To our brains, these are all identical. If we perceive a rope to be a snake, the body reacts to a snake. If we get an angry text message, the body responds as if there were an angry person right in front of us. Here's a rough breakdown: our bodies, being the sensitive entities they are, are constantly scanning our environment for signals about what is most important to us—safety, gratification, and belonging. When the body picks up something meaningful, it generates a general signal that *something* is going on that we need to be aware of. This signal, born in the nervous system, shoots up to the brain. The brain then scans the environment for the most probable (read: not necessarily accurate) explanation for the signal. Once it homes in on the likely culprit, it then spins a story about whoever or whatever that is and how we should react. It all happens in a flash.[1]

This process can be complicated to a great degree when we hold trauma in our bodies (in which case a danger signal lives *inside* us). Our reactions can also be magnified when we are convinced that our subjective perception of a situation is definitely what's going on in objective reality (if such a thing even exists). Our brains are hardwired with what's been called a *confirmation bias*. Meaning, whatever we are convinced to be the case, the brain, in its nonstop scanning of the world for things that matter to us, will seek and find evidence that our subjective perception is true. One particularly heartbreaking example is when we become convinced that there is something wrong with us or that we're worthless in some way and then start seeing evidence everywhere around us that confirms our belief. As we've been discussing, this is not all bad news: we can use this exact same propensity in meditation, as we will explore in greater detail in coming chapters.

The confirmation bias and our inherent propensity to construe meaning out of experience can take us down a rabbit hole to places that are absurd, scary, disruptive, healing, insightful, or just plain deluded. The following is a story about an experience that was all of the above.

DIAMOND DOG

I was recently on a silent meditation retreat when life offered me a teaching I hadn't signed up for. Blazing Mountain Retreat Center is hours away from civilization, way out in a high plains desert of Colorado, off a road that is bordering on impassable. The question had been buzzing in the back of my head for days: *Does Reggie Ray live somewhere on the property? I wonder if he'll be dropping in to offer a teaching.* I have never personally met him, and yet have consumed many of his podcasts and books, and I had been studying intensively all year with Neil McKinlay, one of his closest students.

So, when I went to explore the land beyond the retreat center one day, imagine my surprise when I approached a man in sunglasses who resembled Reggie. It took me 0.5 seconds to realize that the gentleman was a fellow retreatant, but passing him refreshed the question in my mind. Then I passed some bushes and noticed a house. My mind began connecting dots.

This must be where he lives! Who else could possibly be living out here, literally in the middle of nowhere?

I recalled a podcast episode wherein Reggie talks about having a meditation room in the upstairs of his house. I looked, and the house had a finished attic.

What are the chances? Reggie and Caroline [his wife] *totally live here. So cool!*

I swear to you, I am not one to get starstruck or make a fool out of myself around creative people I admire—but then I noticed a red truck sitting in the driveway. Its engine was running. And then the engine stopped.

OH MY GOD. They just got home. Are Reggie and Caroline about to get out of that truck? What do I do?? Do I just say hello and wave? Would it be more polite if I pretend not to see him? He probably wouldn't like to be bothered.

What I really wanted to do was prostrations, right there in the dirt.

The door to the truck opened, and a dog started barking. The dog jumped right out of the truck and made a beeline for me without hesitation.

Perfect! This is how I meet them. Dogs love me, and I love dogs. I'll play with the dog, Reggie and Caroline will come over to get the dog, I'll make some jokes, we'll share a laugh and a heartfelt exchange and then be friends forever.

The dog, practically frothing at the mouth, stopped a foot away from me and planted its paws into the ground in an attack position, fangs showing.

I bent down to pet my new little friend.

Hello! You're so . . .

The dog lunged at me—and bit.

There is a teaching about the moments when our expectations get smashed, when the world delivers a rude awakening from our neat little stories, when we get tossed from our comfort zone into a briar patch and our minds come to a screeching halt. Pema Chödrön talks about this teaching in her seminal work *When Things Fall Apart.* One day she parked her car in her driveway, she got out, and her husband, who happened to be standing outside their home, blurted out that he had fallen in love with someone else and wanted a divorce. Chödrön speaks of the way things went perfectly still and quiet after that moment. In a flash, everything she had based her life on was no longer true, and suddenly her mind had nothing to hold on to.

My friend and colleague Heather Coleman once used this example: Say you're licking an ice cream cone. You're walking down the street on a hot summer day, and the ice cream is delicious. You're *so glad* you got a double scoop! Just then—it drops. Your eyes instinctively follow its fall to the sidewalk, where it is now a splattered mess. There is a moment of shock, of stillness, of open awareness, before the mind can reorganize itself into a narrative of any sort, before you can register disappointment or think "let's go get another one," or construe any story whatsoever. It's a moment of pure experience, unadulterated and unfiltered by the observing ego.

In Buddhism, such experiences are considered to be just as revealing as the expansive moments I spoke of before—moments such as taking in a meteor shower or entering a flow state when engaged in a creative endeavor. In these moments when our limited concepts about things simply drop, having nothing to hang on to, the neurotic parts of ourselves simmer down, the mind opens, and something deeper is made available, even if for a nanosecond. They are pristine moments, easy to miss, during which we briefly taste the richness of experience beyond concept. Of course, such moments arise in meditation practice as well. Our very strong habitual tendency is to let those narratives rush right back in, but we can also train ourselves to recognize these moments when they are happening and abide in them for longer and longer.

The dog lunging at me was one of those moments. The story I was telling myself was so thoroughly thwarted, and the urgency of the situation left no room for another story to take its place. Things felt very still, very quiet. There was no thinking, no panic.

Technically, there was a dog viciously attacking me and my body's instinct to zigzag backward, but in defense, I'm not exactly sure *who* was doing the zigzagging. It certainly wasn't me. Remember the gentleman I had passed on the road before all this? He saw the whole thing. He later told me, "The way you moved was amazing. It was like you were dancing." Somehow the dog only managed to nip the edge of my pants.

The dog's owner (who was, by the way, very much *not* Reggie Ray), finally came running over to intervene. I doubled over in uncontrollable laughter, realizing that the grand story I had been telling myself was just that: a story—one that could not have been more wrong, and one that could have gotten me terribly, terribly hurt. "I'm so sorry," the owner said. "She's a shelter dog we're retraining so that they won't put her down. Six months ago, she would have eaten you for lunch."

8

How We Get Stuck:
Trauma and the Unconscious Mind

Love is what we are born with. Fear is what we learned here.
—MARIANNE WILLIAMSON

PERHAPS YOU'VE NOTICED by now: the moments when the mind fully inhabits the body are moments when, however brief, we are not ensconced in discursive thought. Embodiment necessarily disengages the chattering aspect of mind; it cuts off a big part of its energy source. It moves us away from a left-brained descriptive consciousness and into the open and experiential realm of the right brain. In the beginning, we get glimpses of this, flashes. As those glimpses become increasingly familiar with continued and consistent practice, our ability to recognize and rest within them grows and grows. Yet, despite these moments of relief in embodied meditation, by and large we find that our attention remains unstable. That state of presence within the body slips away from us time and again. We might wonder if something is wrong with us. There isn't. We might wonder if the meditation is "working." It is. We might wonder if there's something we're missing. Most likely there is.

Too few of us hold an awareness of how our emotions work at the deepest level, how we unwittingly come to be conditioned by experience, and how understanding such processes empowers us to get free. Too few of us hold an awareness of how pain is passed down through families, even functional families. And too few of us who come from dysfunctional families realize the power in declaring: THE LEGACY STOPS WITH ME.

A quick overview:

When our fundamental needs for safety, rewards, and belonging are betrayed in some way, we get triggered. The emotions and mental storylines we experience in those moments are actually the result of a cascade of biochemical processes. It might be counterintuitive to conceive of it in this way, but emotions are primarily biological in nature. When we fail to process, metabolize, and resolve such activations—when we cannot, will not, or don't know how to feel things all the way through—those activated chemicals have nowhere to go. In a sense, they calcify. Better yet, we can think of the emotions as liquid that then freezes into an imprint within our nervous system. Thus, the body, the central object of our meditation practice, is like a diary. It holds the totality of our unresolved emotional experiences—our core wounds, our traumas, be they with a capital *T* or a lowercase *t*. You will come to see in this chapter that we all have them. Every one of us.

Imagine you have a gash on your arm and then you touch it. The sting of touching the wound will cause your hand to pull away. There'll be an automatic recoil. There won't be a single thought about it, it'll just happen on its own. Holding unresolved traumas in our body is just like having a gash on our arm. And placing our attention on our body is very much like touching it. There's a saying, related to neuroplasticity: "where attention goes, energy flows." That is, descending our attention down from the head and into the body has the potential to unfreeze the hurts and heartaches held within. Thus, we experience a different kind of automatic recoil: away from the body and back up into the head, back into our own private world of spinning thoughts and neurotic strategies. We can logically posit that the extent to which we are holding unresolved core wounds is the extent to which we will find embodiment challenging. The more trauma that's stored in the body, the more we'll find ourselves in our heads, and the more the monkey will be acting like a feisty beast running wild.

This is what your busy mind is trying to tell you. And it's not bad news. Returning to the analogy of a cut on your arm: the pain of the cut is serving a purpose. The smarting of the wound is your body saying, "Hey, get the antiseptic and the bandages, clean this thing out, and cover it so it can heal." Your monkey mind— your irritating, incessant, confusing, uncontrollable mind; sometimes panic ridden, sometimes depressed, sometimes OK—is the smarting of that wound. It is an alarm. It's been going off for a long time now, and the longer it's ignored, the louder it's bound to get. Our bodies are oriented toward healing, it is not their instinct to hold calcified emotions in our nervous systems. Our brilliant, ever-intelligent bodies just may be choosing increasingly desperate measures to get our attention. This generally takes the form of repetitive and troublesome experiences in our lives. All patterns in our lives are indicative of something deep down that is unhealed, something that is trying to flag us down, something that is screaming, "help!" Repetitive patterns in thought. Repetitive patterns in emotions. Repetitive patterns in behaviors. Repetitive patterns in interpersonal relationships—especially intimate ones. These all share a common source: trauma.

There can be a tendency to become cynical or to minimize such patterns in our lives. We might say to ourselves, "That's just the way I am," or, "The past is the past, I've moved on," or, "This always happens to me. I was born to lose," or, "I'm just unlucky in love." Yet, no one has ever responded to a painful cut on their arm by saying, "that's just the way I am," or anything of the sort. Pain doesn't exist to annoy us. It isn't some senseless, unfortunate fact of life. In fact, there is a rare disorder that causes people not to feel physical pain, and those people are at high risk of self-inflicted injuries and premature death.[1] Pain is part of the body's maintenance system at both the physical and the psychological level. It is part of our ecosystem. It is part of the body's unstoppable drive toward well-being, which, again, looks one way in the presence of stressors and yet another way in the presence of safety and warmth. Pain is the very sensation of the body attempting to restore harmony. If anything, it's evidence of our basic goodness, our deeper nature.

This forms the rationale for going deeper with our meditation practice. We can absolutely use our practice to safely and methodically unfreeze deep-seated wounds. When we do so, we clear room for more joy, compassion, and purpose in our lives. In the coming chapters, we will explore two categories of heart-opening and healing practices. The first of which, maitri, is centered on building our inner resources, bolstering our ability to experience visceral warmth, and strengthening our resilience. It's designed to deepen a continuous, underlying sense of safety, feel-good rewards, and belonging within us. This then gives us the fuel to do the deep dive presented in part three of this book.

Just as with our universal drives and needs, it's important that we understand exactly what's going on here. This way we can begin to discern what's been going on in our experience and know how to best respond. Allow me to back up and tell this story from the beginning.

THE BODY-MIND ICEBERG

For over a century now, psychologists have theorized that we possess an aspect of mind that we don't experience directly: an unconscious psyche. The cliché analogy is of an iceberg, wherein one can view but the smallest part of the ice structure floating above water while a colossal mass lies beneath the water and out of view.

Sigmund Freud posited that the unconscious mind is a veritable Pandora's box of erotic and aggressive drives that form the basis of all our conscious action. For Freud, this accounted for humankind's capacity to enact cruelty upon one another on an unspeakable scale as a product of disconnection and objectification. Within his model, we humans are stuck navigating powerful subliminal urges, both sexual and destructive, which then get enacted through behavior in disguised ways. Freud's best hope was that we might learn to channel these energies in a mature fashion, but even that hope was terribly thin. He wrote, "I have found little that is 'good' about human beings on the whole. In my experience, most of them are trash . . . "[2] *Thanks, Dr. Freud! Clearly you weren't worried about alienating your readers by calling us all trash.*

Contemporary theories regarding the unconscious mind are not only more scientifically verifiable than Freud's but also more empowering and more accessible to our subjective experience. Turns out, the hidden parts of our personal icebergs aren't irredeemably dark or corrupt. They are just storehouses of the totality of experiences we've absorbed since birth. We are also figuring out that the unconscious mind, that storehouse, is actually the body—again, the very places we are tuning in to in the forms of meditation presented here.

Where else could our experiences be absorbed and stored other than our physical being, other than the vast and sophisticated neural network that is spread throughout the body? Back to the iceberg analogy: the part of the ice structure above water, therefore, would correlate to the consciousness centered in the head, and the exponentially larger part below the surface would correlate to the body consciousness. Although our conscious minds are excellent at pruning away most of the barrage of stimuli we constantly receive through our senses, the unconscious body-mind is a radically open entity. It has no filter, it has no opinion, it cannot say no. Our body-mind functions like a dry sponge in the wetlands of our complex, multilayered, dynamic experience.

MODEL SCENES

Our wild unconscious does become organized as we develop. It organizes around significant moments from our life known as *model scenes*: meaningful experiences that then condition every-thing about our personality and the expression of our primary drives. A model scene is a significant moment from our past that, in a way, we never left. For instance, you might have had a painful experience with your father or your first grade teacher that, when you think about it, still makes you upset today. Perhaps it was such an intense experience that it'd be more accurate to say you relive it rather than just remember it.

Model scenes are expressed in our life as repetitive thoughts, patterns, behaviors, emotional experiences, relationships, work situations, political beliefs—really in all of our tendencies. They are not negative by nature, but the painful scenes do persist until they are met with and resolved. It could be an experience you remember clear as day, something you have blocked out, or a memory you consider to be negligible. While the domain of model scenes is the unconscious, they are constantly appearing in our experience.

Here's something that Freud got right: model scenes give rise to something in us he called the *repetition compulsion*. We become *compelled* to recreate them in symbolic ways. That is, the experi-ences we've had that mattered most to us, positive or negative, are what form all the cyclical patterns in our lives. Their influ-ence ranges from simple daily choices we make to dictating the very complex, dynamic patterns of bonding, our subjective needs in intimate partnerships, and the confused (if not labyrinthine) manner in which we attempt to get these needs met. A model scene is a dress rehearsal for reenactments that will play out a thousand different ways—even in the way we breathe. Our per-sonal model scenes are what inform our individual (often mis-matched) emotional reactions to circumstances, which are then expressed in behaviors.

Damaging model scenes are synonymous with trauma—moments in which our need for safety, warm feelings, and belong-ing was threatened in some way. They embed themselves in our

implicit, emotional memory systems according to the particular sensations (sights, sounds, smells, tastes, tactile sensations)
that were present when we experienced them. Our system wisely
stores these sensations in an enduring way so that if the body
should pick up a similar constellation of sensations, it can quickly
engage our reptilian fight-or-flight response to give us the energy
to defend ourselves. This all happens in a flash; just like the automatic recoil involved in touching a wound, it is quite automatic.
You will see in an example below about a foster child with PTSD
that we can find ourselves triggered in such ways without even
consciously knowing what the trigger is or why we're suddenly in
an agitated response.

Such activations fall into three general categories, and how
we experience them often correlates with the intensity of the
trauma we've embedded. The three categories are *hypervigilance
and avoidance, hyperarousal* (pronounced emotional responses),
and *reexperiencing*.[3] If an experience was extreme enough to create
and embed true traumatic stress (acute trauma) or even traumatic stress *disorder* (chronic trauma), the activations related to
that model scene are amplified.

We can find avoidance, hyperarousal, and reexperiencing
all in the innocuous experience I spoke of in the last chapter,
wherein the model scene of my babysitter shaming my eating habits was evident in my breath cycles. Because, naturally, I wanted to
avoid the frustration of having a similar shaming experience, my
system had generated a *hyperaroused* response (feeling I need to
rush through everything I do). The response repeats itself in any
situation wherein I am feeling like I have to keep up in order to
be good enough. Thus, on any given day I might *avoid* appearing
to move slower than others by rushing about or by behaving in
a competitive manner with those around me. This, however, is a
fool's errand. It's only a matter of time before something happens
that will force me to slow down and make it appear to others that
I'm unable to keep up. In fact, that's exactly what was going on in

the yoga class I took. Slowing down and moving out of sync with the instructor's *vinyasa* (a fast-paced form of yoga), the memory came hurtling back—I *reexperienced* it. Fortunately for me, it wasn't a terribly intense ordeal I had gone through, and I know how to work through such memories. Thus, I could contain my reaction, feel the emotions coming up, process the memory, and integrate the insights it led me to.

The paradox is, I developed a predilection for putting myself in situations where I feel I'm not doing enough. If you recall, I discovered this model scene of mine following a period when I had worked myself into a state of radical exhaustion. I so often have an underlying, unconscious feeling that I have to burn the candle at both ends in order to be a sufficient person. I tend to not even see this until the tendency has put me in a painful situation. This is the repetition compulsion. Yet, notice that the pain of the repetition compulsion also put me in the exact situation I needed in order to recognize, feel, understand, and gain insight about the part of me that was stuck reliving the model scene. The repetition compulsion is actually a mysterious yet functional part of our natural propensity for healing.

A capital-T-trauma example: A colleague of mine once worked with an adolescent in foster care who was exhibiting aggressive behaviors at what seemed like random intervals. This young woman, ordinarily friendly in demeanor, had been labeled a "bad seed" and had been bounced from home to home and from school to school as a result. Her diagnosis of oppositional-defiant disorder (ODD) alongside post-traumatic stress disorder (PTSD) reflected this. She was put on several strong psychoactive medications, but to no avail. She herself didn't understand why she so often felt driven to go on the attack, yet the need to do so felt very real and urgent in the moments these episodes would take place. When she physically assaulted a bus driver, for example, she had felt disrespected and belittled by him, though later she couldn't place her finger on why. In hindsight, she could see that her behaviors were largely unwarranted, and no part of her wanted to experience the consequences she was getting. "Make better choices," everyone said, as if she wasn't trying to.

Finally, someone sat down and did a moment-by-moment sensory assessment of the traumas she had experienced, which included being attacked as a younger child. In such an assessment, a clinician probes specifically for what sights, sounds, smells, tastes, and tactile sensations were present in the experience. Such sensations form what are called *traumatic reminders*, which can powerfully trigger the fight-or-flight response. When the youth described what her attacker looked like, she reported that the man had a moustache. This was a detail that no one, in all her years spent in the child welfare system, had ever known about. No one had ever asked her what her abuser had looked like. It turned out that the bus driver she had attacked had a moustache. Various school teachers she had been in altercations with had moustaches. Men with moustaches took her body back to a moment when unspeakable things had occurred, and her body responded with an impressive efficacy. It began to dawn on her treatment team: The world is *filled* with men who have moustaches. *No wonder* this teen is flipping out all the time. Her aggression wasn't the least bit random. Nor was it her fault. Armed with this awareness, she could then work with her therapist to resolve the unnecessary activation. Not until she had this awareness could she make better choices. And with this awareness, she could then have what's called a *corrective experience*, an experience wherein someone responds with care and tuned-in attention to the precise way we are hurting. The repetition compulsion was trying to get her to this place all along.

The Life Cycle of an Emotion

The emotions we experience in response to stimuli are just like anything else in our world: they have a shelf life; they are impermanent. There is a time when they aren't present, there is a definite moment when they come into being, a moment when they peak in intensity, and then they fade out until they are no more. That is the trajectory they naturally follow, that our emotions themselves *want* to follow and will follow if we allow them. If we don't or can't let them—that is, if we repress or distract ourselves from present feeling-states, we choke off the progression of their life cycle, and they have nowhere to go. The biochemicals that have become activated in us are left just sitting there in our system. If we were only willing and able to feel things through and allow their natural duration, they would, in a sense, remain liquid and pass through our system rather than become frozen.

THE LIFE CYCLE OF AN EMOTION

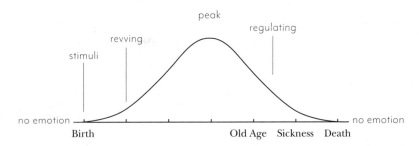

This is one of the reasons why we have funerals and are given time off of work when someone in our family dies. It's part of why Jews commonly sit *shiva*, literally doing nothing but sitting in remembrance for a full week after a loved one dies. It is simply understood that we need time to grieve and process; to sift through memories; to recall what the person meant, what they taught us; to make meaning of the experience and grow in some way. Yet, this opportunity does not always present itself, or the grief can become repressed in all kinds of ways. For example, my dear friend and bandmate, Pandora, died when I was at the deepest point of my addiction. My response was to numb the pain with drugs. Meanwhile I went through the motions of grieving publicly because I felt guilty for being so numb. Some four years later, I came across a recording of one of our rehearsals and the full wave of grief crashed down upon me. I cried for days on end. It uncannily felt like it had all just happened. And it continued until all the grief was gone, until I came to a place where I could see how lucky I was for knowing such an incredible being.

Going toward pain and difficulty with compassion is actually easier than trying to get rid of it. The problem is, this is in the opposite direction of our instinct. It's also a response that's impossible for children to have. As kids, we didn't have the knowledge, resources, or capacities developed for such a response. Yet, childhood is when we are the most tender, when distressing, frustrating, and heartbreaking experiences make their deepest imprint on us. How many of us would rather just "move on," "let it go," and proclaim, "the past is the past," not realizing that the past is sitting here, now, in our bones?

In the absence of corrective experiences, material held in the unconscious mind is bound to seep into our conscious experience and behaviors in subtle, symbolic, and metaphoric ways. This is much like the warmth and vapors that exude from a radiator: we don't see the vapors, we're not aware of the fuel source underground, but we do feel the heat in the room. We may not be aware of the experiences we've internalized that are informing our lives, but we certainly see and feel it when yet another panic attack, anger attack, lonely spell, or depression comes on. When we can't put down an addiction we know is terrible for us, when our minds are a mess, when another relationship fails for reasons eerily similar to the last one, we are experiencing the reflection of a model scene.

POSITIVE EXPERIENCES AND EMOTIONS

All of this begs the question: What about the positive experiences we've taken in? Don't our bodies hold those as well? The answer is yes. However, Daniel Kahneman won a Nobel Prize for demonstrating that our bodies and brains devote far more resources to the afflictive experiences we've had than to the rewarding ones. When we go on default mode, our psyches are organized far more around what has hurt us than around our positive experiences. Dr. Rick Hanson commonly points to evolutionary psychology to describe why this is so. To paraphrase Hanson, imagine you are back in hunter-gatherer times and you are out to trap lunch for the tribe. You hear a rustle in the bushes to your right. That rustle is most likely one of two things: the wind or a predator. Let's say you assume it's a predator and you run off. If you're wrong about that, no big deal. But what if you assume it's the wind and you're wrong? *You* become lunch. Not only that, you don't live to pass down your genes. Thus, natural selection has favored those who developed a negativity bias: those who were more paranoid, organized around negative experiences. By logical extension, it further favored those who held on to negative experiences in a deeper way so as to quickly discern danger in future situations.[4]

The actuality of modern life for most of us is contrary to this: What we struggle with pales in comparison to the leisure and fortune we enjoy. The internalized beliefs we might hold regarding our worthiness can't hold a candle to our potential for self-actualization.

Hanson's theory states that we can indeed internalize the positive experiences we have just as deeply as we do the negative ones; it just takes our systems longer to do it: ten to fifteen seconds, to be exact. Although negative experiences sink right into our implicit memories instantly, we must learn to linger in the gratifying times we commonly experience for a quarter of a minute in order for them to impact us. Do this: Take out your phone and open the stopwatch function on the clock app. Press "start" and sit while fifteen full seconds go by. Now you have an idea of how long you'll need to linger in positive experiences to make model scenes out of them. This is yet another place where working with the distress tolerance inherent in being present pays off.

THE BIG BANG OF NEUROSIS

Astrophysicist Carl Sagan wrote, "If you want to bake an apple pie from scratch, you'll have to start with the Big Bang." Similarly, if we are going to resolve the core wounds that are the very fuel our monkey minds run on, we are going to have to get at their root. We've got to start with the Big Bang of our neuroses, if you will.

It's important to remember that neurotic cast of characters that frequently visit us in life—anxiety, depression, worry, panic, compulsions, problematic patterns in intimate relationships—did indeed have a Big Bang of their own. Just like our individual emotions: there was a time when they didn't exist, a moment when they came into being, and a series of later moments that shaped our neuroses into the unique way they play out in our lives today. (It's true that many of us are born with a genetic predisposition for certain emotional characteristics and pathologies, but the word *predisposition* is important. Relatively few people are born with guaranteed disordered traits. Rather, one may be born with the *potential* for certain traits to arise, and when that potential meets with the right constellation or intensity of stressors, that characteristic will more or less "switch on."[5])

Just like the raw materials of the universe—the once-simple elements that grew to form intricate stars, planets, and galaxies—our psyches and their constellations continue to grow in complexity: expanding, exploding, imploding, and changing shape indefinitely. The six-million-dollar question in astrophysics and cosmology is "What came *before* the Big Bang?" and we have a similar question on our hands here. What came before our hurts and our subsequent struggles for safety, before we developed sub-jective complexities and patterns that tend to ensnare us? Thank-fully, we have much more information about the origins of our afflictions than science has about what existed before space and time.

Think about newborn babies for a moment. What are they like when they come into this world? What sort of qualities do they have? They are born playful, spontaneous, unfragmented, and empathetic, full of love. Fun fact about empathy: babies are born hardwired with facial recognition software that can interpret the facial expressions associated with the six main human emotions—happiness, sadness, anger, fear, surprise, and disgust. This is because the face of a newborn baby's caregiver, the primary object of their focus, is the only indicator they have of what is going on around them and whether they are safe or not. Babies are born with an ability to sense the feelings of others.[6]

In Buddhism, we would refer to the love we were born with as our natural state, or *Buddha nature*. This aspect of ourselves never goes away, though it does become covered over, causing us to lose the experience of it.

Not All Mammals

Being born with such positive qualities was made possible by some other qualities we were born with: radical vulnerability, complete openness, utter dependence, and an inability to fend for ourselves. Here is where the trouble begins. As infants we were highly sensitive, constantly molded and conditioned by what our baby minds perceived and also totally dependent on caregivers for absolutely everything we needed, unequipped to deal with a single thing on our own.

As humans, our wholesale reliance on caregivers goes on lon-ger than for any other species on the planet. What other mammal is hitched up to its parents (or surrogate parents) for fourteen to eighteen years before being sent off to fend for itself? The truth is, our natural state, the pure love we were born with, isn't exactly capable of handling the challenges that confront us when we are children. The pure relaxation of Buddha nature would not be capable of keeping our eight-year-old self safe in the face of bullies at school. The open, fresh presence alive at the core of our being would not be the right candidate to govern things for a child who's newly coping with a world rife with perceivable threats. After all, the problem isn't that we have defenses, the problem is our neurotic overreliance on them. Furthermore, a child's developing brain isn't capable of abstract processes, such as feeling and processing an emotion all the way through to integration. This would be especially true in the inevitable moments when they are faced with a caregiver failing to provide a felt-sense of safety, rewards, and belonging.

Contemplative psychotherapist Dr. Miles Neale often cites the example of how newborn sea turtles contrast to the dependent situation we're born into. Mama Sea Turtle simply buries her eggs in the sand on a beach and she's done. *Peace out, hatchlings. Best of luck.* From those eggs hatch fledgling mammals already hard-wired to find their way to the ocean and begin caring for themselves. By contrast, we human animals are born so tender, so open to influence, so available for conditioning, *and* so very dependent on others who are most likely holding their own unresolved traumas and confusions. It's a situation primed for folly.

As if being born both radically vulnerable and dependent wasn't enough, our situation is complicated by the subjective nature of experience. That is, it wasn't the objective accounts of events that we internalized as children. We internalized what our child minds perceived.

Looking closer at that last point, do you remember what it was like to be five years old? Think back to all the fantasies you lived in and often believed were true, all the absurdly skewed perceptions of the world you had. When I was five years old, I actually believed that I was capable of flying when I wore my Superman Underoos. *And I had proof!* I would test this by leaping from one living room sofa to the next, and was convinced that this was the early stage of a bourgeoning capability. It was true that I still needed to develop this amazing talent, but I had the basics down. With a little work, I would soon soar like a rocket. I never even had a moment of reckoning with this fiction, of having to admit to myself it wasn't true. I simply outgrew my interest in it.

Now consider that same fantastical mode of perception in a painful situation. Specifically, consider how that child's mind might exacerbate or otherwise see and feel events as being more catastrophic than they actually were. Even experiences that are actually happenstance can easily be internalized by a child as abandonment, neglect, or abuse.

How Model Scenes Work

Imagine a young kid riding a bike without training wheels for the first time, totally proud of herself, exhibiting that endless hunger all kids have to be seen and validated. She shouts, "Look at me!" not knowing that, two seconds before, her dad had received a text message about something extremely distressing—say, another family member having been hit by a car, or having lost a multi-million dollar contract at work, putting his job in peril. Hearing no response, the kid registers disappointment, feels unseen, stops the bike, and turns around to look for Dad. Dad, in his panic doesn't even hear her and appears to be absorbed in his phone. The child's sense of being unimportant and unseen grows. Due to her hardwired negativity bias, the disappointing aspects of the experience take precedence, and the feelings of pride, competence, and autonomy she was on the brink of internalizing as lasting parts of her personal psychology simply vanish.

To borrow another example from Dr. Miles Neale: say a newborn child is safe and sound in his crib, sleeping. Mom is home alone and hasn't had a minute to herself all day because she's been absorbed in lovingly tending to her baby. Finally, she can go to the bathroom. She'll be gone for all of ten minutes, but the infant wakes up hungry after just two minutes. He cries out for Mom's breast or a bottle. The bathroom is downstairs, and Mom forgot to bring the baby monitor with her. She doesn't hear her kid, who's beginning to sense he's alone (read: terrifyingly vulnerable) and becoming increasingly distressed. Mom is usually so attentive that she's always quick to discern when the child is hungry and feeds him right away. As this situation isn't unfolding like the infant is accustomed to, Mom's excellent response record actually works in reverse. That Mom isn't responding, for the first time ever, means an established pattern has been thrown into uncertainty for the infant, which is cause for further alarm. Hello, negativity bias. His cries intensify and for eight full minutes the child is perceiving a life-threatening situation he can do nothing about. His nervous system is flooded with cortisol and adrenaline. The result is an internalization of this *empathic failure*. This internalization is intensified not only by the vulnerability inherent in his young age but also because it is happening pre-language. He is the furthest thing from having a capacity to resolve or understand such matters. An imprint has just been made at a deeply unconscious level—one of abandonment, neglect, and sheer terror. All the while, Mom is a fantastic parent doing her absolute best.

These are the Big Bang moments of our monkey minds. Undoing the negative imprints of such moments is literally what the path of conscious evolution and personal development are about—for most of us, a necessary means to accessing our deeper nature. That said, the evolution of our neurotic patterns is hardly finished. The model scenes we experience are always met by a series of complicating factors.

COMPLICATING FACTOR #1:
PREJUDICE IN THE SOCIAL ENVIRONMENT

We've been working with the attitude of the holding environment as essential groundwork for a fruitful meditation practice. We've seen that environment is everything. The way in which we automatically and unconsciously shift in response to our perceived setting is quite strong. This is true in situations wherein we feel safe and cared for, and it is true in contrasting situations. This brings me to the topic of the kinds of model scenes commonly experienced by people who are not of the dominant race, class, gender, sexual orientation, or able-bodied status in our society. Stop and think of anything threatening, disappointing, or heartbreaking that's happened to you. Now, imagine that happening in a violent neighborhood where drugs are sold. Or in front of parents who are faced with the unspeakable and constant survival-stress of poverty, and are expressing their own complex reactions to that reality. Or at a school that feels more like a prison, complete with metal detectors and underpaid (i.e., bitter and short-tempered) security guards and teachers. Or when you live in fear of being assaulted for your sexual preference. Or when your best friend was attacked for wearing a hijab and you wear one, too. Or when you deal with being catcalled every day. Or when you need a wheelchair to navigate public spaces and wouldn't be able to run if you were attacked. *Or all of the above.*

Traumas that are stand-alone experiences are difficult enough. Traumas that occur in a continuous fashion or within a matrix of other traumas create situations and reactions within us that are even more fraught and difficult to untangle. If this in any way describes your experience (even though I am describing it from the outside, and my acknowledgments are cursory at best), I want you to know you are seen here, and your experience matters.

Our discussion might seem like it's growing away from the subject of meditation and the monkey mind. There are many meditators out there who insist that meditation, Buddhism, and the spiritual life have nothing to do with our personal psychologies or with greater social issues. We will see in the next chapter that nothing could be further from the truth. As we are all interdependent with one another and our environments, we must include the struggle of all beings if we are to recover our experience of intrinsic wholeness and joy. One of the most enormous outcomes of trauma is our propensity to disconnect, objectify, and detach from the humanity of others. We cannot expect to address what's *really* going on in us without developing a sense of connection with how it is for others.

COMPLICATING FACTOR #2:
WE BELIEVE THINGS ARE PERMANENT

We've all had an experience of depression after a heartbreak or loss that felt as if it would go on forever. When we are at our depths, we tend to become convinced that it'll be like this from here on out, and we become as hopeless as Ken Baldwin felt the day he jumped from the Golden Gate Bridge. There's a reason why we need to be reminded of the adage "This too shall pass" when we are in the thick of difficulties.

Similarly, we've all had the experience of being genuinely shocked when something good came to an end. I might know rationally that someday my laptop will suddenly no longer work, but when that day comes, you can bet money that I will be surprised by it, let down, even angry. On some level, I haven't acquiesced to the truth that that day will come. Our capacity for losing sight of how temporary things are is huge.

We are rather convinced that things are permanent, and we act accordingly every day of our lives. Despite a lifetime of direct experience to the contrary—that instead, things are impermanent, constantly changing, constantly in flux, constantly being born, peaking, and dying—on some level we remain in denial of this. This is true of our personal computers, and this is true of the moments when hurt and distress befall us. The same was true for us as children, even more so. Thus, when we feel we are not good enough or that we've been abandoned, we internalize that as if it is a permanent, fixed, never-ending, unworkable situation. Our reasonable distress in response to this perception freezes part of us in time, in the model scene, and in the developmental stage at which that belief developed.

COMPLICATING FACTOR #3: CHILDREN ARE NARCISSISTS

Children are egomaniacs. All of them. They are hardwired to be entirely self-referential; they frame literally everything within The Story of Me (we'll be talking much more about this very compelling story). In other words, it's not just the pain of what we go through, it's what the experience says about us, which is why core wounds always seem to funnel into matters regarding our worth and value. Because if *I'm* obsessed with me, and I have an unconscious, survival-oriented drive for *you* to be obsessed with me, and then you're *not* obsessed with me for even eight minutes—it must be a message about the person I'm obsessed with: me.

Especially in the earliest stages of life, it is highly unlikely for the message a kid receives to say something negative about their caregiver. That's a perception far more intolerable to hold. If I need you for food and safety and my mind spins a story about how you're not good enough, that puts me on very dangerous ground that I am powerless to address. Contrarily, if I run with the interpretation that the experience means *I'm* not good enough, I can do something about that. I can become anxious and clingy. I can figure out how to shut down my need for you and shift toward ambivalence. I can start developing the characteristics of an anxious perfectionist. I can embed the state of narcissism I currently live in and never grow out of it to mask myself from the pain of how insufficient I believe I am.

Finally, in the earliest stages of life, empathetic failures can't be perceived as what they most likely are: inevitable mistakes or human shortsightedness or lack of resources. That's too complex a situation for a small child's brain. They aren't yet able to discern that Mom/Dad/whoever is sometimes "good" and sometimes "bad" because, *surprise! they're human* and therefore complex. In fact, coming to the point of discerning such complexity in people and things is a pivotal developmental milestone in maturation in later adolescence. Sadly, it's something that many people never fully work out.

COMPLICATING FACTOR #4: WE KEEP EXPERIENCING A CARBON COPY OF THE MODEL SCENE

Here, we return to the paradox, a schism, really: our bodies hold on to traumas because we unconsciously fear if we let go, we'll forget to defend ourselves should a similar situation come our way again. Yet, our bodies simultaneously want to shed the trauma so we can return to our natural state of balance and ease. In order to do that, the emotions from the original trauma must be reexperienced in some way; they must return to liquid form so they can become unstuck and move. Thus, our unconscious minds instinctively look for situations that reflect our trauma so we can become triggered as a necessary step toward healing, but in the same breath, we are hardwired to defend ourselves. I believe this is a wrinkle in our evolution as a species that is simply yet to be ironed out. Nonetheless, as with all traumatic situations, that things are this way is not our fault, we are only accountable for what we do with them.

In other words, one part of us gets very excited by situations that put us in familiar distressing situations, and another part of us concocts a story about how that situation is everyone else's fault or how it's some cosmic tragedy ("Why me?"). This makes it very difficult for us to get curious about what's going on or to notice that we ourselves are the common denominator in all of this—which means we stay stuck. It means those frozen emotions become liquid, get frozen again, become liquid again, and become frozen again. All the while, we are deepening and reinforcing the experience's message to us about our worth. A classic example of this: A person fears being seen as unworthy, and so they cling tightly and neurotically to others for validation and are deeply disappointed when they don't get it—thus their clinging drives others away.

To know this and to begin discerning that we are the common denominator in all the repetitive patterns in our lives is empowering. It is doubly so when we can begin to trace these patterns back to their point of origin, the model scene(s) from whence they came. Armed with this level of self-knowledge, in the heat of triggered moments, we then have the opportunity to stop reacting and make a better choice that moves us in the direction of well-being (this is what chapters 13 through 15 are all about). Armed with this level of self-knowledge, we can resume taking responsibility for our own happiness.

Our Unconscious Formula

Thus, it isn't just what has hurt us that haunts us. It's the hurt of whatever was experienced *plus* the painful message it sends our unconscious minds about our worth *plus* the survival terror that comes with those beliefs *plus* the notion that this is a permanent, unfixable situation *plus*, through the repetition compulsion, experiencing the same hurts and frustrations over and over again. Is it any wonder that model scenes have the potential to endure for so long and impact us so deeply? Is it any wonder why our stuckness tends to take so long to work out in therapy?

All of this serves a perfectly good purpose in our personal ecosystems. Yes, you read that right. All of this is part of the monkey's message: poison in the beginning, nectar in the end. It is perhaps the most important message we could ever decode. In part three of this book, we will look at innovative practices that can help us do that decoding. By listening to the monkey mind, we can make our way into underlying model scenes, then correct any lessons we might have learned from them that no longer serve us.

First, however, I want to discuss the biggest impact that difficult and distressing experiences have on us, which has as much to do with our society, culture, and environment as it does with our personal lives and psychologies. If we are going to decode the messages fully, then we've got to understand the corrosion of empathy and its surprisingly far-reaching effects on our lives. Stay tuned.

9

What We Lose
When We Lose Empathy

Only connect.
—E. M. Forster

MINDFUL PRESENCE is a state of being wholly and actively available for one's experience. It is a calling to evolve into our full humanity. Presence, defined in this way, entails growing into unconditional acceptance of what is, and true acceptance necessarily cannot include neutral disinterest or negative regard. Acceptance, then, must entail positive regard—genuine appreciation and welcoming of our experience, the quality of human warmth. This kind of presence is quite enjoyable, though not necessarily easy. To step into this kind of presence is to open to a sense of delight in the world, accompanied by an ability to respond well to situations that are difficult. Without the energy of emotional warmth, such active receptivity would be a form of torture. No monkey mind would willingly sign up for that. And if we're interested in dissolving the repetitious situations in our lives, we must, little by little, become open to experiencing them. We can only do that with warmth. We can only do that with a genuine sense of care for ourselves. Again, to do it otherwise would be quite harsh.

Empathy is like a tortilla. For me, there is no food that is not made more delicious by wrapping it in a tortilla. Similarly, there is no human experience that isn't made more delicious when wrapped in the quality of human warmth. Families, friendships, sex, politics, comedy, art, counter service at a coffee shop, education, exercise, music, Instagram posts—such things are always more satisfying when imbued with a quality of warmth. When we sense this, we naturally connect, identify, or sense belonging, safety, or gratification—it just feels better.

A life lived with empathetic connection or, instead, a life that's cut off, claustrophobic, reactive? Fresh nourishment or stale potato chips? They are both on the menu.

We were born with the qualities of empathy and warmth. We were born totally available to our subjective experience, with a mind that could not say no, a mind intrinsically and wholly connected to things. This most precious experience is the most substantial thing we lose to trauma, though our capacity for it can always be reclaimed as we dissolve the hurts held in our bodies. Such a reclamation is perhaps the chief benefit to engaging in meditation, especially in the ways we are about to explore. I'll offer more on that last sentence in our next chapter. For now, I want to give a full view of the price we pay for ordering the stale option. I believe grasping this will motivate us to continue the journey.

Disconnection Equals Objectification

Disconnection is our habitual relationship whenever we judge the value of something to be neutral or negative. We can ground this in our observable, everyday experience. When we enjoy something, we judge its presence as positive and we lean in with interest. We might even absorb whatever it is into the fabric of our identity. This is perfectly evident in how so many of us put tattoos on our bodies to symbolize things and people and places we want to feel connected to forever. Or, if tattoos aren't your thing, I'll bet you have some T-shirts in your closet that bear some sort of statement that you connect to and identify with. We identify with our political party because we connect to what it represents;

we feel what it stands for will promote desirable situations and eliminate undesirable situations. These things, places, and ideas are alive to us in some way and thus we show them respect and affection.

Yet, once we have judged something as not serving us in some way, unless we've developed a clearer understanding, we'll want it tossed out the door as quickly as possible. We might even pay good money to get the tattoo of an ex-lover's name erased from our arm. Strangely enough, that is actually a form of connection as well, just an inverse one. Similarly, when things don't do much for us, when we perceive things as ho-hum and neutral, we also detach. When the color fades on the shirt in our closet, it goes in the garbage without a thought. When the flavor of the bite of food we just took starts to fade, we simply take the next one. The friend that we've grown away from, even though there was no disagreement or falling out, we simply cease talking to. It might even be years before we stop and realize that this person still exists. We've disconnected.

To disconnect is to assume something is irrelevant, undesirable, adversarial, to be taken for granted, or merely to be used toward our own ends with no further consideration. This is possible only when we consider something or someone to be an object as opposed to a living presence with sovereignty and sentience. (I recognize it might be confounding for me to say "things" have "sovereignty and sentience." Later we will discuss how things such as emotions and the planet we walk on deserve to be treated as if they are living, discrete entities. That is, they are more than mere objects and we definitely have relationships with them. Great understanding can arise from this awareness, and there is empirical evidence to support this.[1] For now, I'll ask that you continue to think within the myth here.) We are capable of treating that which is alive as objects only when we feel no sense of empathy, warmth, or identification. Or perhaps it's the other way around: it is only when we withhold human warmth and decency that the vibrating world around us becomes deadened, flat. Disconnection is synonymous with objectification, the loss of empathy, and desensitization. When a person's feelings cease to matter to us, when their inherent value as a being seems irrelevant, we have objectified them. When we disconnect, when we cease to feel how our actions affect ourselves or others, the unspeakable becomes possible. We are surrounded by so many examples of the cruelty that is possible when we live in a disconnected state.

It's why we have prisoners shave their heads, don a uniform, and replace their names with numbers. To strip someone of their individuality and uniqueness is to strip them of their humanity, which makes it easier for them to be despised and placed in deplorable conditions. It's why combat soldiers are often trained to think of the enemy as animals (hell, this is often the rhetoric even on the national news). When a soldier kills an enemy soldier in combat, that person is referred to quite simply as a "kill." To consider the humanity of such a person would be too traumatic in this situation.

Politicians notoriously employ rhetoric to manipulate us into objectifying entire populations. People from other countries are "rapists" or "animals," and therefore we are absolved of caring about what happens to them. People voting for the other guy are "deplorables" and irrelevant. Sensitive humans quickly become "other" and therefore their pain doesn't count; our hearts need not tremble should they encounter unspeakable atrocity.

Such desensitization and dehumanization aren't confined to prisons, battlefields, and politics; it's universally present in our ordinary, everyday life. We reduce living, breathing people to objects, or we neglect to acknowledge their existence at all. The lives of those we feel connected to are precious to us—we would be devastated if something terrible were to happen to them— and we fear our own deaths tremendously. The extent to which I can write you off as a "loser," or simply as someone who does not belong to my circle, is how much less I will care what happens to you.

Consider that objectification is a principal mechanism in sexism and other forms of bigotry. We are most familiar with hearing the word *objectification* in feminist arenas, where it refers to the ubiquitous social tendency to reduce women to sex objects. The result of this objectification is sexual assault and harassment inflicted in widespread and myriad ways. Objectification is present anytime we allow ourselves to stoop to a reactive level of relating that erases the inherent value and dignity of a person from our minds. We shut out that they, just like us, have dreams and frustrations and things that keep them up at night and a favorite flavor of ice cream and that they mean the world to someone. We may even judge someone as deserving to be in pain in some way; we may even rationalize that we deserve to be the one to deliver it. We no longer listen. We attempt to erase our sense of connection from our awareness; that what impacts this person explicitly impacts us implicitly. After all, our experience of such states of disconnection and desensitization is a hell all its own. Our ability to go there is borne of trauma and multiplies trauma.

At the level of society as a whole, we've enacted a disconnection from and objectification of the earth itself. Our inherent connection to the earth is undeniable. Literally everything we need for survival springs up from the earth: The food we consume forms the building blocks of the living and dying cells that compose our bodies. Our bodies are made of the earth. The raw material for clothing, shelter, and heat all come from the earth. In our industrial and technological age, we've lost sight of this. In a way, we're all convinced these things come from the store. *These new cotton sheets on my bed didn't come from tiny life forms that grew from the nutrients in the soil and the light of the sun; they came from Amazon.com!* Our implicit consciousness is not that such things are provided by the earth; they're provided by the money we earn at our jobs and the marketplaces where we get them.

Of course, the results of our disconnection from environmental reality are starting to become more and more apparent. In 2017 California saw the wettest winter on record, followed by the largest wildfires on record. Texas was devastated by a record-breaking hurricane. Florida was hit by the worst hurricane in its recorded history. Puerto Rico set records for the longest blackout in U.S. history. British Columbia, Canada, had the worst wildfires in its recorded history.[2] In India, the annual monsoon took the lives of 1,200 people, following a trend of steady incline in related mortalities over the past fifteen years.[3] In the United States, requests for emergency funding were ten times higher in 2017 than in 2016.[4]

Our disconnection has led to objectification, and that objectification is what has allowed us to use up the earth's resources and pollute the atmosphere with little to no regard for what impact it is having. We are living in the result of that disconnect and objectification today. Literally in it. Environmental catastrophe, mass incarceration, warfare—these are pronounced results of the kinds of disconnection each of us engages in all the time, no matter who we are or how we see things. It's actually not our fault. We simply cannot help but to internalize the conventions of modern society, which see disconnection as normalcy. Acting in the same way as those we see around us is part of how our minds and bodies work. We are, however, responsible for, and will bear the consequences of, what we choose to do about it.

As I contend throughout this book, we cannot fix disconnection with more disconnection—we cannot heal it with shame, rejection, resentment, neurotic anger, and aggression. Instead, the response always needs to be rooted in compassion (which sometimes even entails a wise form of anger). I also believe that, if we want to address the large-scale forms of disconnection and objectification we see in our communities, in our society, and on the earth, we will need to recover the skills of connecting and relating to the basic ingredients of our own lives: our emotions, our relationships, our bodies—the subjects our monkey minds are so often screaming about.

OBJECTIFICATION OF EMOTIONS EQUALS OBJECTIFICATION OF PEOPLE

Freud coined the term *affect phobia* to describe the way so many of us are consciously and unconsciously afraid of letting our emotions arise and be felt, acknowledged, expressed, and processed. Just like food, they need to be tasted, masticated, digested, and metabolized in order for us to move on. Yet that's the exact trajectory our emotions need to follow in order not to go "underground" in our bodies and psyches, where they cause all kinds of other, more insidious problems. We could even say our emotions themselves have a will and desire to complete such a process. When they do, they tend to provide "nutrients" in the form of insights, lessons, and an expansion of both our distress tolerance and our ability to discern and relate to the emotions of others (the opposite of sociopathy). Yet, our habitual relationship to emotions is one of disconnection: to treat them as either boss or enemy, we either repress or let them take over. Neither of these options do us any good. Neither of these options respect the power and utility of our emotions, which is often made evident when we honor them and allow them in (more on that in chapter 13).

Paradoxically, indulging our emotions can be yet another form of disconnection—and often it entails both disconnection from our emotions themselves and from the people around us. When strong feelings flood us, our habitual tendency is to allow them to dictate our actions and decisions, often to disastrous ends, and this is actually an unconscious strategy to displace them onto someone or something else. As the saying goes, "Hurt people hurt people." We tend to try to pass on the pain we feel to others instead of connecting to it and holding it ourselves. Sadly, this never works. The pain simply grows and even multiplies with each person we impact with our afflicted state.

This relates to the ways in which we feel disconnected from one another. We feel independent rather than interdependent, but the truth is much closer to something Dr. Martin Luther King Jr. once said: "Before you've finished breakfast, you've depended on half the world." When was the last time you walked down the street with a true awareness that every person you pass has a life that is precious to them, that they struggle to keep afloat in some way or another? As the famous saying goes, "Be kind, for everyone is fighting a great battle you know nothing about." We live disconnected from this reality, from anyone who isn't within our circle of relations, and often from many who are.

We operate this way with good reason: we intuit that it might be overwhelming to actually live with such a sensitive and open awareness. We might *feel* too much. We might be torn to shreds if we were to allow ourselves to open fully to the pulsing, feeling, often struggling humanity that surrounds us. Furthermore, we've been burned before. We've been hurt, insulted, betrayed, and treated like objects ourselves. Shutting down and narrowing our world seems like the logical response when this happens; the imperative of our limbic stress response demands it, and we are inclined to obey. We make rules for other people to follow, then decide what people deserve from us if they fail. We get paranoid we might be left high and dry in intimate situations; we fear that too much closeness will come at the expense of freedom. We might even treat moments of joy with suspicion, perhaps out of fear of our vulnerability.

The inner outcome of our unconscious and pervasive tendency to disconnect and objectify is twofold. For one, we begin to live in a world that is quite narrow, closed off. The extent to which we have disconnected and objectified is the extent to which we live in a world in which very few people feel dear to us. Objects, after all, are dead. The extent to which we objectify others is the extent to which we are unable to give or receive love and warmth; to feel things like gratitude and appreciation; and to touch the deep inspiration, awe, and wonder each of us were born with a capacity for. To go without these things is untenable to the human psyche. It is starvation to the heart. To reconnect and disrupt the illusion of objectification, then, is to begin to untangle the confusion and fear that is the monkey mind's very fuel.

Chögyam Trungpa Rinpoche referred to this closed-off experience of life as "the cocoon." It might be cozy and warm to live in a cocoon, but it's very dank, very dark, and there's not a lot of room for possibility. It's perfectly reasonable to choose this option: it's safe, less vulnerable, a comfort zone. But it is also a prison. "What insulates isolates," as my former psychotherapy supervisor used to say. What feels like a womb is actually our tomb.

The second outcome is that the objectification turns inward, and we suffer our immense capacity for self-abuse.

OBJECTIFYING OURSELVES

Our traumas and resultant beliefs lead us to disavow parts of ourselves and become fragmented. Consider the common view that being hard on ourselves—even hating parts of ourselves—is how to go about making progress. We seem to be genuinely convinced that ignoring or even going to war with ourselves is going to lead us to the lives we want. Yet, to quote again from the great Martin Luther King Jr.: "Hate cannot drive out hate, only love can do that."

At the other end of the worthiness spectrum, we have narcissism, self-aggrandization, and the like—what we all know are masks we put on to compensate for our own insecurity and sense of unworthiness. Egocentricism is a special, inverse kind of pain—so often we grasp for lifelines that turn out to be daggers.

These inner dynamics certainly show up in the way many meditators approach practice. All too often, we sit down not even realizing that we're already disconnected from and divided against ourselves. The subtle intention held in the back of our minds is to shut the monkey up, to get rid of our anxiety and difficult emotions, and somehow to replace the experience of our ordinary selves with a more enlightened one. As we saw in chapter 4, there's a way to bring a clear and decisive energy to meditation, which is necessary in order to establish a disciplined practice. But we don't need to go to war with ourselves in order to do that. All too often, our approach to meditation involves treating the body and breath as if they were objects, and thus blinding ourselves to their natural wisdom and vitality. We judge our minds for being so busy, or our emotions for not being as peaceful as we imagine they're supposed to be during meditation. We get angry at our anger. We hate ourselves for not being more loving. Anytime we abandon, ignore, or struggle against any part of ourselves whatsoever, we are enacting aggression. We become bullies in the playground of our practice, unconsciously believing that this is somehow a way to buddhahood. As my first meditation teacher, Vinny Ferraro, puts it, "We try to hate ourselves into enlightenment."

How wild is it to realize that the very same propensity to disconnect, the very energy that allows people to engage in activities as horrific as terrorism and trafficking in persons, is alive and well inside us, too? That it can be present even in the midst of our meditation practice?

Meditation will only bear the meaningful, transformative fruit we all desire if we engage in it with the intention to recover the experience of connection. There is no presence without opening, albeit little by little, to the vast aliveness in us and all around us. Awareness and selective blindness are mutually exclusive. How can we expect to feel truly connected if we conceive of our meditation as being an act *against* the monkey mind? Thus, we must concede right away that sitting down for practice is an act of self-love, not just self-care. Presence, empathy, and connection are inextricably intertwined. In fact, *attention is the vehicle of connection.* That's one of the reasons why meditation necessarily involves paying attention.

PRACTICING COMPASSION

Compassion, the antidote to disconnection, is often misunderstood at the conceptual level. We tend to think of it as being synonymous with love, empathy, kindness, sympathy, or even pity. Although I would say that, except pity, all of those are ingredients in compassion, compassion is something more. The classical definition of compassion aligns with the etymology of the word: *compassion*—"suffering (*-passion*) with (*com-*)." It is indeed synonymous with empathy, to feel someone's pain as if it were your own. As I stated before, we are born hardwired with this capacity, though we develop sophisticated ways to shut down this and other natural responses. The word the Buddha used for compassion, *karuna*, is sometimes translated as "a quivering of the heart." These two definitions take *compassion* as a noun, as an emotional state. Compassion, however, must also be a verb. It can be psycho-emotional in nature, but it necessarily must lead to action for it to be genuine. If you feel the sting of a cut on your arm, you naturally get up and get a bandage with some urgency. If compassion means you feel someone's suffering as your own, then it logically follows that you will act on that feeling. Therefore, if I am to treat the cut on *your* arm as if it were my own, it follows that I would have the same sense of urgency to get a bandage for you as I did for me. So, compassion is opening to our natural capacity for feeling into the hurts of another and taking the healing course of action that grows out of this—rarely the action of fixing things, giving advice, or feeling torn down because we empathically feel too much of someone else's struggle, but always the activity of being with and feeling into what's needed.

Chögyam Trungpa Rinpoche offered a contrasting view of

compassion that I find to be most uplifting and empowering. He defined *karuna* as having a genuine appreciation for the world and the beings in it. He also stated that compassion has the quality of delight to it.[5] When we have a true, felt-sense of appreciation for the world around us and the beings in it—which necessarily means that we have dropped our defensive objectifications and are willing to feel into the pulsating, living qualities all things have—acting with sensitivity organically follows. To me, this is synonymous with taking the world as a holding environment: offering our warmth unconditionally so that experiences of all kinds can arise and not have their existence denied. What I like most about Trungpa Rinpoche's definition is that there is energy to it, inspiration. It offers a very lighthearted approach to resolving what is a heavy dilemma. It is genuine appreciation and delight coupled with a realness about suffering, taking action toward the relief of suffering *because* the world is worthy of our appreciation and everyone deserves the opportunity to delight in it.

Part Three: Heart

WITH THE CRUCIAL NATURE of empathy and connectivity firmly in mind, we now move into discussion material and practices designed to uncover the natural empathy and warmth within us. We've established what goes wrong when empathy corrodes; it is now time we talk about what goes right when such qualities of the heart are roused. This is literally the direction the monkey mind has been trying to point us in all along, its ultimate message. As you will see, such a journey begins with discovering a wellspring of gratification and growth lying within us, and ends with the opportunity to apply these strengths toward healing our painful relationship to stored traumas and wounds. The monkey's call has always been for us to heal our life at the deepest level.

In the opening chapters of part three, we will focus on what is considered to be the natural outgrowth of shamatha meditation: maitri, or lovingkindness meditation. I'll unpack exactly how this practice undercuts all our narratives by getting to the brass tacks of what we're *actually* thinking about, beneath the surface. In chapter 12, I'll discuss why healing our life is the most important work we could ever do. In chapter 13, I'll offer a straightforward model for understanding our emotional lives, and a practice for healing our model scenes. In chapter 14, I will offer some clarity around the intrusive thoughts and voices so many of us struggle with, such as the inner critic. In our final chapter, we will combine all the work we've done together into something that's never been put together before: an integration of Buddhist practice with the "parts work" of an evidence-based therapeutic modality known as Internal Family Systems.

10

The Challenge of Self-Love

Fear is a natural reaction to moving closer to the truth.
—PEMA CHÖDRÖN

It's not so much that we're afraid of change or so in love with
the old ways, but it's that place in between that we fear.
It's like being between trapezes. It's Linus when his blanket
is in the dryer. There's nothing to hold on to.
—MARILYN FERGUSON

MEDITATION CAN BE like turning on the lights in a dark room we've managed to take up residence in. Perhaps we've lived here so long our eyes have adjusted to the darkness. We may have gotten used to finding our way around by feeling for the familiar textures of certain things. We may have memorized the number of paces from one end of the room to the other and how many paces from the bed to the door. Perhaps darkness feels like home, and we've gotten cozy living like a mole. Maybe it's even the only home we've ever known. But when the lights turn on, we may be aghast to discover piles of debris in the corners, a secret mess in the closet, cracks in the support beams, a trapdoor that we never knew existed leading to god-knows-where. We may suddenly want to turn the lights back off and go back to the way things were. But we can't unsee what we've seen. We'll never be able to get comfortable in this place again—until we clean it up.

That's the bad news. The good news is, cleaning it up just might become the most satisfying thing we've ever done.

It feels burdensome at first, tending to this place. Now that we see, we don't really have a choice. But we begin to realize: "This is where I live. Every bit of energy I invest here is energy invested in where I lay my head at night and what I wake up to in the morning." We may notice the fact that we couldn't tell how asleep we were, before we started to wake up. Sooner or later, we discover pure gold underneath the dust in the ashtrays and light streaming from lamps we'd never noticed. We might get curious about what other wonders we're still blind to. Doing this work may begin to make more sense than anything we've ever done before. We might even discover a strange sense of joyful enthusiasm about the uncomfortable work that lies ahead.

No one enjoys living like a mole. People sometimes talk like they do, but that's just a story they tell themselves.

MEDICINE FOR THE COMATOSE HEART

It was startling in my earliest days of practice to realize I felt dead on the inside. Frustration would overcome me in therapy appointments. Here I was, finally aware of all my traumas, wanting to work them out, but then I'd go blank every time we'd approach emotional intensity. I had done too good a job of numbing myself for too many years. My emotional repertoire was pared down to the most primitive options: anger, cynicism, restlessness, insatiable hunger, and occasional bursts of absurdity (pretty much the only emotions I ever experienced coming from my father). I began to wonder if I was broken for good.

I was fresh out of rehab when I took up a practice called *maitri*, or lovingkindness. It's a set of practices that represent the natural outgrowth of shamatha meditation. Having formed a foundation of attention, warmth, and embodiment, the next step is to further awaken the heart. The instructions aren't difficult: one simply repeats phrases imbued with benevolence in one's mind while developing an ability to feel their essence. The phrases I first worked with were, "May I be happy. May I be healthy. May I live with ease. May I be free." With these phrases, we reintegrate the linguistic left brain in a smart way: as the servant of the right brain.

I can see in my mind the window on Fulton Street in San Francisco where I'd sit, repeating the prescribed phrases to myself, daunted by how mechanical they felt. The instructions in Jack Kornfield's *A Path with Heart* warned me of this. He had advised to simply keep going until something shifted. There were mornings when I rose from my seat more frustrated and depressed than when I had first sat down. It just didn't seem to be working. The practice felt inauthentic. Everything in me resisted. The monkey mind screamed. Part of me resented the saccharine quality of the practice. It all seemed so flimsy. *I'm a recovering junkie, for Christ's sake. "May I be happy"? Really?!* Another part of me resented myself for having such little sincerity. Another part of me insisted that I was damaged goods, a hopeless case, and I should save myself the trouble. And yet, another part of me trusted Mr. Kornfield, trusted that meditation had already helped me so much, and trusted the science behind the practice. So, I heeded the call: keep going.

I remember the exact morning something broke open in me. I can still feel the actual sensation I had in my chest, face, and belly on the day when the lights came back on. Genuine, warm feelings astonished me when they arrived. The maitri phrases, once dull and rote, now felt alive in some way. *May I be FREE.* It was as if the sole window in my own personal dark room had been painted black, such that I had become convinced that the sun no longer existed. But on this day, a chip of that black paint fell off and a ray of light streaked in. On this day I felt as if the maitri phrases were the very force chipping away at that paint—slowly, slowly, one by one.

The sun had been there all along. I had just lost my experience of it.

Meditation Is Medicine

I began teaching a workshop series called "The 30-Day Self-Love Challenge" based on my experience. The original idea of the workshop was to disseminate self-focused maitri by guiding participants to simply stay with the practice until something shifted for them. I was surprised to discover that the voices of resistance, shame, and doubt I had experienced were just as strong, if not stronger, in those I was teaching to, and these were people who hadn't done time under the needle with hard drugs. My internal reaction to this practice wasn't the result of my numbing myself all those years. It was much more universal than that.

The voices that tell us we can't, we're no good, we're unlovable, we're fake, and it's only a matter of time until they figure us out—these voices reflect people's deepest hurts and negative beliefs about themselves. And, with great consistency, all of these voices get triggered by lovingkindness practice. *Lovingkindness*, of all things. The practice is like throwing a purifying agent into a vat of toxic chemicals: the impurities come right to the surface. But these aren't just meaningless garbage, voices we should push past. These thoughts represent parts of us that have been abused, neglected, abandoned, pushed around, shamed, hated, and belittled for far too long. These thoughts are essentially the voices of our inner children, perhaps the ones who need and deserve our maitri the most. Today I am convinced that, when these voices arise, we shouldn't ignore them or try to force our way around them. These are the deeper echoes of the monkey's message. There's treasure to be found beneath their surface appearance, beneath the dust in the ashtrays.

If you've ever done a juice cleanse and found that you became sick or developed a rash or a screaming headache from the detox, you'll get this. If you've ever made clarified butter or warm milk and have seen how milk solids rise to the top in response to heat, you'll get this: The psychosomatic energy of maitri is purifying. It pushes our emotional toxins right to the surface. Then, just as the skin on warm milk can be removed, our afflictions and limiting beliefs can be dealt with.

CHARNEL GROUNDS:
THE FIERCE ORIGINS OF MAITRI MEDITATION

Before we even get down to the practice, I want to dispel any subconscious gossip that meditating on love is just emotional bosh—"boring hippy shite," as Johnny Rotten snarls in the movie *Sid and Nancy*.

For many of us, the Buddha represents serenity. We like to think of him as a round-bellied laughing man sitting "Zen-like," without a care in the world, atop a hill someplace. To the contrary, the Buddha was a consummate badass. He lived in the jungle, where eagles dare, where uncertainty prevailed. He eschewed the classist and sexist norms of ancient India and taught freely to everyone—including members of the lower castes and women (both of whom were barred from receiving spiritual teachings). He also instructed his students to practice in some pretty wild places so they could work with their fear, work with their hurts, and work with their *ghosts*.

The mythos goes that the Buddha sent some of his students to practice meditation in the local charnel grounds, the place where dead bodies were cremated. Big surprise: the joint turned out to be haunted. The poltergeists hanging around these fearsome places came at the meditators with their worst ghost antics and ran them off. The students went back to the Buddha and threw their hands up: "Meditating the way you've asked us to— it's impossible!" (Sound familiar?) The Buddha said, "No, this is utterly possible; I wouldn't ask you to do it if it wasn't possible." The monks and nuns returned to the charnel grounds only to be met with intolerable hauntings once again. They returned to the Buddha, full of the same complaints. Finally, the Buddha, like a doctor writing a prescription, gave them the earliest form we have of lovingkindness meditation.

The meditators were told to steady their concentration on feelings of empathy, warmth, and benevolence. The instruction was to get them to stimulate the energies of the heart: love, compassion, sympathetic joy (i.e., perceiving others' happiness as a cause for one's own), and equanimity (resilience). He encouraged them to wish these things for the specters they met in their practice and to offer them, the most unwanted of experiences, the energy of caring. The students returned and followed the instructions. Through the practice, it's said that they generated a field of lovingkindness that was so strong that the ghosts themselves were transformed by it. Once the meditators' enemies, the haunting spirits now found themselves inspired to become their allies, and they began to bring the meditators food and supplies and to protect them from the elements.[1]

Thinking within the myth, we can ask, "what sort of charnel grounds do we have inside ourselves?" So many of us feel haunted by the ghosts of resentment, lack of confidence, self-hatred, the never-ending need to achieve, feelings of worthlessness when we fail, unresolved anger, memories of traumatic and hurtful experiences, insatiable longing, cravings, loneliness, emptiness, hopelessness, and callousness toward others. How many attempts have we made to evict these ghosts? To avoid and deny them? How long have we tried to numb and distract ourselves from them only to find they don't budge? How many of us have conceded that this is "just the way I am"?

It's just like in the 1980s Jim Henson movie *The Dark Crystal*. When the Crystal of Truth splits in two, the race of peaceful beings inhabiting the planet Thra also splits into two: the Skeksis and the Mystics. The Skeksis get power hungry, become tyrannical, and send the Mystics into hiding. A once harmonious planet falls into the oppressive rule of the Skeksis for a thousand years. The ages-long split, however, is resolved after a heroic effort by members of the slave race, the Gelflings, who recover the split-off crystal shard and reunite it with its source. When the Crystal of Truth is restored, the Skeksis and the Mystics reintegrate. They merge because they were ultimately the same beings all along. Despite a millennium of living as fragments of themselves (which is what made tyranny and slavery possible) we find in the end that the terrible Skeksis and the meditative Mystics never stopped belonging to one another.

The inner ghosts we meet with both in practice and in daily life are not anyone or anything other than parts of ourselves. We have simply split off from ourselves, and our deeper wisdom has been sent into hiding. The defensive and managerial "ego" aspects of ourselves have become tyrannical, convinced that they need to hold the power, because our inner Mystics are just too vulnerable. We have a subconscious narrative that Skeksi-monkey energies like stress, anger, control, self-reliance, neediness, numbness, and even self-hatred are much better at manifesting the versions of ourselves best equipped for dealing with life—even though they usurp our well-being. This may have been actually true in childhood, but *whoa*, is this an outdated myth.

This split is maintained by the fact that we have hurts and weaker parts of us—Gelfling parts of us—that we sense we must keep from being exposed at all costs. We must keep them locked up; to allow them to run free would be too overwhelming. That this way of going about things may seem to be the only option for us.

Like the Sakyamuni in his early days of searching for truth, we ourselves have gone to therapy that didn't work, we've done all the yoga, tried to find the perfect partner, got a better education, got a better job, tried seeing healers, and yet these parts of ourselves that assail us still seem to be stuck in place. What we will be exploring in the chapters to come are processes by which we can get unstuck. Processes whereby we can fully process and fully integrate; whereby our ghosts can become our allies; whereby we can relieve the slaves of sorrow and hurt of their burdens; whereby we can align with our inner tyrants—retaining their power and protective qualities, but working for, not against, our wisest self— whereby we restore the harmony we were meant to have, and did have for a brief while as infants or children; whereby we can recover our experience of the sun, our experience of intrinsic wholeness.

Despite what you may have heard or tried before, self-love and healing don't entail trying to fix or get rid of the haunted parts of ourselves. When we attempt to disavow these parts, all we accomplish is creating an inner struggle. Such an approach follows the logic of cutting off our finger because we don't like the way it looks. It is only when we mindfully shift our relationship to our inner ugly fingers that we can be in harmony with ourselves. Thus, we begin the courageous and transformative work of bringing our unwanted parts front and center in our awareness. We will make them the focus of our practice, the focus of our lovingkindness.

Neurotic Judgment and the Comparing Mind

Our propensity to look out at others and compare ourselves to them is bound up with judging ourselves harshly. Our nagging sense of not being good enough, not being able to keep up, not belonging, not being loveable—these tense expressions of survival terror are comparative in nature. Someone can claim they are good enough only compared to someone else who is relatively not good enough. Someone can be a coward only when compared to someone who is relatively brave. A person can feel social redemption only in a world where so many others are rejected, outcast, unbelonging. These ideas and feelings do not exist independent of comparisons, so they do not exist objectively in the world. Please read that sentence again and absorb its implications. No matter what our confirmation bias tells us, our most common stories about ourselves—"not good enough," "unworthy," "failure," "unlovable," "I'm shit"—do not actually exist in the observable world. That is, we cannot hold in our hands a value judgment regarding our worthiness (or anyone else's for that matter). As real as such narratives may feel to us, and as utterly valid as they always are, they exist only in the realm of the mind. Ultimately, they are stories, nothing more. *Ghosts.*

It is as if we sleepwalked into a beauty pageant, talent contest, or some dismal year-end employee review in our minds. *Charnel grounds.* Winning at such imaginary competitions temporarily pays off: we can privately reduce another person or people to the status of unworthiness; we can objectify someone or some group and then project onto them our worst fear. We feel safe, secure, and powerful, and for the moment this falsely satisfies the primary imperative of psycho-biological survival—it's like eating candy instead of dinner. And yet this is just a cocoon. It's only a matter of time before someone comes along who shreds us to pieces in a category of life where our perceived mediocrity is exposed. Almost instantly, we descend from OK-ness into despair. This is the price of admission to the "good enough contests" we so innocently enter.

True self-worth does not come through telling ourselves, "I'm good enough." Such affirmations do little to liberate us from the mind games in which at some point everyone loses. Knowing this, the self-loving person simply puts down the game. The self-loving person can experience a sense of "not good enough," can even receive criticism and endure failures, but they can discern them accurately and not be triggered into judgment and emotional deflation. Such a person is adequately in touch with the intrinsic worth, value, dignity, and love within themselves—in touch enough not to enter the "good enough contest" in the first place. This is the potential of self-maitri practice.

Such intrinsic worthiness and love are not the opposites of hate and unworthiness. They lie beyond the realm of judgment and ordinary affection. They represent a truth, an experience that can only come from touching the ground of our natural state. They are what's left when we undo the tension in our lives, the deepest root of which is trauma and unresolved emotions born of adverse experiences. Genuine dignity and self-love are never generated, only uncovered.

To drop out of the oppressive mental talent show requires discernment. The ability to pause in the face of the stress that accompanies insecurity and apply discernment—this is the habit we are building and strengthening in earnest meditation. It is part and parcel of the neocortical functions we are wiring with each return from distraction, with each release of the exhale, with each repetition of a maitri phrase. The nature of such an ability is in contrast to that of our more ordinary habits. It comes from decidedly favoring the risk of openheartedness over the cozy cocoon of the monkey mind, the deadened domicile of habitual responses.

Paradox #4,537: If we want to fix our life, we'll need to stop trying to fix it. When we learn to simply *meet* our life in the appropriate way, life tends to fix things in ways we couldn't have conceived in the first place. Again, the nature of the human organism is to heal itself when in the presence of the appropriate conditions. What are those conditions? Presence, warmth, and generosity. That is, H.E.R.E. + time. Holding environment, Embodiment, Returning from distraction, Easy breath + *simply keep going.* When we add the energy of maitri to this mix, it can be like tossing gasoline on a fire. It is amplifying the essence of shamatha. (In the beginning, it may feel more like tossing lighter fluid on a stove burner, but I digress.)

Self-Maitri Prep

The elegance of lovingkindness practice lies in its simplicity. We will return to a form of embodied mindfulness of the breath (set in its natural rhythm), but with a twist. We will incorporate four phrases of maitri directed toward ourselves, working with the same four phrases for the entire practice. This will be very much like working with a mantra—a meaningful phrase repeated over and over again—except we are looking for *feeling* to eventually arise here. We are excavating the heart.

One might be tempted to think of this practice as flimsy, "granola," unicorns and rainbows, but don't be fooled: it is quite fierce. It's very common for it to be triggering—all kinds of self-doubt and self-loathing may come to the surface. Do not be dismayed, and do not be surprised. Again, keep going. You can even choose to send the lovingkindness phrases to the voices that are assailing you. I will discuss this at length in the chapters to come.

STAYING ON TRACK

To aid in continuity, I recommend that you obtain a *mala*, a string of prayer beads, which are easily available online if nowhere else near you. Alternatively, you could use a rosary or, hell, even a string of Mardi Gras beads will do. If you don't have any of these, no sweat: you still have your hands. If you have a mala, simply hold one bead between a thumb and a finger on the same hand (traditionally, it's supposed to be your third or pinkie finger, but feel free to ignore that) as you repeat one maitri phrase for one breath cycle. Then, move to the next bead with the next phrase and breath, and so on. If you are using your hand, simply press your thumb against your index finger for the first phrase, your middle finger for the second, your ring finger for the third, and your pinkie finger for the fourth, then begin the cycle again at the index finger.

Some phrases that I find to be powerful:

- May I be filled with love
- May I feel safe
- May I feel inspired
- May I awaken and be free

If mine don't work for you, please choose your own. You can find phrases from a teacher, or simply create ones that work for you. It's important, though, that once you choose your phrases, you keep them exactly the same throughout the practice. Let whatever needs to come up in response to them come up. Here are some more examples:

- May I feel held in great lovingkindness
- May I be well
- May I feel peaceful, serene
- May I be at ease
- May I be happy
- May my heart heal
- May my heart open

You can practice along with the audio available on the website, for training wheels, or practice silently on your own. When practicing on your own, always set a timer. The timer on your phone will do.

PRACTICE: *Self-Maitri*

PRELIMINARIES

Try setting the attitude of the holding environment before you even sit down. Sit down already mindful of your body and movements, already aware that this is a safe, connected situation. Relate to body and earth by finding a stable and aligned posture.

Practice an appropriate breathwork as needed (as described on pages 103–6 of chapter 7).

Practice Sun Meditation (as described on page 53) three times briskly to relax and to place the majority of your awareness beneath your shoulders.

Set the breath in its natural rhythm. Feel the waves rising and falling in the space of the heart. Then begin.

As you inhale, mentally repeat one phrase. As you exhale, allow the phrase to resonate. Do this with each phrase below. Go slow.

> May I be filled with love
> May I feel safe
> May I feel inspired
> May I awaken and be free

Repeat continuously for the length of your practice.

To end your practice, spend some time dedicating your efforts to others by very simply turning the phrases outward:

> May all beings be filled with love
> May all beings feel safe
> May all beings feel inspired
> May all beings awaken and be free

11

The Monkey Is a Mensch

Admit something.
Everyone you see, you say to them,
"Love me."
Of course you do not do this out loud,
otherwise someone would call the cops.
Still, though, think about this,
This great pull in us to connect.
Why not become the one who lives
With a full moon in each eye
That is always saying,
With that sweet moon language,
What every other eye in this world
Is dying to hear?
—HAFIZ, "WITH THAT MOON LANGUAGE"

THE GREATEST STORY EVER TOLD

OUR THOUGHTS TELL a compelling story: the Story of Me. It's no wonder they've come to rule our lives. Thoughts spin stories about what we love and what we hate, how great we are and how horrible we are, all the places we want to go, all the things we'd better not forget to do, all the things we want to see and eat, and everything we must avoid. It's a 24/7 podcast titled *Me*. The great Indian sage Ramana Maharshi pointed out that every single thought we have begins with "I" in some way. Our inner narratives are 99.999 percent self-referential. Even when we think about others, we tend to think about them in relation to ourselves and our feelings about them. Even if we want to help or give to others, we tend to think about what we ourselves feel other people need and what we'd like to do for them. Or maybe our motivation is influenced by how helping someone out will make us look to others, how "spiritual" we'll become, or how worthy a generous act will make us feel.

In the outtakes of the movie *Pulp Fiction*, there's a scene I cannot believe didn't make the final cut. When Vincent Vega (John Travolta's character) arrives to pick up Mia Wallace (played by Uma Thurman) for their night out, she interviews him on a camcorder before they leave. Her first question for him: "When in conversation, do you listen or wait to talk?" After a brief pause Vega responds with unusual honesty: "I have to admit that I wait to talk, but I'm trying hard to listen."

How many of us barely listen while waiting to talk in conversation? How many of us find it challenging to wait until the other person is finished? How many of us stop and take in what is being said to us when in dialogue? It's as if we can barely wait to get back to the Story of Me. Equally poignant is that Vega says he's "trying *hard* to listen." It's difficult to surrender ourselves for even a few moments. It's hard to give people, even people we love and hold dear, the kind of attention and receptivity we ourselves so long for. I find it ironic that our default mode is to retell the same old Story that we've heard a thousand and one times before, whereas directly experiencing the fresh and vibrant world and the fascinating people right in front of us takes effort. Even the people we can't stand are, from a certain vantage point, far more interesting than the stale laundry lists we keep cycling through.

This discussion finds us back at a familiar juncture: the Story of Me is simply the safer choice to our reptilian and mammalian brains. Taking in the vast and uncertain world—giving our whole attention over to other people for more than a few moments—leaves us vulnerable. Better to relate to things from the edge of our cocoon, so we can retreat at any time.

It can be alarming to wake up to just how extreme our tendency toward self-referential thinking can be. It's like we are snagged in a neurotic net of our own needs, wants, and strategies. It's like the monkey is strung out on a drug called "self-concern," fiending for the next hit the moment we lose the full attention of our own minds. Is it any wonder this tendency is often taken as a basis for recrimination? Religions see this situation as evidence that human nature itself is inherently evil, narcissistic, and even violent. Entire cultures have become rooted in guilt, shame, and the need to repent and punish ourselves for apparent selfishness that is actually rooted in our drive for safety. It is heartbreaking to consider the depth and breadth of such imposed self-aggression. Especially when we consider that such attitudes only serve to reinforce the Story of Me. "I'm a shameful sinner" is just a different performance of the Story in which "I" is still the star.

I will continue to insist: the mind is not our enemy. The chaotic and self-centered mind is not our foe, nor is it something to cling to. It is an encrypted message, hand delivered by the monkey. One that actually isn't too hard to decode.

THE TWO CATEGORIES OF THOUGHT

Take five minutes to write down everything you can remember thinking about today. Then notice that every single one of them follows two basic themes. When we look underneath the contents of our thoughts and stories, it isn't hard to see that everything—absolutely everything that we think about—can be collapsed into one of two categories: "How Can I Be Happy?" and "How Can I Avoid Suffering?" Take a look at your list again and tell me it isn't true. You can also go back to the universal examples I laid out in chapter 4 and see if there's a thought that *doesn't* relate to our basic drives to go toward what feels like growth or a reward, or to keep ourselves safe from what would be painful, difficult, or dangerous.

Simplified in this way, does anything about this sound evil or petty to you? I find it impossible to judge anyone who is just try-ing to feel safe and loved. Beings naturally want to feel good and not be in anguish. Of course, there are complex, confused, and aggressive expressions of these two fundamental motivations, and we must contend with these. Yet, even the most narcissis-tic and malevolent person out there is thinking and behaving in a manner that their monkey mind is claiming will take them toward fulfillment and away from dissatisfaction and danger. Even suicidality is an expression of our survival instinct and drive toward well-being. Suicidal ideation is, at its core, an extreme expression of wanting the pain to stop. If the pain were to be removed, that person would no longer have thoughts about want-ing to die. How can we conceive of something or someone as pathological when the basic motivation is wanting to not suffer? I must remind us here of Ken Baldwin, the Golden Gate Bridge jumper who realized mid-air that what seemed impossible (deal-ing with his problems) was utterly possible. Shifting from "the pain of my problems will never go away," to "it might be hard, but these situations are totally workable," he found the will to live while in the most terrifying of situations.

Once Again, Meditation for the Win

You can take it as a coincidence or as a stroke of brilliance that there's a traditional meditation from the Buddhist canon that speaks directly to these matters. Maitri practice dives beneath these surface-layer expressions of our grasping and aversion and gets right to the point. It meets us exactly where we're at: thinking in a self-concerned fashion. We begin maitri by essentially say-ing, "May the good in me increase, and may my confusions and sufferings decrease." The name of the practice implies that these express the essence of what love is. Ultimately, our deepest nature is love itself. Everything else about us comes from some form of longing for love, and our fundamental need to be safe and well.

The traditional instructions for this practice offer an important distinction. The phrases traditionally offered in the practice don't stop at "may I be happy," for example, but rather, "may I be happy *and have the causes of happiness.*" This final, more nuanced aspect of the root thought acknowledges that our ordinary attempts at attaining pleasure and avoiding pain generally come up short. Nectar in the beginning, poison in the end. The thoughts we have around attaining happiness are generally about how we'll feel complete when we get _____ or get rid of _____. And we're convinced that what we seek is just around the corner. It always seems to be contained in the next thing we'll acquire or the next experience we'll have. This has been dubbed "I'll Be Happy When Syndrome." And in the words of Vinny Ferraro, "When we think things need to be some other way in order for us be satisfied with the moment, we've already missed the *only* moment satisfaction could ever be experienced in."

So what would it mean to have not just happiness but the causes of happiness? What does it look like to have not just well-being but the root of well-being?

Getting What You Want by Giving It Away

I cook a great deal. Despite living in New York City, where cuisine from almost any ethnicity is readily available within blocks of my apartment, I prefer to know exactly what I'm putting in my body. Yet, as someone who lives alone, I can't help but notice that the meal I make for myself is *not* the meal I'd prepare if I had guests over for dinner. When I cook for others, it's a multicourse situation. There's likely to be a salad, some fresh form of protein, and a side dish. I may go all out and make an appetizer. Wine and dessert are generally involved. The cloth napkins come out. If I'm eating by myself, dinner very well could be a bowl of cold cereal eaten standing over the kitchen counter. At best, it's a single course, and it rarely feels like an event. I go further—much further—any time other people are involved. And I'm not just talking about dinner—it's true in my meditation practice as well.

When we practice lovingkindness for others, it is actually in service of our own well-being. When we make the better meal because it will be enjoyed by guests, we get to enjoy that meal, too. When we practice giving away what we want, wishing for happiness to increase and suffering to decrease in the beings around us, we ourselves receive the lion's share of the benefit and strengthen our ability to live in higher emotional responses. Tibetan Buddhist teacher Charlie Morley calls it a "Happiness Paradox." When we wish others well, quite often we are the first ones to feel good about it. And this isn't just wishful thinking: there's a ton of science to suggest that there are physical health benefits to the practice as well.[1]

In addition to showing positive impacts in the neocortex, generosity practices, when earnestly employed, benefit the vagus nerve. How exactly the experience of positive emotions leads to better physical health remains somewhat of a mystery to scientists, but it's posited that the vagus nerve is a key factor in this. It's the longest nerve in your body and one of the most important ones. It starts in your brain stem and connects with every one of your organs except for your adrenal glands. In fact, your adrenal glands are responsible for producing and regulating stress-related adrenaline, but the vagus nerve is involved in the opposite biochemical process: relaxing and restoring your system. The stronger the function of your vagus nerve, which is determined by your degree of vagal tone, the better it can do its job of helping you stay healthy and warding off stress-related diseases.

These claims come from the work of Barbara Fredrickson as well as Bethany E. Kok, who have developed the Upward Spiral Theory through their research on the emotions that are evoked by lovingkindness meditation. They've found that the more positive emotions you experience, the healthier you'll be physically, which subsequently causes an increase in positive emotions, which then causes an increase in health, essentially creating the most desirable feedback loop that ever existed.[2]

Lovingkindness can be such a powerful practice that it is being used in all sorts of treatment modalities for things as heavy-duty as PTSD, addiction, and schizophrenia spectrum disorders.[3] It has also been shown to slow down aging processes at the level of your DNA and to be effective in addressing physical complaints like migraines and chronic pain.[4]

Again, we were biologically built to practice lovingkindness in some form or another. We are hardwired for it, despite its going against the grain of our most outdated, overused instincts. Its benefits push forward our evolution as a species, and the monkey mind, and all the worldly frustrations we experience as a result of following that monkey around, is leading us right to it. Though the Buddha might not have anticipated Facebook addiction, it is stunningly obvious that he brilliantly deduced our contemporary neurotic mental patterns, unearthed their hidden wisdom, and gave us a practice that starts where we are and then takes us deeper than we thought we wanted to go.

PRACTICE: *Maitri Proper*

The practice of maitri has three general parts:

1. Visualization
2. Contemplation
3. Offering

PRELIMINARIES

Sit in a comfortable position. Connect to the earth and your body by finding an upright posture. Check in with yourself. Remember why you're doing this.

Practice one of our three breathworks as desired (pages 103–6), followed by the Sun Meditation (page 53).

Spend some time feeling the breath in its natural rhythm. You can feel the whole body breathing or feel the breath in the center of the chest the space of your heart.

THE BENEFACTOR

Visualization

Imagine someone from your life whom you care for. Someone who's been good to you, someone who understands you, someone who it's easy to feel warmth for, perhaps someone whom you admire. (These instructions are for a human recipient, but feel free to adapt them to a nonhuman if you like.) Once you have settled on your person (many might come to mind, but just settle on one—it doesn't have to be the perfect person), make them real. Bring them into the room with you. Acknowledge their name. See their face, their eyes, their clothes, their cheekbones. You might even be able to hear what their voice sounds like or smell their scent.

Contemplation

Notice how it feels to be in this person's presence. Think about their good qualities briefly. Notice that, if this person were to have something fantastic happen to them, you would celebrate alongside them. If tragedy were to befall them, you would feel deeply concerned for them. In a way, their victories are your victories, and you would never want to see them in pain. This is the essence of maitri.

Offering

From that natural place of caring, begin to offer them thoughts of lovingkindness connected to your breath. As you breathe in, think the first intention I recommend below. As you breathe out, allow the energy of that intention to resonate. Let it go out into the atmosphere toward this person. You can even visualize them receiving the intention, and their face lighting up as they do so. Moving down the list, breathe in the next intention, then breathe it out to the person and let it resonate.

> May you be filled with love
> May you feel safe
> May you feel inspired
> May you awaken and be free

Take a breath and let go of the image of the benefactor.

Your Self-Image

Visualization
Now imagine you're looking in a full-length mirror. Here you are with yourself. Again, make it real: see your face, your eyes, your body, everything about your self-image.

Contemplation
How does it feel to be here with yourself? Do you feel good about it? Do you want to run and hide? Do you want to change something about yourself? The latter is the case for most of us. But notice something else: You work hard at having it good. You choose clothes that represent yourself well. You choose friends that you identify with in some way. You work hard at having a good home, a good income, at enjoying yourself in your free time. You're even here in this practice right now, working to evolve yourself—this challenging work is something that most people don't bother to do. And anything that's painful, you work hard to avoid. Whether or not you think you love yourself, you've been engaging in the essence of maitri all along. Take a moment to sit in the recognition of that.

Offering
Breathe in to relate to the phrases of maitri, breathe out to feel their resonance:

> May I be filled with love
> May I feel safe
> May I feel inspired
> May I awaken and be free

Then, take a breath and let go of the self-image.

THE STRANGER

Visualization
Think of someone who is in your life but whom you never think about. This could be a neighbor, a coworker, the last person to serve you a meal in a restaurant, or your doctor. They're in your life, but they're not that big of a deal to you. Again, make them real. See their features. Bring them right here, sitting with you. Acknowledge their name if you know it.

Contemplation
Consider that this person is much more like you than they are *not* like you. Just like you, they have a birthday, a favorite flavor of ice cream, dreams for the future, regrets about the past, a difficult relationship with a family member, financial worries, and a favorite song. Just like you, all day they want to feel pleasure and avoid pain. Even though you hardly know them, they're just like you.

Offering
Breathe in as you relate to the phrases, feel them as you breathe out:

> May you be filled with love
> May you feel safe

> May you feel inspired
> May you awaken and be free

Take a breath and let go of the image of the stranger.

The Enemy

Visualization

Now, picture someone you don't like. If you're new to this practice I recommend that you avoid selecting someone who has deliberately hurt or traumatized you. Choose someone who gets under your skin and pisses you off. (I usually practice for my least favorite politician.) Again, see their face, everything about them. Hear their voice and know what their name is. Bring them into the room with you.

If it's getting uncomfortable, you're doing it right. This is the part of the practice that strengthens the prefrontal cortex. Feel the burn of the resentment, irritation, or whatever it is for a moment. Here, we'll skip the contemplation and allow ourselves to be with the feelings this person evokes. And in the face of that discomfort, we train ourselves.

Offering
With the breath:

> May you be filled with love
> May you feel safe
> May you feel inspired
> May you awaken and be free

Take a breath and let go of the image of the enemy.

Expanding Maitri

Begin to open your mind to the environment around you. Consider the beings who surround you in the immediate sense, in your home or your neighborhood. Think of the things they might be doing.

Extend the following intention to them: May each of you be filled with love. May each of you awaken and be free.

Go further. Think of your entire city. Begin to fold nonhuman life forms into this intention: plants, animals, even insects. Every creature who works hard to be satisfied and to avoid pain.

Extend: May each of you be filled with love. May each of you awaken and be free.

Keep going. Think of the state you live in. And then expand to consider your part of the country. At this point we are truly considering countless beings, all possessed of the same drives toward freedom and well-being that you have.

So, extend to them: May each of you be filled with love. May each of you awaken and be free.

Consider your entire country, the land crowded with beings who are just like you.

Extend: May each of you be filled with love. May each of you awaken and be free.

Finally, consider the whole of the earth. All seven continents. All the oceans and bodies of water. All the creatures who fill the sky and live beneath the earth's surface. Take one last moment to recognize that each of these beings, no matter who or what they are, are just like you.

Extend: May each of *us* be filled with love. May each of *us* awaken and be free.

Take a moment and rest in that vision. A world filled with love. A world without war. A world where no one goes without the basic things we all need. A world where people trip over themselves to help one another. That other world is possible. How does it feel to consider this? Celebrate this vision, basking in any feelings that have arisen for as long as you like.

Return to the breath when the feeling fades. Rest your mind on the breath for a minute or two. Transition from your practice in a way that doesn't disrupt the state of mind and body you've cultivated.

Congratulations. You've just done something more profound than many people do their entire lives.

On-the-Spot Practice: *Mini-Maitri Bursts*

So simple, so beneficial: periodically throughout your day, on the train, in your car, at work, out to dinner, wherever, secretly send lovingkindness to someone near you. Pick a person, clandestinely tune in to them for a moment (i.e., don't stare at them). Briefly consider that they, just like you, face endless difficulties and long for a rich and healthy life. Then send them some well wishes via a maitri phrase: breathing in the phrase and exhaling the feeling over to them. This can take as little as a few seconds. And, practiced multiple times daily, it will change your life. You can even set a reminder in your phone to do this.

Interlude

Love, Level 10

When I speak of love I am not speaking of some sentimental and weak
response. I am not speaking of that force which is just emotional bosh.
I am speaking of that force which all the great religions have seen
as the supreme unifying principle of life. Love is somehow the key
that unlocks the door which leads to ultimate reality.

—Dr. Martin Luther King, Jr.

Love demands expression. It will not stay still, stay silent, be good,
be modest, be seen and not heard, no. It will break out in tongues of
praise, the high note that smashes the glass and spills the liquid.

—Jeanette Winterson

Yongey Mingyur Rinpoche, who gave us the three categories of relationship we can have to our experience, is sometimes
called "the happiest man alive." To meet him is to believe it. He
was also among the first cohort of Buddhist monks to be put on
a functional MRI (brain scan) machine by Richard Davidson at
the University of Wisconsin.[1] Twice now I've had the pleasure of
hearing this story in person, but I'll have to paraphrase.

"They put me in the tongue, and then the tongue went back in
the mouth." This is Mingyur Rinpoche's description of the con-
cave table one lies on when getting a brain scan. One lies on a
rounded cot resembling a tongue curled at its sides, which then
slides into a larger structure ("the mouth") that houses the brain-
scanning device. "And then a voice said, 'Mingyur Rinpoche, now

do concentration meditation: level 4 . . . now bring concentration to level 8 . . . Now do compassion meditation: level 6 . . . level 9 . . . '" And Mingyur Rinpoche would intensify his meditation, cool himself down, or switch practices altogether according to the instructions given.

Prior to this, the researchers at the University of Wisconsin had operationalized the different mind states they hoped to study. In other words, first they determined what parts of the brain they'd most likely see light up when a specific state of consciousness would be generated by the monks. Not only that, they were able to anticipate what the levels of intensity, 1 to 10, would look like for each of those states. They did this for states of mindfulness, concentration, compassion, and, yes, lovingkindness. Next, they asked Mingyur Rinpoche to bring his mind and body to these various states of meditation, delineating the level of intensity as well. Over and over again, the researchers found that Mingyur Rinpoche and the other monks they studied were able to demonstrate astonishing agency over their inner worlds. They would ask Mingyur Rinpoche to bring himself to "Love, level 6 . . . now down to 4 . . . now love, level 10," and they'd watch his brain light up on their screens in tandem.[2]

Stop and imagine your life with a mind capable of love, level 10, on command.

I tell you this story not as a fanciful anecdote about a cool Eastern monk getting involved with cutting-edge Western research, but to inspire your own confidence. We are faced with the reality that a deep fulfillment of the heart is available to each of us through maitri practice and is utterly possible for us to realize.

12

The Gifts of Difficulty

The most beautiful people we have known are those who have known
defeat, known suffering, known struggle, known loss, and have found
their way out of the depths. These persons have an appreciation,
a sensitivity, and an understanding of life that fills them with
compassion, gentleness, and a deep loving concern.
Beautiful people do not just happen.
—Elisabeth Kübler-Ross

ONCE UPON A TIME, I went to a high spiritual teacher and asked
to be saved. With one eyebrow firmly raised she found a deep and
dark chasm and threw me in it. She shouted down into the abyss,
"Here you will find your salvation," and turned and walked away.
And now my gratitude knows no bounds.

I was in the throes of kicking dope. Again. I had withstood the
notoriously excruciating detox a half dozen times that year, which
had become its own cycle. I'd kick, endure the sleepless nausea
for some days, enjoy a clean life for a couple of weeks, and then
my depression would resurface and I'd find myself tortured by
intense thoughts of self-hatred again. As I had failed to develop
any sort of daily practice in my life—self-care, spiritual, or otherwise—I'd become willing to throw everything I had away just
to get some relief. The samsara of kicking and relapsing had
become a strange, masochistic addiction in and of itself. I was
scared of this development. Scared for my life. Scared of myself.

So, when Amma came to the Bay Area, I went to her and
pleaded for her to excise the addiction from my life—lock, stock,

and barrel. Amma was and is a complete mystery to me; she is no ordinary woman. Despite my agnosticism, I must tell you that I have experienced so much inexplicable synchronicity around her (such as the night in Washington, D.C., when I asked Amma a question in my mind and a woman sitting right in front of me turned around and answered it). My twenty-six-year-old self was convinced she could lift the addiction from me if she wanted to. If anyone could save me, she could. I told her as much. Her response went something like this:

"I would never do that to you."

To me?

"Yes. If I were to lift this from you, I would be doing you a disservice. I would be robbing you of something precious. The hardships and struggle you're about to face all on your own are going to give you so much. You're going to have to give your entire life to it, and it is perfectly so." I was aghast, confused. The magical thinking that felt rock solid turned to dust and laid at my feet. A thousand *fuck yous* circulated inside me. I felt abandoned, done for, left for dead—by my teacher. My *teacher*. I didn't believe a single word she had said.

My drug addiction had been lived out side by side with my spiritual aspirations for the better part of a decade. Having a foot in both worlds had caught up with me. I had been engaging in something called *spiritual bypassing*: attempting to use contemplative practice to go around my problems rather than through them. I had been using *bhakti yoga* (devotional Vedic practice) just like a drug—but a more respectable way of getting high. As a friend said to me recently, "There are chains of iron and chains of gold. The challenge is to attach yourself to neither."

I was back on dope within the week. I overdosed and woke up vomiting in an emergency room soon thereafter. I was dope-sick six more times over the next six months. Endless trips on a merry-go-round from hell. I couldn't die, and I couldn't live.

Without hitting that bottom, I would have never gotten desperate enough to turn around and face myself. I would have never admitted that my approach to spiritual practice was arrogant and that I actually had no idea how the path worked. I would have never surrendered. I would have never gone to rehab, where I fell in love with psychotherapeutic process, yoga, and mindfulness meditation. I would not have become inspired to give my life over to offering those very things back to the world. I would not be typing these words to you right now.

I honestly don't know if Amma actually had the power to give me what I was asking her for, but I do know that she gave me more than what I asked for. I also know that everything she said made no sense to me in the moment, and it makes perfect sense to me now. Having to claw my own way out of the bottomless pit of heroin addiction was the best thing that ever happened to me. I wouldn't wish it on my worst enemy, and I wouldn't trade it for the world.

Follow Your Heartbreak, Find Your Purpose

I'm going to say something controversial, something that needs to be said carefully. In particular, I want to make sure to say that this is not always the case but is *potentially* the case: trauma can and does serve an adaptive, positive, evolutionary purpose; a purpose that is very much in service of our personal ecosystems as well as that of human civilization. *If* someone has the resources, both material and psycho-emotional, to make it out alive and to face the reality of what happened in the appropriate way, there can be no greater blessing than trauma. This is not true for someone currently experiencing trauma, it is not true for someone who hasn't been able make it out in some way or another, and it is often less likely to be true for those with less material resources and whose healing is met by the forces of institutionalized oppression. But for those of us fortunate enough to find our way to the other side of the nightmare, the potential for benefit is incomparable.

One of the biggest gifts difficulty could ever lay at our doorstep is the hunger for truth. When hurt and struggle corner us to the point that we ask, "What is it that I'm missing? What is it inside of me that needs to be healed? Why am I still stuck?" we are starting to ask the right questions. Trauma begins serving its adaptive purpose when and if we find the wherewithal to start wondering if there's something important to be learned here, if there's more to this existence than the story that our limited perceptions have told us. Such daring, courageous, self-effacing questions are never asked in comfortable conditions. So long as life in the cocoon is working out fine, we'll remain convinced that we've got this life thing sorted out, which couldn't be further from the truth. Comfort can be toxic, and trauma can be precious. *Welcome to Paradox City—population: infinite.* Poison in the beginning, nectar in the end.

But the most significant gift trauma could put in front of us is life purpose. Spiritual activist and author, Andrew Harvey once wrote three words that changed my life forever: "follow your heartbreak." That is, if you find yourself lost with regard to what you are meant to do with your one wild and precious life, consider what has torn you down the most. Consider your own healing journey and then go and help others who are in similar situations you were once in (or are still in). There, you will find you have insider knowledge, insider language, and a passion for the work that cannot be taught or otherwise acquired. When we go about asking, "What is it I want to do?" our thinking tends to get very tight, very circular, very samsaric. We often end up in what's called *analysis paralysis*: considering the options over and over again from various angles until we find ourselves helplessly stuck in indecision. When we begin to ask, "What is it that I have to offer? How can I help?" endless doors open up before us. The need is so great for wise and courageous hearts to begin addressing the unspeakable despair in the world, the opportunities know no bounds. When we surrender to the call to address the suffering of others, our own liberation is close at hand.

BROKENHEARTEDNESS BECOMES BRILLIANT HEARTEDNESS

Susan Piver, who so generously wrote the foreword to this book, also authored the remarkable work, *The Wisdom of a Broken Heart.* I once saw her give a talk with the same title at the Shambhala Meditation Center of New York, wherein she pulled off something of a brilliant stunt. Toward the end of her talk, she had the crowd break up into pairs to discuss the last time we were devastatingly heartbroken after a failed love relationship, and how we dealt with it. Shortly thereafter, she had the room come back together to discuss what we had learned from our dialogues.

One after another, hands went up and people shared stories of how they were forced to respond when backed into a corner by a traumatic breakup. Every single story followed an identical trajectory, which went something like this: "It hurt like hell, but once I was done wallowing, it drove me to things I'm grateful I did and that I wouldn't have done otherwise." Recovering from the trauma of heartbreak had compelled one person to go back to therapy to figure out why this pattern was repeating itself in relationships. It had led another person to do a monthlong Spanish-language immersion in Mexico City. Another person started playing the guitar again to channel their hurt feelings. Brokenheartedness compelled one person to start a meditation practice, and it had inspired yet another person to finally take their practice seriously. Someone else decided that they needed to invest more in their close friendships rather than in fleeting relationships. Over and over again, people shared how heartbreak had pushed them to engage in life-affirming, creative, and satisfying practices in order to recover homeostasis, the balance they had previously enjoyed.

True, this wasn't anyone's first reaction to the pain, but sooner or later everyone had gotten up, brushed themselves off, and done something truly positive for themselves. It was incredible to watch a room of over a hundred people "spontaneously" reach this conclusion together through sharing their direct experiences.

I put *spontaneous* in scare quotes up there for a reason. It wasn't spontaneous at all. Susan knew exactly what conclusion we'd arrive at. She was able to trust that our stories would mirror one another's in terms of theme and trajectory because this is simply how we work. It's similar to the stages of grief outlined by Elisabeth Kübler-Ross: following a significant loss, we all tend to go through a sequence of shock/denial, anger, bargaining, and depression before we can get to acceptance. But when acceptance arises, it is almost always accompanied by a victory lap, a substantial change for the better in one's life.

Make no mistake: we don't grow *in spite of* the obstacles in our lives, we grow from them. There is even a Tibetan practice whereby one prays for difficulty to come one's way. But not just any difficulty: the right kind of difficulty, one that isn't so severe that it hijacks our life and tears us apart, but also that isn't so minor that we can just rest on our laurels and space out. Rather, the prayer asks to be pushed to the growth edge by the kind of challenges that will test our limits of patience, forbearance, mindfulness, and lovingkindness so that those limits can expand and invaluable insights can emerge from overcoming difficulty.

Without the gifts of trauma, abandonment, assault, alienation, depression, and addiction, I would not be doing what I do in the world today. I would not have the high satisfaction of doing deep work with people. I would not taste the supreme joy of a life dedicated to healing, growth, and awakening. I would not have the fire in my belly that I do today, the zeal for authenticity, art, music, literature, and science. I might be stuck like so many others, not knowing what direction their life is meant to go in, unable to discern the calling that is already in them. Without experiencing rehab, sleeping next to ex-cons, I would not have been so desperate to meditate and work things out with my therapist. Without experiencing a dog attack, I would not have had a penetrating insight about the stories we tell ourselves. And I would not have it to give you.

I tell you this because, as we head into the deep end of the pool together, turning toward the difficulty in our lives rather than away from it, we can generate a cynical response. What's the point? Why should we even bother? Isn't the past in the past? Can't we just "let that shit go" and move on? Isn't that what Buddhists do?

I'm here to tell you there is much more to the story.

Say it with me one last time, real loud for the people in the back: the monkey mind is not the problem, and it was never the problem. It was always a symptom of a larger dilemma. The monkey is on our side. It is our wake-up call, the adaptive sting of a wound that does not wish to fester, a message written in bold: **It's time you healed your life.** The monkey is nothing short of a blessing.

The Original Pain and Its Carbon Copy

Again, the cascade of events our model scenes and wounds compel us to reenact are actually the products of our system's natural urge to heal and restore balance. Everything described in the examples above and the case study below are analogous to the stinging of that cut on our arm.

We can only heal a hurt when hurting is present. We have to be feeling the pain, not just aware of its source, in order to do something about it. We can't analyze it from a safe distance or develop a mere intellectual understanding and expect a meaningful and lasting unburdening to take place. Despite our attempts in life not to have this material triggered, we find that it invariably does get triggered, and this is literally our unconscious mind offering us the opportunity to heal and dissolve the distortion. Here, I will highlight two things that are essential to helping this come about:

1. We must be in touch with the original pain within ourselves, not the carbon copy.
2. When triggered, we must make new choices that are in the direction of well-being.

The patterns that we tire of repeating, that eventually lead us to this work, are the alarm, the sting, the call to action, but they are not the real thing that wants to be healed, the wound. I cannot underline this enough. Our reenactments of our model scenes in symbolic ways are what gets our attention, and so we make the mistake of thinking they are the problem. They are not. The *essence* of the original pain is felt in the reenactments and neuroses, but it is the carbon copy. You cannot heal the cut on your arm by disinfecting a picture of it. We must get in touch with the original pain, the original model scene, and the part of us that never left that moment. We must feel *through* the original experience that could not be felt at the time, absorb the insights embedded in it by understanding the story of what happened, and apply the disinfectants of presence and warmth until we shift our relationship with that part of us. That is how our deepest hurts become our richest treasures. That is how we recover the experience of connection and end the inner objectification that has amounted to disaster in our lives and in our world. That is how we resolve our monkey mind. This is actually what all the training in shamatha and maitri is for.

Case Study: Jean

Jean (whose name and personal details have been changed) came to work with me during an episode of a recurrent depression. It had grown so intense that she couldn't be alone with the shadows of hopelessness and disappointment anymore. She is thirty, Caucasian, heterosexual, able bodied, and from a middle-class mid-western family that, from the outside, is more or less an embodi-ment of the so-called American Dream. She has many resources: smarts, savvy, education, good social supports, emotional intelli-gence, and creativity, for starters.

Jean's father's life and interests were centered around sports. He championed Jean's two brothers for their athletic abilities and the trophies they'd sometimes come home with. Jean found her-self far less interested in and adept at sports, but of course she craved her father's attention and approval. She also perceived that her father would sometimes treat her as if she were a boy, and she picked up that he had a negative attitude toward activ-ities and hobbies that are commonly considered feminine (but that she wanted to engage in). Dad, completely dismissive of his daughter's feelings, predilections, personality, and needs, was most likely to play with her if she agreed to a game of catch or other sports-related activity with him, such as watching football on TV or going to a game. She took this and other experiences as signals that her father wished she had been born a boy and resented her for not being so.

Jean was born with a highly sensitive temperament, but like many of us she spent much of her childhood trying to keep such parts of herself at bay in order to fit in. Instead, she overrode her natural inclinations to participate in soccer and baseball, which were her only avenues to feeling seen, belonging, getting rewards, and not feeling left out. This was the obvious choice, but it was to no avail. She was always trying to reach a bar that had been set very high by her competitive brothers. Having a mother who was too wrapped up in her own drama to tune in to Jean's needs left Jean with no one she felt she could confide in, get support from, be validated by, or identify with.

Jean's mother was emotionally erratic, unpredictable, and often unavailable for Jean. But at other times, starting from the time Jean was ten, her mother treated her as if she were an adult, confiding in Jean about her adult problems. This very well could mean that Jean's stress response was constantly firing, albeit at a low level. We know that when kids don't perceive a consistently safe and stable environment, their systems, informed by negativity bias, tend to assume the worst. Jean also had to endure Mom's opening up to her about problems in her parents' marriage in particular, something that tends to be deeply distressing for kids and adolescents; it tends to create a schism in their minds regarding the parent being complained about. (Holding the truth that people are complex, with both wonderful and terrible parts, is simply beyond their stage of development.) To hear Mom badmouth Dad, whom Jean loved and sought attention from, could have easily created confusion about what was OK and not OK to think, feel, and say about him.

Mom's unpredictable emotions created a sense in Jean that she never knew who she was going to get. One day Mom could be fine, the next day she could be scolding her for something that had never been a problem before, and then the day after that, Mom could be in tears and imposing on Jean for counsel. Thus, Jean never felt she could drop her guard and relax. She constantly had to override the natural feelings we have when our boundaries are crossed because she in no way felt empowered or supported. For Jean, as a highly sensitive person (which, by the way, is not a mental health diagnosis, but is definitely a term a lot of people identify with) all of this registered more deeply than it would for the average person. That she feels things so deeply but could observe that no one else around her did contributed to a sense that something must be wrong with her. She learned to keep this part of her personality a secret, maintaining a stiff upper lip.

Everywhere Jean turned in her family home, her identity had been invalidated. She received the message that she couldn't be a girl from her father, the message that she couldn't be a child from her mother, and the message that she'd never measure up from her brothers. Her emotional sensitivities were not valued or nourished, and instead she was constantly met with the message that she did not belong and perhaps that she wasn't loveable just as she was. Jean grew up in what many consider to be ideal and fortunate conditions, but her unconscious, subjective, and primitive brain absorbed the message that she had no place in the world, and that love was always just out of reach. A sense of unworthiness became her enemy, and no matter how hard Jean fought to avoid feeling unworthy, the message was already frozen in her nervous system. It was bound to keep rearing its intolerable head.

Jean's most recent depression was triggered when she sustained an injury while running. She used running to cope with the feelings of isolation and unmet needs she would often have. It was also an attempt to address things on a deeper level than she was aware of. She was running toward Dad's affection and approval while running away from her mother's presence. However, when Jean became injured and unable to run (in more ways than one), her core wounds and beliefs and model scenes caught up with her. She could no longer bypass them with the endorphin rush of exercise. Thus, she was cornered into seeking help, cornered into ending the bypassing of her problems, cornered into facing herself.

Jean had been to another therapist, who was quick to diagnose her and suggest medication as a solution—to my mind, yet another invalidation of her personhood and yet another message that there was something wrong with her. Our work together gives this highly intelligent, emotionally connected, empathetic, altruistic woman a space to identify and own her feelings and struggles and to have them be received without judgment or expectation. Every so often we even get to make contact with Jean's anger: like many of us, she grew up in a situation that naturally triggered anger in her, but it had nowhere to go except inward, toward herself. (Unfun fact: Depression is not sadness. It is anger turned inward. We can think of depression as the intense energy of anger that has been stymied and stifled into a squashed, cloudy angst.)

Thus, Jean's outward expressions of anger are encouraged in our sessions as therapeutic as they represent a step forward in her evolution. I can remember one session in particular when, stuck in a dehumanizing, entry-level social work job, Jean uttered the words, "I'm better than this." I asked her to repeat those words even louder: *"I'm better than this!"* upon which we celebrated her burgeoning sense of self-worth.

Yet, the most powerful and transformative sessions Jean and I have together are when she has been able to make contact with inner child aspects of her psyche in a process called "parts work." (Parts work is an evidence-based practice that creates a welcoming arena for the unconscious mind, thus inviting it into conscious experience. For this reason, I sometimes refer to this process as "hypnosis without the me-hypnotizing-you part." We will be talking about parts work much more in the chapters to come.) In these sessions, she is given a safe, well-informed space to make contact with the *original* painful experiences she endured. We don't just do this by talking about and feeling through the narrative of what her experience has been; we also work with her inner world in an even more direct way.

We start this process when she strikes upon a strong emotion connected to her history (all strong emotions we experience are connected to our model scenes and core wounds in some way). I ask her to stop and feel where it is in her body. I ask her to describe the sensations: whether it is sharp or dull, cooler or warmer, pulsing or constant, heavy or light, hollow or full. Invariably, there is a heaviness in her heart. (For others, it might be a tight jaw or a hollow feeling in the belly or some other sensation.) I ask her to stay with the sensations but not to be *in* them. In order to make the process more substantial, I'll ask her to engage with this feeling as if it were another person. After all, these feelings are a part of her, and thus they are alive, feeling entities. They aren't our deepest self, but all parts of ourselves are still valid. They have perfectly sound reasons for existing, despite all the trouble they may cause us. I'll ask Jean to take a step back from this part of her, to not identify with it so closely. I check in with Jean's relationship to this part. She usually resents it in some way, which is universal. I ask her to relax her reactivity to this part's presence. It might take some time, but eventually she gets to a place where she at least feels willing to be here with this part of her.

Quite often in this work, parts of ourselves will appear in mind as images. Given that the unconscious mind's language is metaphor and symbolism, any imagery that appears in Jean's mind as a result of this process is always potent and meaningfully connected to her formative experiences in some way, even if it feels like an act of imagination at the time. The images can range from cartoonish to quite literal. This doesn't always happen, but when it does, it makes the work that much more meaningful.

Jean's child self often shows up in her psyche as a malnourished little girl in a closet (trapped and left out), who is very timid about engaging with Jean. After all, that child part of her has basically been in solitary confinement all her life, being sent painful messages about her worth all the while. It's as if a crew of court jesters were standing outside her jail cell poking fun at her misery and isolation. I'd be timid in that situation, too; anyone would be. But, here, in this triggered state full of feeling and in touch with a child part of her that is frozen in time, I can guide Jean to validate this kid's feelings in all the ways she missed out on. Jean can offer herself (in the form of these sensations and images) the love, attention, and support she never got. She can become her own best parent, her own therapist.

Over time Jean has shifted the relationship with this closeted, neglected part of her that holds many of her hurts, disappointments, frustrations, and limiting beliefs. This little girl represents a wounded and defensive schema that was once unconscious within Jean and has now become conscious. Such a shift means that Jean has agency over her relationship with this part of her. She has choices whereas (even if only in her body-mind complex) she previously felt randomly hijacked by her feelings and all the rumination and spinning thoughts that came with it.

Together, Jean and I have also been able to do further symbolic work within her unconscious mind. For example, Jean has entered a scene that hurt her and taken the little girl she once was out of the situation and to a place where she feels happy and loved. Here, she has been able to ask that child version of herself what she'd rather do, as opposed to hiding in the closet. The answer for Jean—and for almost everyone who asks a hurt part of themselves this question—is *play*. Since usually we were children when most of our hurts were accumulated, it is the child parts of us that get frozen in time, and lose their spontaneity and sweetness in the process. This is why people talk about losing their innocence or growing up too fast. Parts of them got stuck experiencing and re-experiencing model scenes and lost their childlike qualities in the process. We can absolutely recover this.

Most importantly, in the days and weeks after our sessions, Jean has a process of working with her emotions in a tangible, conceptual, and embodied manner. Now she has a conscious relationship with this part of her, and she has an image to relate to when that part of her gets triggered. This part of her is no longer an object but is respected as a living energy. One could argue, and many do, that this is all the work of imagination. And it partly is. That's the beauty of it: the brain doesn't know the difference between imagination and reality. We do keep things grounded in the somatic experience and Jean's sensory world throughout the process, but it's through imaginary interactions with the genuine sensations of the original pain that true healing becomes possible. Any fictions involved will work themselves out in due time if the process is sincere.

PRACTICE: *The Holding Environment*

Chögyam Trungpa Rinpoche once gave the meditation instruction to "place the heart of fearfulness in the cradle of lovingkindness." At a glance, these eloquent words might smack of a platitude or just a nice thought, but they actually describe how healing works. Trungpa Rinpoche's offering here is identical to that of Winnicott's holding environment, which I discussed in chapter 3.

This next meditation we're going to explore employs this concept and incorporates a traditional Buddhist practice for cultivating compassion known as *tonglen. Tonglen* is a Tibetan word that translates to "sending and receiving," which is often interpreted as "exchange of self and other." It is usually taught as a process akin to lovingkindness meditation, wherein one works with various people from one's life. Whereas in maitri we send out love and warmth, in tonglen we seek to take away another person's pain and confusion. In the version of tonglen we'll explore here, we will just be working with our emotional parts, which, again, are exactly like people. Because we'll be working with ourselves and our parts exclusively, I'd like to propose an alternative definition of tonglen here: "exchanging hurts for compassion." This will serve as a bridge to the parts work meditations to come and give you a new context in which to work with your emotions.

WORKING AT GROWTH'S EDGE

Before we get to the practice, we must note that compassionate work, whether it is done for oneself or for others, must always be tempered by a respect for one's own boundaries. What matters more than anything else is that the work be sustainable over time, because we do not heal all at once but incrementally. Turning back to our earlier discussion on distress tolerance, each of us has what neuroscience calls a *window of tolerance:* a finite degree (though mutable over time) to which we can handle distress in any given moment. Picture, if you will, a two-dimensional box, like a drawing of a window. Outside the left side of the box is chaos, outside the right is rigidity. Within the box is our capacity to hold distress and difficulty. When our degree of distress fills the box and goes beyond, outside the edge of the window, we collapse into either chaos (the situation becomes our boss, and we get angry, panic, act out, or engage in addictions and compulsions) or rigidity (the situation becomes our enemy, and we make rules, shut things down, become very "tight" about things). We either freak out or clamp down, basically.

WINDOW OF TOLERANCE

Chaos			Rigidity
Acting out	Growth Edge	**Zone of Optimal Functioning** **a.k.a.** **Comfort Zone** Growth Edge	Controlling
Addictions			Numbing
Tantrums			Manipulating
Dissociation			Perfectionism

All healing and compassionate work must be done within our window of tolerance. That said, the window of what we can handle does not have set boundaries. For example, the cultivation of distress tolerance can widen that window, the knowledge that one has resources and is resilient can widen that window, the attitude of establishing a holding environment can widen that window. We might also find our window of tolerance is smaller on a day when we don't feel well or broader after we come home from a vacation. The type of work I am proposing we engage in will also expand that window if we work to the edge of it. That is, we want this work to bear some intensity, but not so much that we lose our grip on things. We need to find the "Goldilocks zone" between the coziness of our cocoon and biting off more than we can chew. This is often referred to as *the growth edge.* It's the place where we are expanding our comfort zone and ultimately expanding our capacity to enjoy life.

Holding Environment Meditation

Take a comfortable seat. Find the appropriate posture. Settle in, check in with yourself, and step into mindful presence. Relax and enter the body with the Sun Meditation (page 53), and practice a breathwork (pages 103–6) as needed to help you calm down and open space in the mind.

To help you settle further, place your attention in the space of your heart, and allow the breath to find its natural rhythm. Feel one breath at a time, and note the settled quality that lies in the space between breaths. Begin to invoke the sense of a holding environment by attending to the breath with a sense of care and warmth, with an attitude of lovingkindness. If you don't feel that warmth, just keep doing the practice with a patient and friendly attitude toward yourself.

Once you are relatively settled, begin to inquire of your system, of your body, if there is some part of you that wants to come forth into the holding environment. Perhaps there is an emotion that's right there on tap, or something you've been trying to keep at bay that is longing to be recognized. You don't have to force anything to come up; simply inquire and see if something starts to shift in you.

It's optional to think of a specific recurring problem in your life and to allow whatever feelings are there to arise, **but please don't intentionally think of something that's very intense or traumatizing to begin with**. Start mild, and work your way up.

If, after some time, what you find yourself sitting with is resistance to the practice, feeling like you're "not getting it," feeling numbness or blankness, then simply work with these parts of you. Any mind state is fair game in this practice, and there is no right or wrong, no better or worse.

Let the feelings you have about this situation come to the surface, whatever they may be. They're welcome here, and you are in a safe space for experiencing them. Invite them.

As the feelings begin to arise, notice the shift in your awareness. Acknowledge what emotions are becoming present. Anger? Hurt? Abandonment? All of the above? Notice there is also a shift in the body. In one region, maybe multiple regions, various sensations have become present: perhaps a heaviness in the chest, a knot in the stomach, an ache in the heart, a clenching in the jaw, or something else. Discover what is true for your body, and become increasingly aware of these sensations. Allow the story in your head to fade away.

Begin attending to these feelings and sensations as if they were a hurt or upset child who's right here in the room with you. What will you do with this child? Tell them to shut up? Lock them in a closet? If that's how you feel right now, take some time to breathe and stay with this child. Over time, allow your breath to relax you out of your reactivity until you can see: this energy inside you is indeed childlike in nature. Practice holding these feelings with your attention just like you would hold a child—with warmth, with tenderness, with mercy. You can visualize this happening or just have a sense of it happening. An image associated with this part of you might have already emerged on its own as well. If it would feel good to do so, you can say to this child, "I am completely here with you. You are not alone. I've got you."

This part of you can manifest in any number of ways. There might be a sense of the child resisting you, yelling at you, or having a tantrum. They might start telling you their troubles, or seem comforted by your attending to them. Whatever is true for you, allow it. Let it in and simply hold it with care.

From here, we'll employ tonglen and begin working with our

breath to unburden this part of you. Begin breathing in the part of you that is upset, feeling the affect on the way in. When you breathe out, imagine you're offering the warmth of compassion. Breathing in again, imagine the upsets are like thick, black smoke. Breathing out, bring even more warm, nurturing light to the situation. You might like to think of it as a golden energy. Breathing in again, it's as if your in-breath is a vacuum, pulling this part's troubles away from itself. Breathing out again, your out-breath is like a ray of the sun, bringing more and more space and warmth, which begins to surround this child. Stay with this process for some time, alternating with each breath, taking and sending.

Gradually, so much holding space develops that it becomes like swimming in an ocean of compassion. As you continue, notice what, if anything, is shifting in this part of you. This hurt part of you is now getting smaller and smaller in relation to how much compassion it is surrounded by.

To close the practice, say goodbye to this part of you. You can even let it know that you'll be back. Take a big, deep breath, and as you exhale, let the practice go entirely. Let it fade out. Return to the space of the breathing heart for a minute, then transition gently out of your practice. If you are still triggered, a quick Sun Meditation (page 53) and a 15-second fake smile will help you restore balance.

13

The Family Within

> "I" am a crowd, obeying as many laws
> As it has members. Chemically impure
> Are all "my" beings. There's no single cure
> For what can never have a single cause.
> —ALDOUS HUXLEY

> You think there's some essence to who you are that will
> endure no matter the situation or context, but this
> is not the case. . . . You have a vocabulary of the
> self; a range of people you become.
> —DR. LISA FELDMAN BARRETT

YOU HAVE the traits of every clinical disorder there is. I'm not making that up. We all do. Every one of us has the seeds of each disorder in us, and we experience them all the time. They are not extraordinary. The only difference is how pronounced some of those traits are in an individual, and the degree to which they disrupt their life across the general lines of love, work, and play. That's all a "disorder" is: when the volume on a particular set of traits and propensities in a person gets turned all the way up.

Everyone gets stressed out sometimes, but if you get consumed by stress to the point that you have an episode of intense anxiety that feels like a heart attack and/or a bad acid trip, we call the emotion *panic* and the episode a *panic attack*. And if this happens to you repeatedly, which will interfere with your ability to perform at work, maintain meaningful relationships, and enjoy your life, then you probably meet the criteria for *panic disorder*. It is natural to have had a period of feeling heartbroken, disillusioned, and cloudy. And if this gets to the point where nothing you ordinarily enjoy seems worth the effort, you start to feel hopeless, and if this lasts long enough to impact love, work, and play, we call it a *depressive episode.* If an episode turns into *episodes*, plural, and you get fired for not coming into work, and if it gets so bad that life itself ceases to feel like it's worth the effort, so you start to think about killing yourself, we've invented a phrase for that called *major depressive disorder.*

The same is true of multiple personality disorder. Each of us, in a way, actually has multiple personalities. Who we are when we're at work is a completely different person than who we are when fighting with our significant other. Who we are when we're on the phone with a customer service representative is a very different person from who we are when we're out to dinner with friends. Our experience of who we are in the morning often contrasts greatly with the moods, behaviors, desires, and activities we find ourselves enacting at night. And who we are when we're with our friends actually depends on which friends are present, because every person in our life evokes different parts of us. The difference between this experience and the criteria for *dissociative identity disorder* is that these parts of myself are not so pronounced that I break from reality and lose track of my continuous, more solid sense of self. That is to say, these personalities remain subpersonalities and not alternate personalities.

"I" Am a Crowd

An aspect of our universal psychosomatic setup is that we have parts. We even talk like this: "One part of me wants ice cream while another part of me wants to avoid sugar." It's as if we all have a committee with many members living inside us, and who we are at any given moment depends on which committee member is holding the microphone. And just as with committees, each of our parts is just like another person. That might sound bananas at first, but think about it: the part of us that gets anxious and edgy when things feel uncertain is a whole different subpersonality than the part of us that feels hurt and deflated whenever an Internet date turns out to be a complete waste of time. Our worry has a whole different set of variables and traits than our grief and loss do. They are quite distinct.

Not just that, but our parts have volition, voices, stories to tell, a logic they respond to, and insights to share with us, just like people do. They have wise aspects, and they have neurotic aspects, just like we do. And they have distinct histories. For example, my angry parts have been shaped by experiences with my father. When an angry part gets activated for me and I'm not careful, I can act in an intimidating manner just as my dad used to. I start to have different thoughts—what is arguably the "voice" of this part "telling" me things. It was shaped primarily in childhood and adolescence, and in the moments when I am able to stop and investigate my experience of anger, I've seen that it has a juvenile mentality and feel to it. The angry part of me has desires. It wants to yell, say nasty things I'll regret later, cut people off, go on the warpath—and in the past, it's wanted to (and did) break things and get extremely wasted. That angry part of me also responds to my experience. When activated, if that angry part feels heard and understood in a way, it's likely to calm down and maybe let another part of me take center stage.

I also have a relationship to this angry part that isn't so dissimilar from the relationships I have with other people in my life. It's my boss sometimes, in the moments when it takes over and calls the shots. Yet, as the old punk song by Heavy Vegetable goes: "*Breaking things makes it feel OK, until you need what you broke that day.*" When I wake up in the morning and behold the mess I've made, when I have to apologize for sins committed on the warpath, I'm more likely to relate to an angry part as my enemy. I might wake up hating my anger, ashamed of it, exhausted by it.

But this doesn't mean anger doesn't have wisdom in it. It absolutely does. This angry part of me arises when my boundaries have been crossed in some way, when I have been disregarded as a person or treated as an object. It arises in experiences that are actually quite painful, but specifically ones in which the pain either would be intolerable to admit to myself or would leave me too vulnerable to admit to someone else.

Anger is what we call a *secondary emotion*. It's never the first emotion; it's always a response to hurt. We often don't experience the hurt of feeling disregarded, because anger is so quick to step in to protect us. This is actually very intelligent. Hurt and disappointment are very deflated states to be in, with little energy to them. These would be terrible states to remain in if we were in the presence of someone actively hurting us. We would be that much less equipped to defend ourselves. So, anger steps in when we get hurt to make sure we have the energy and the intensity to extinguish potential threat. The problem is, anger is *so* fierce that it tends to eclipse all reason and go too far. But, what if we could have the sort of relationship with such an angry part of us whereby we could agree with one another? Where anger could trust our deeper self, and would serve as an adult bodyguard rather than as an attack dog? What if we had a volitional relationship with anger as opposed to an automatic one?

The lonely part of me has a different history. It's been informed by a set of experiences when I felt abandoned and rejected. Those experiences actually form a narrative arc in me, a set of stories I've told a million times in therapy but have seldom felt my way through. Loneliness has a distinct voice that takes the shape of thoughts like, "Why am I still single?" "Why didn't I get invited to _____ ?" "Maybe everyone actually hates me and they're just being polite when I'm around." My loneliness gets very compulsive about being on dating apps, because it's convinced that if I keep checking and swiping, maybe "the one" will finally be there waiting for me. I have a relationship to this lonely part. I treat it like my enemy. I perceive its presence in my life as evidence of some sort of failure. Evidence that I'm not good enough. The energy of this part of me can seem so needy and neglected that when it comes on to the scene I can hardly bear it. So, I drown it in a shot of whiskey. I put it in front of Netflix like so many parents do with their children. I find some way to numb or distract myself. Anything to not relate to this part.

And yet this part has wisdom to it. After all, it's been holding my loneliness for me so that I don't have to experience it all the time. It's a part of me that's frozen in childhood, frozen in experiences where I felt unseen and uncared for. It's stuck in moments when I was left alone and my child mind couldn't understand why. If it weren't so weighed down with hurt, it might express itself creatively and playfully, with joy, lightheartedness, and humor. This child part of me is closer to the love that I was born with than many of my other parts. I would do well to resolve this relationship, help this part feel felt, listen to its story, and see if it can lay down some of its burdens to free up its energy.

THE INNER HOUSEHOLD

As kids, each of us had an external family with multiple members who all wanted the same things: to feel seen, heard, respected, understood, loved, held, listened to, and like they have a parent who is empathetically attuned and trustworthy. So, here's a myth to live into: at all stages of life, each of us has an inner family with multiple members who all want the exact same things. Our parts actually look to us to be the head of our inner household. The first problem is, we've been in an abusive relationship with them. We treat our parts in ways we would never, ever treat another person (I hope). The second issue is, we were just kids when all our parts had to start absorbing our wounds and betrayals. In the natural state we were born in, we did not have the capacity to manage, feel, and process such experiences fully. What our parts don't seem to know is that now, as adults, we are far stronger and more resourced than we once were, and in their blindness to this they don't trust us to run the show. Rather, they are convinced that they must step in and hijack us in the name of survival. This is precisely why our emotions tend to lead us astray and baffle us the way that they do. This drama has been taking place in the unconscious waters of our being since we were babies, and now that we have some insight around it we can address it effectively. That is, we can bring harmony, integrity, and healing to our discordant and mistrusting inner household.

This is a theoretical lens, so I am not actually asking you to believe me or to unconditionally accept this set of ideas. I am only asking you to suspend belief and disbelief alike and look through this lens for a while. See if it functions to bring about useful results and deepen your experience of your life. That's the only point anyhow.

The concept of the inner household forms the basis of the preliminary healing meditations we are about to embark upon. Here, I will break down the most basic tenets of this model. I'll also describe the practices we're about to embark upon, and then we'll dive into the actual work.

THE INTERNAL FAMILY SYSTEMS MODEL

Internal Family Systems (IFS), created by psychologist Richard Schwartz, is among the newer modalities of evidence-based psychotherapy. We have already been discussing many ideas that are core (though not native) to this radically nonpathologizing approach. IFS is based on the acknowledgment that each of us is composed of parts that have sovereignty and sentience. Again, each of our parts is just like another person: they hold information, have motivations and feelings, and try to tell us things all the time, and we have relationships to each of them that is often fraught with reactivity. From the point of view of IFS, the objective of healing is not to rid ourselves of these parts (such would be impossible) but rather to heal our relationship to them. It is through the process of shifting toward empathetic connection with our parts that they become "unburdened." That is, the painful model scenes and exhausting defense strategies our parts get caught in begin to dissolve over time as our parts begin to trust what's called *self-energy*, our deeper wisdom. Parts work, then, is a process of learning how to purposefully interact with our hurt and defensive parts from the vantage point of our deeper, wiser self. The result of doing such work is a release of tremendous amounts of psychosomatic energy ordinarily eaten up by the repetitive patterns in our lives, be they cognitive, emotional, behavioral, or interpersonal.

Too often, delineations of how consciousness works are either quite nebulous or too complex for us to really sink our teeth into. If the key to clarifying our experience of life is clarifying our relationship to things, we need a model that allows us to explicitly identify the moving parts within us and learn how they dynamically shift in response to one another.

IFS is not unique in thinking that we are each essentially a dynamic system of interwoven parts each enacting a function in service of our being. This thinking is present in Jungian psychoanalysis, gestalt therapy, Psychoanalytic Energy Psychotherapy, Voice Dialog, Co-Active coaching, and in ancient aboriginal, animistic, and shamanic traditions the world over. In fact, IFS's model closely resembles *soul retrieval*, an esoteric healing practice that's present in West African shamanism and in the indigenous medicine of cultures of the Andes mountains.[1] It is also nearly identical to the *Vajrayana maitri* ("esoteric lovingkindness") and *chöd* ("feed your demons") practices of Tibetan Buddhism. At its core, IFS, a newer model that fairly recently gained status as an evidence-based modality, is actually millennia old.

Essentially, IFS is just wrapping contemporary language and concepts around a universal reality that has always been there. Similar to the neuroscientific studies of meditation that began in 1992, science is confirming what countless generations before us already knew. Nonetheless, all theoretical models are the menu, not the meal, of experience. IFS, Vajrayana maitri, chöd, soul retrieval—these are maps, and all maps are myths. All that matters is whether the map helps get you somewhere. Although we will not be exploring IFS in earnest in this book, I find Richard Schwartz's four basic categories of the various aspects of our psyche to be useful, accessible, and accurate.

THE FOUR DIMENSIONS OF PSYCHE

Managers

Managers are the parts of ourselves that we "live in" most of the time. They are evident in a mindset that seeks to preempt disaster. They anticipate potentially painful and difficult situations and strategize how we might steer clear. They are the parts of us that prompt us to give good face in social situations, to organize our calendar and finances so something crucial doesn't slip through the cracks, and to remember birthdays. Less benign than this, they are the parts of us that have us avoid people, things, and situations that are out of our comfort zone. Their most important job is to make sure none of our most hurt and vulnerable parts come to the surface, where they might be exposed to further hurt. Managers are ultimately working for our good, but that doesn't mean they steer us in the most fulfilling directions. A manager will preempt you from taking a risk at work or in your relationship, even if it could ultimately lead to fulfillment and growth. A manager will tell you perhaps it's not the best idea to write the book, take the salsa lesson, or hop in the car and take the spontaneous road trip. A manager will tell you perhaps it's better to stay home, to stick to the routine, to default to the safest choice—

which is usually the most lifeless choice. Sadly, there are many people who live in such states their whole lives.

Hurt Parts, or Exiles

Causes of distress for a child could be as simple as Mom being in the bathroom for eight minutes but I don't know where she is, or being nicknamed "dummyhead" on the first day of kindergarten, or Dad giving an excessive admonishment following a bike accident. Nonetheless, to bear and process the full brunt of such experiences—that is, to stay with them long enough to come to a cogent understanding and absorb the insights such experiences could provide us with—is not a capacity we had as children.

Exiles are the parts of us that absorb all that has not been fully processed through our system, all that at one time was too hot to handle, too painful to look at. Due to our survival instinct that compels us to circumvent pain, these are the parts of us that we attempt to keep locked up and out of view, hence "exiles." Richard Schwartz sometimes refers to these parts as "basement children" because we tend to hold them down in unconscious regions of the mind in hope that they might wither away and disappear entirely. Yet, to paraphrase Schwartz further, we often hear them calling up to us through the floorboards.

Imagine trying to hold a cork underwater. You can push it down just fine, but if you take your hand off of it, it pops right back up to the surface. Now, imagine trying to hold ten corks underwater. You might manage to get your hands and arms over them all for some time, but sooner or later one of them is going to slip past you. Now imagine trying to keep fifty corks down. And then a hundred. Now imagine you have to keep any number of corks down twenty-four hours a day, seven days a week, 365 days a year. The corks represent all the parts of us that hold our core hurts for us. There are two drains on our energy inherent in this activity that we should not underestimate. Obviously, the amount of exertion that it would take to keep the corks submerged would drain us. Less obvious is that the hurts themselves, the submerged corks, are eating up our psychosomatic energy. It takes much more effort to manifest pain than it does ease. And the whole charade is a fool's errand, as sooner or later an exiled cork will break free and find itself exposed at the surface. In this analogy, our manager parts are the ones attempting to keep the corks submerged, and it's our firefighters (extreme defenses) that come out when a vulnerable cork becomes exposed.

Firefighters

Think back to the beginning of this book, when I told you about the annoying customer service experience that got my system unnecessarily overheated. This was due, in part, to my own trauma history, which has resulted in my feeling threatened any time I feel contained or restricted by another party—in this case, being made to wait for help while my word processor was held hostage. The parts of me that became activated in those moments were my firefighters, my defenders; these are the parts wisely driven to keep me safe but that, like our managers and exiles, also tend to be a bit misguided. My firefighters manifested in the form of irritation and anger in a futile attempt to push back at the situation. In a more extreme situation wherein core hurts get more substantially triggered (think: fighting with a lover), these parts could compel me toward drug use (in the past, at least), aggression, overeating, and other forms of self-medicating to smother the "fire" of my exiles busting out of the basement.

Ultimately, our defenders are very wise parts of us, but they tend to manifest as problematic. Why? Two main reasons: (1) They were programmed in childhood when we were defenseless and vulnerable. These parts of ourselves are often frozen in time. (2) We tend to have poor relationships with these parts of ourselves. We might hate them, be ashamed of them, or simply wish they'd go away. Their hidden wisdom can be uncovered when we can (1) update these parts of ourselves on how well resourced and strong we are now that we're grown up, and (2) step into a friendly, and even loving, relationship with them.

Who We Truly Are

The most essential aspect of our inner family is our natural state, our original nature, the love we were born with. This correlates with "Buddha nature" (or in Sanskrit, *tathagatagarbha*) in Buddhism, "Self" (with a capital *S*) in Vedic religions, "Source" in many Native American traditions, and in IFS it's called "self-energy." The natural state is what we experience when all other parts of us relax and dissipate. The experience of the natural state emerging can feel just like the sun coming out from behind the clouds or like a clear and warm center revealed as our inner tussle seems to fall back. In Buddhism, it is sometimes pointed to as the natural warmth of awareness itself. Self-energy is what's most likely present in the expansive moments when we feel connected in the flow or spontaneously warm toward another being.

In IFS, this aspect of you (notice I'm not calling it a part) consists of four main qualities—"the four Cs." In fact, we can use the presence of these qualities to gauge whether we're in the natural state: calm, creativity, curiosity, and compassion. If you've ever experienced any of these states of mind in an earnest, uncontrived sort of way, then you've tasted the goodness of the natural state. All the practices in this book are designed to give you glimpses of this state, deepen your experience of it, and train you to remain there for longer and longer. It's important that we get clear and specific about what the natural state entails now, because this is the aspect of self we'll need to access in order to do the healing work to come. Thankfully, it is not a state of consciousness we have to cultivate, or work to achieve. It is not necessarily esoteric or hard to attain, and it certainly doesn't call for putting pressure on ourselves. Again, it is what is revealed when all else falls away. We simply undo our tension and reactivity and relax into it.

Our natural state is never marred by anything that we've experienced. It remains intact no matter what. Like the sky, it is the background, the substratum of our experience. It is the space that storms and model scenes and tornados and core beliefs all dance within, but the sky itself is never affected. It is always there, though our experience of it becomes obscured. Upon hearing this you might ask, "If that's true, then how am I in the condition I'm in now?" That's precisely where "parts" step in. We're born with Buddha nature *and* born with parts of our psyche that intervene to help us function because, again, the natural state would never be able to survive this world totally on its own.

The natural state is in the domain of *absolute reality*, that is, the aspect of reality that is marked by oneness and transcendence, what some might correlate with notions of divinity. In this, our current myth, it is the substratum of reality itself, the unchanging backdrop against which everyday experience is enacted. It's like the space of a room or the inside of a tea cup; it is self-existent, and it accommodates whatever you want to fill it with. On the other hand, everything manifest that you can perceive with your senses is in the domain of *relative reality*, the aspect of reality that is in constant flux and that gives things their uniqueness. Absolute reality is the ocean, whereas the waves of that ocean—individual, unique, constantly changing, constantly rising and falling—are relative reality. The absolute is one, the relative is many. Our being is the ocean, our parts are the waves.

THE WORK TO COME

The next practice is an adaptation of the "parts work" of IFS. It's a powerful process for evolving our inner relationships. It's sort of like self-hypnosis without the being hypnotized part. Basically, we'll be creating a safe and supportive arena—a holding environment again—to allow the unconscious mind to come forward into consciousness, which takes a lot less effort than you might think. I personally do something pretty close to this practice most mornings, and it has paid dividends in clarity and freedom.

First, for clarity's sake, I want to give you a play-by-play of what we'll do together. This is work we'd ordinarily do in a one-on-one setting where I'd dialogue with you throughout the practice and give you prompts accordingly. We won't have that opportunity here, which is better in a way, because ultimately I want you to become your own guide in this practice. For now, there's no need to worry about remembering the series of steps, as I'll guide you through them on the recording. Eventually, through the magic of repetition, you'll be able to let go of these steps and act as your own healer in a more spontaneous fashion.

1. Settling In: Shamatha Meditation and Declaration of Practice as a Holding Environment

You'll transition into the practice with some breathwork and by reminding yourself that this is a perfectly safe space for doing this kind of work. You do this to let your limbic system know that it's OK for the defenses to drop a little and for your exiles to at least peek outside the closet.

2. Triggering an Afflicted Emotional State

As in the last meditation, we'll need an upset part of you to be present so that we have something (someone) to work with. If that's not already the case, you'll need to trigger an upset by thinking of an experience you've had recently during which your firefighters or exiles came out of the woodwork. You might suddenly find that you want to work with several scenarios at once or figure out the ultimate one to work with, but that's not necessary. As my own therapist often says to me, "I have a feeling that, whatever we talk about, we'll be dealing with the same thing."

Although it might be tempting to go straight to the big hurts in your life, especially if you've been in therapy for some time and are aware of what they are, I ask that you not work with a situation in which you were traumatized or when someone was purposefully very hurtful to you. That might be appropriate after some practice, but it will be a much more successful venture after you're familiar with the process. Start with something big enough to feel but not so big that it's overwhelming.

3. Grounding Emotional Awareness in the Body

Same as it ever was: if we're not embodied, we're in la-la land. Perhaps more to the point: the emotions we experience in the mind correlate to chemical processes in the body and show up as tightness, density, throbbing, tingling, hollowness, or one of many other sensations. You'll feel for where it is and what it is.

4. Unblending

We can't stay "in" the feeling if we're going to relate to the feeling. We need to establish some space between us and the feeling. It might be helpful at this stage to acknowledge that what's been activated is a part of you that is like another person. Then you can think of simply taking a step back from that person. For some people it is just a matter of being present and breathing until there is a sense of space. Ultimately, you will discover your own intuitive way of doing this step.

This step alone has tremendous therapeutic value. Do not be discouraged if the unblending doesn't come easily. You're still doing great work. There's a chance this part of you doesn't want you to unblend because it thinks that you're going to repress it, shame it, or try to "heal" it (too many of us engage in "healing" that is riddled with shame and repression). It might prove useful to remind this part that you're just here to get to know it a little better.

5. Recovering the Natural State

Unblending gives us the opportunity to notice how we feel toward the part we're working with. Generally speaking, there will always be some aversion or impulse for this part to be other than it is. You'll simply ask these *other* parts of you to relax and stand to the side. They don't have to go away entirely, but we'd just like them to move away from the center. This is what you'll need to keep doing until your self-energy emerges, until the sun comes out from behind the clouds.

Again, working on this step alone is a fantastic investment of your time and energy. If unblending goes more slowly for you than the guided meditation does, don't worry. Just stay on this step and keep asking the other parts to relax.

Important: You might sense that another part in particular keeps imposing itself and just won't budge; most likely this is one of the defenders trying to keep you from experiencing the hurts down below (see step 6). This is perfectly natural and good. Our defenses are the gatekeepers to our hurts. Simply switch your focus to working with this part. Make sure there's space between you and it, and then ask your judgments about this part of you to stand aside.

6. Discerning the Nature of the Part

Parts are generally either defensive in nature or they're holding hurts. You'll be able to sense directly what type of part you are working with, and that will determine where we go next.

7. Engaging

This is the heart of the work, and everything about the way you approach this step must be informed by what type of part you are working with and, by logical extension, what its needs are. If the part you're working with is defensive, you will heal your relationship by befriending it. If the part is hurt, you will heal your relationship by acting as a benevolent parent would toward it. In either scenario, you will enter into an interaction with the part, either verbal or symbolic. Furthermore, and this aspect of the work surprises me every single time, you will also get answers and responses from the part itself. This is another reason we want to be embodied for this practice: we are engaging with our intuition, which is the domain of the unconscious and thus the body. We want to allow space for the answers to come from the depths of the body, not from our heads.

Defensive Parts

Can you sense how hard they've been working on your behalf? Can you sense how very judgmental you've been to this part when it's just trying to help, albeit in a misguided fashion? Rather than going to war with this part of you, wouldn't it make more sense to befriend it so it can be fully on your side? Perhaps this part of you even sees something that's putting you in harm's way that you've been missing. Perhaps this part of you is holding an insight that, if you continue in enmity, you won't ever get. Is there something you can do to help this part relax? You can literally ask this.

Hurt Parts

Is it possible to sense how this part of you is just like a child who's hurt, freaked out, and feeling abandoned? In acknowledging that, can you see how you so often take the wrong approach to dealing with this part—trying to make it go away, judging it, hating it? How does it feel to consider the burdens of this child? Is it possible to open to empathy for this little one? A good question to ask here is if whether this part has a story it's been wanting to tell you, whether there's anything it would like you to know.

An important note: Defenders can step in at any time during this process and make it seem like you can't access parts of yourself. You might have been feeling blocked from the onset of the practice. You might be in the process of working with a hurt and then go numb or have too much resistance arise to continue. If this happens, simply switch to the defensive part of you that has imposed itself. It is doing so for a reason, and working with this part of you has just as much value as any other part you might encounter in this work.

When Parts Don't Want to Interact with Us

I brought my first cat, Emma Goldman, home from what must have been New York City's most overcrowded and horrific animal shelter. (I was bitten by a dog while I was there. The guy running the place was chain-smoking. My girlfriend at the time cried. I don't know how I didn't.) But there Emma Goldman was, hissing in the back of a kennel. I was told she was damaged goods for life, that she'd hide behind my couch forever. Being who I am, this made me want to bring her home all the more. At home she acted traumatized and was distrustful of me. Who could blame her? I was a strange giant to her, and all the other strange giants before me had been awful. She would hiss from under the bed every time I came around. She was incapable of even eating, her danger alarms were firing so loudly.

I was studying child trauma during my clinical year at grad school at the time. So, I put on my therapist hat and did some research on how I might create a holding environment for this tiny being. I read that cats feel calm when the variables in their environment are consistent. I also read that they feel safer if you don't look directly at them and if you happen to yawn around them. After all, if you're a predator, you wouldn't be taking your eyes off your prey, nor would you want to show any sign of weakness, such as being sleepy.

I put Emma Goldman in a spare room where she could be alone. I began visiting her every hour on the hour for exactly ten minutes. For the entire first day, I just sat across the room from her, looked in another direction, and fake yawned from time to time. Emma hissed and hissed. I went on yawning. I needed to give her time to figure out that I wasn't any threat to her. We continued the regimen for three days. Slowly she stopped hissing so much and started to relax more. Incrementally she came to accept food and treats from me and play with the toys I brought her. The moment eventually came when she allowed me to pet her, and soon after that she burst out of the spare room, ready to explore her new domain.

What sort of inhumane treatment have we unleashed on our anxiety, sadness, loneliness, anger, and their familiars? Doing this work can be very much like me bringing Emma Goldman home. Why on earth should our parts trust us at this point? If someone is enough of a jerk to me, I'll eventually block them on all my social media accounts. Our emotional parts are no different. They've unfriended us. When we suddenly approach them with this new intention, they're often not quick to be trusting. Do not be dismayed. What's needed here is for you to simply sit in the same room with them as a safe and stable adult. Let them hiss at you. *You* hold your new intention. Eventually they will get the message that you're a good person to be around. It is when our parts begin to trust us to lead, to be the adult in the room, that this work truly opens up. Once we can become a decent parent to ourselves and display that to our parts through our interactions with them, they begin to set their baggage down. This is what's often called "getting out of our own way."

Winding Down

If you're going to open a wound with the intention of applying antiseptic to help it heal properly, it's just as important that you close the wound back up properly. Similarly, we always want to seal up our deep emotional work with care. I simply make sure to use some of the techniques at the end of the shamatha meditation instructions in the first part of this book. Invoking that fake smile, scanning the body with the sun, dedicating the merit of your practice to others who are suffering—these all can go a long way to help you restabilize post-practice. Some extra self-care—such as long, warm baths or going for long walks—may be in order as well. When you're doing deep work like this, treat yourself.

Practice: *Parts Work Meditation*

Sit upright and take some time to review the points of posture. Check in with yourself. Invoke somatic awareness by scanning the body. Balance your system with breathwork as needed. Let your attention land in the center of the heart, and feel your breath rising and falling there, allowing it to find its natural rhythm, honoring the spaces between breaths.

Think of a situation from your recent history that upset you. Please don't pick a traumatizing event, but rather something mildly intense; pick a time when your feelings were hurt or you were worried, ashamed, or angry. Don't worry too much about finding the "perfect" scene. It's all connected anyhow. Once you settle on a scene, allow it to play out in the theater of your mind's eye.

Let the feelings come. This is a safe space for them to emerge, and they are welcome here. Notice that they arise not only in the mind but also in the body. What are the characteristics of those sensations? Heavy or light? Sharp or dull? Pulsing or constant? Warm or cool? Feel into the somatic dimensions of this emotion, allowing the story in the mind to fade away.

Acknowledge that this is a part of you and not the real you. It's a part of you that is just like another person. Check to see whether there's any space between you and this part or whether you feel like you're "in" it. Notice how quickly you blended with this part. In a friendly manner begin unblending from this part, like taking two steps back from another person. It might help to say to this part, "I'm not going to push you away or beat up on you—I would just like to get to know you."

Take all the time you need here. If unblending is all you work on with the rest of your allotted meditation time today, fantastic. This much alone is a tremendously useful skill.

Once there's a feeling of space between you and the part, notice how you feel toward this part. Hate it? Ashamed of it? Sick of it? Wish it would go away? Get honest. It's perfectly logical for you to be averse to unpleasant feelings. And at the same time, I want you to ask these other parts if they would simply relax and stand to the side. They don't have to go away, but rather move aside. This may take a few tries. A friendly tone helps. It might also help to let these other parts know that you're perfectly safe and that you're simply trying to get to know what I'll now call the "target part."

Notice whether there are any residual negative feelings toward the target part. If so, simply keep asking these other parts of you to relax and stand to the side. Spend as much time as you need to on this step.

If one of these other parts of you—whether it's numbness, anger, shame, or something else—has come front and center and doesn't seem to want to go anywhere, honor the wisdom of your system. Make this insistent part the target part. First take a moment to make sure you're unblended from it, then continually ask any negative feelings you have about this part to relax and stand aside.

Look for a place inside of you that feels kind of clear, perhaps warm and kind, and open to working with this part of you. You might already be sort of leaning in, really curious about this part, or you might be feeling empathy for this part and its struggles. If you can't find this aspect of your self-energy, keep asking anything that's in your way to simply relax and stand aside.

Once you have recovered the energy of your true nature, discern whether this is a hurt part that you've exiled or a defensive part of you that's trying to keep you safe in some way. What comes next will be determined by the type of part you are meeting with and the intuitive sense you get of its reaction to you.

If this is a defensive part of you (which is most likely the case, but not necessarily), can you see how hard this part of you has been working on your behalf? Can you find any gratitude, any respect? Can you see how you've had a misinformed relationship with this part of you all along? If so, express those feelings and revelations to this part and see if you can sense its reaction, which might come as a subtle change in how you feel, or it may come in words. Take your time. Then, use this next little while to converse with this part—a conversation that asks, "How can we be better friends? Is there anything I need to do to help you relax?" You can literally ask those questions, or express anything else that seems appropriate within your intention of healing the relationship. Amends may need to be made. Please note that this part may distrust you and want nothing to do with you. If so, respect that and maintain a steady, warm presence for it. Take as much time as you need to be with this part of you.

If this is a hurt, exiled part of you, approach it as if it were a child who is freaked out, alone, and afraid: with tenderness. Acknowledge that you see that this part is hurting. Check to see if any empathy, compassion, or remorse is arising in you. If so, express this toward the part and see if you can sense any sort of response—perhaps as a shift in body feeling, perhaps in words. The conversation that needs to happen here should have the tone of, "I am completely here with you and you are not alone. How can I help you? Won't you tell me your story? I'm so sorry for keeping you locked up for all these years. Is there anything you would like me to know?" These questions might be a good place to start, or you might sense that this part wants to have a different sort of interaction with you. Take as long as you need to interact with this part. Whatever happens, you are here to understand the part, not the other way around.

When it is time for the meditation to end, either because you are out of time or because it just feels right, say goodbye and express thanks to all of your parts, to your entire system, for being willing to work with you today and for all that they consistently do for your well-being. Take a deep breath and let the practice go.

Settle back into the space of your breathing heart for some time. End your practice with a big, stupid smile or some calming breathwork, or both.

Transition gently out of your practice. Congratulations. You've just done some extremely courageous work.

14

Working with the Inner Critic and Other Harsh Inner Voices

Meditation is not a matter of trying to achieve ecstasy, spiritual
bliss, or tranquility, nor is it attempting to be a better person.
It is simply the creation of a space in which we are able
to expose and undo our neurotic games,
our self-deceptions, our hidden fears and hopes.
—CHÖGYAM TRUNGPA RINPOCHE

There's a lot of different Annes in me. Sometimes I think that
is why I am such a troublesome person. If I was just the one
Anne it would be ever so much more comfortable,
but then it wouldn't be half as interesting.
—ANNE OF GREEN GABLES

I'VE BEEN WAITING, daydreaming about this moment for
months. Now that it's come, I'm lying on the floor of a back office
filled with anxious dread. "Why does it seem to work this way so
much of the time? Why must I be sabotaged by panic right when
the dream-come-true moments present themselves?"

I never get nervous teaching anymore, but everything about
this gig is intimidating. I'm about to teach as a substitute for the
brilliant and adored Vinny Ferraro, the first man to deliver meditation instruction to my ears over a decade ago. There are two
hundred people here. *Two hundred people.* Including the therapist
I worked with in rehab (who, in a strange twist of events, has
become my colleague). It's my first time teaching in San Francisco. It's my first time teaching from a stage. It's my first time

being amplified over a PA system. It's like a dog pile of crazy-making variables. I start thinking that being able to leave my body in meditation is a talent I should really work on, because there's no back door to this venue.

At T-minus five minutes, my inner critic goes nuclear. "Everyone is expecting Vinny and they're getting you? They're going to be pissed. People are either going to get up and walk out or spend the next two hours wishing they had. Don't you remember how bummed you used to get when you'd come to Vinny's class and a sub would show up? That's what everyone in the room is going to be feeling about you. You're not even a real dharma teacher, just some social worker with some half-cocked ideas that sound good on Facebook. You blow it in real life every time. You stutter, and your jokes aren't funny. You still use filler language after all these years. You still haven't taken a teacher training or seen a voice coach. This is it: the moment you're exposed as the fraud you are. *To two hundred people.* Who told you this was a good idea? And now you're so nervous, it's almost certain you're going to screw everything up. I hate you. We should've just stayed home. You're not ready to teach at this level."

Lying there, having done a ton of breathwork, my thoughts are still screaming. I am powerless to make anxiety go away. With two minutes left till showtime, I remember—duh: *I'm dealing with a part of me.* A part of me that feels like it has to scream. A part of me that is berating me because it doesn't want me to faceplant like a fool. A part of me that remembers the time I peed my pants in front of my entire third-grade class. A part of me that is protecting a less resilient part of me, most likely a younger part of me, and one that is *so afraid.*

Recognizing the terrified child standing behind my inner critic, now a sense of compassion became available to me. I shift my attitude toward friendliness. I tell the defensive critic that its concerns are completely valid. It is indeed possible that I could screw up the talk. That's always possible. I tell the critic that we share the same motivation to do well out there, and that I definitely don't want the scared part of me to get hurt either. I then ask the part if we could go out and give the class together as opposed to against one another, if we could be on the same team. The tension in my body begins to release. The volume of my mind turns down a couple of notches. The critic is conceding. I thank it. This defender still hangs around for the first few minutes of the talk, but once it becomes obvious things are going well, it recedes entirely. The class is fruitful and satisfying.

Too many of us live with harsh inner voices that range from self-sabotaging to outright abusive. Over and over, and somehow in the moments that matter most, we find ourselves assailed by defenders who tell us we're no good, we're imposters, we're doomed to fail, that humiliation and rejection are inevitable. They cause our bodies to contract and tremble. Our voices shake. We feel stuck and helpless, and yet so often there is no choice but to show up and do the dreaded thing anyhow. The nervous jitters are even likely to stick around to take jabs at us while we're presenting or performing. And then the moment it's finally over, we get hit with a wave of shame and embarrassment. We'll find ourselves approached by others telling us how well we did, how they got so much from it, how proud of us they are, and all the while the nagging voice inside is completely certain that they're just saying that to be polite. They're just trying to make us feel better after we bombed so hard.

The truth is, it would be safer to stay small, to not try, to not accomplish anything. If we have something, it can be taken away from us. If we have nothing, at least we can't fall farther.

The inner critic is, of course, only one example of parts that wield harsh voices. Intrusive thoughts could be related to trauma, addiction, obsessiveness, worry, shame, or depression. But regardless which part it is, several things remain true: they don't listen when we ask them to just leave, they are not without some level of logic, they are trying to protect us in some way, and (this is important) they don't have all the facts.

BEFRIENDING THE DEFENDER

I've used what I learned that night in San Francisco to develop a method for working with harsh defenders. It's rooted in both IFS and Cognitive Behavior Therapy and has been met with great success. The best part is that it's not rocket science.

I use the acronym DAD to describe the three principal steps involved, which are Discern, Affirm, and Debrief.

1. Discern the motivation of this part.

This part of you has been activated by the risk involved in being seen by others, or by something else that feels emotionally dangerous. Understand that it's ultimately trying to keep you away from the pain of failure, being rejected, or something along those lines.

2. Affirm this part's feelings.

I often call this step "radical validation." Here, we want to go completely over to this part's side and try to see things through its eyes. After all, there's a rationale behind what this part is saying to you that makes sense at some level. We want to let this part know that it is perfectly right to feel the way it does. It's crucial that we give this part some solid examples of how it's so very right.

This step is counterintuitive and can freak people out at first, because it seems like we're reinforcing our negative beliefs by validating them. If you're thinking that, your logic is sound, but only if we take this step out of the context of the entire process. Therefore, I ask that you suspend your disbelief for a moment and think within the myth that parts are just like people. Isn't it true that people scream only when they don't feel heard? That there's no reason to scream when someone's agreeing with you? Well, this part of us is screaming. It sees us going toward threat and nothing more. When this part starts feeling heard, it will begin to soften and become inclined to listen to other things we have to say, just like anyone else would. Affirmation is what opens the door to step three, Debrief, which is where the real medicine is. But hang on to your hats here; this will all make more sense soon.

First, we'll review some of the more universal things inner critics and their associates tend to say and some affirming responses you could use in talking with this part:

- "You're not good enough."

  Response: It's definitely true that I'm not the best at everything. There'll probably always be someone better than me, and I'll always be a work in progress. I want to live up, but sometimes I just don't. It's called being human. I have some pretty great parts, and I definitely need to improve, too. You are perfectly right for feeling this way.

- "You're a nothing, and you deserve for bad things to happen."

  Response: Even though I try not to think about it, it's true that I've done some pretty terrible things in my time. I've been unfair. I've cheated, told white lies, and even been cruel in some of my least savory moments. Perhaps way worse. If karma bit me in the ass here, it wouldn't be shocking. Thanks for pointing this out to me. Maybe I have some amends to make.

- "You're going to fail."

  Response: You're absolutely right. It's totally possible that I might fail. I've blown it in the past, and it could happen again. That'd be pretty painful. I can see how you'd feel that way. I don't wanna fail either.

- "You'll be rejected."

  Response: It's also true that this is totally possible. I've been rejected in the past, and that really hurt for a long time. Feeling like I belong is essential to having a life that feels good. It makes absolute sense to want to avoid this.

- "You're a fraud."

  Response: You're right: I've faked it in the past. I've felt like it was necessary to puff myself up, cut corners, or exaggerate things when I've felt insecure. I'd hate for that to be exposed right now—or any of my shortcomings, for that matter.

Notice how in each of these statements I've done two things: I've found and stated reasons why this part might feel this way, and I've made sure to include a statement along the lines of, "You're completely right." There is nothing that goes through our minds that doesn't have an explanation somewhere, and it is usually not that hard to find. Also, it's important that when we do this, we affirm every one of the part's main complaints. This is radical validation.

3. Debrief.

I also refer to this step as a "loving confrontation." Although it's true that there's some level of logic to this part's complaints, it's also true that this part is a bit misguided. It doesn't seem to have all the information about the situation. For instance, you'll recall that parts are often frozen in time, never growing past the moment in which a painful model scene was absorbed. I often have my clients ask their parts how old *the part thinks the client is*, and much to their surprise, they'll get "four" or "sixteen" or some other young age. This means that this part still thinks we're as defenseless and poorly resourced as we were when we were kids. No wonder it's so freaked out by our having to contend with our adult situation. What follows are three reality checks we can kindly deliver to the defender we're working with:

The Tour of How Things Are Now. This plays out a lot like Ebenezer Scrooge's sojourn with the Ghost of Christmas Future, except that the part gets taken on a tour of how safe and well resourced you are now. You can tell your parts about (and even imagine mental images of) your friends and social supports, how intelligent you've become, how you're working on skills to evolve and take care of yourself—at this very moment, even. You can update your parts as to any successes you've had in the meantime, which might include your job and even your bank account—all to display that you are relatively materially secure and not facing a survival threat, at least in this department. (In the event your job isn't going so well or your bank account is a ghost town with tumbleweeds rolling by, you'll likely want to avoid that part and skip to the narrative on resilience.)

You might say, "I want you to know that I'm twenty-eight now (for example), all grown up. I don't live at home anymore and I can provide for myself. That scary situation I used to face all the time—that doesn't happen anymore. I got out. I have great people in my life now who care about me and have my back. I'm strong, smart, and working to heal everything that hurts. I meditate and go to therapy and read books and do all the things I need to do in order to have a good life. I'm much more resourceful and able to handle stress and challenges and difficulty way better than before. I'm wondering how you feel now that you're seeing this."

You're Resilient. Isn't it true that you've been down before, but you were able to pick yourself back up eventually? Isn't it true that you've even been strengthened by some of your most serious scrapes? Isn't it true that the last time you got your heart broken (for example) is when you eventually turned to therapy, started learning to play the guitar, started seeing your friends more, learned meditation, or something else life affirming in nature? Therefore, you can truthfully say to this part, "You're right. I just might fail. I just might get hurt. I can see why you'd be screaming at me about that. I've been hurt before, and it was terrible. *And*, you know, I'm also pretty resilient. I'm pretty sure that, even if that happens and it really sucks, I'll be able to bounce back in due time. I've even grown from having faced adversity in the past. I'm not sure I'd be going to yoga or salsa lessons right now if not for that."

We're on the Same Team. Just as in situations of human-to-human conflict, when one party begins to yell, the other party yells back. It's totally reasonable to resist, even hate, the inner critic, *and* it's also true that the critic actually wants the same things that we want, to not get hurt or feel threatened. Putting together the Affirm and Debrief steps can look like, "It makes so much sense that you think I might fail and that you want me to avoid the situation . . . but you know what? When you yell at me like this it actually makes it more likely that I *will* fail. We're actually on the same side here. Can you help me avoid a self-fulfilling prophecy? Is there something I can do to help us be on the same team?"

When I do this work on myself and others, I generally find that all three debriefing methods are necessary.

Something I really enjoy about this method of working with parts is that we can skip the processes that come before actually talking to the part. Once we become aware that we're working with a part, we can start affirming and debriefing right away, and then our inner system begins to open up as a whole. Generally, after the first round of affirming and debriefing, the critic will sort of relax, though it will still be incredulous and distrusting of us in some way. That's just fine. Simply repeat the process. For example: "Of course you feel that way. We were just arguing with each other a minute ago, and it's new for you to be hearing these things from me. I just want to check: we're still on the same team, right? Do you think you can give me a chance here?"

After two to three rounds of this process, a more vulnerable part begins to emerge, the part we can logically assume the critic was protecting all along. I find that the openness and curiosity of self-energy also becomes more immediately available with this shift if we simply look for it. The opportunity of this situation is to engage with the exile in some way—at the very least, to give it a little bit of lovingkindness for a moment.

As with all practices, doing this may feel wonky at first and may yield mixed results, but every time you return to it it'll be more familiar and effective.

PRACTICE: *Relating to the Inner Critic*

For this practice, we will skip the preliminaries. If the inner critic or another harsh voice isn't already active inside you right now, please think of a recent situation in which a part of you was activated. Allow the feelings you had about the situation to emerge, including all the harsh thoughts that came with those feelings.

Discern that this is a part of you and not the real you. Listen to its "voice" and what it has to say. Discern this part's motivation: Is it trying to protect you in some way? Is this critic trying to save you from failure? Heartbreak? Humiliation?

Affirm this part's feelings and point of view. Radically validate this part. After all, there is some logic to what it is say-ing. I want you to say to this part, "You are totally right for feeling the way that you do. You're right. I have failed before. I very well may fail again here, and that would really hurt. And you're right: sometimes I'm just not good enough when compared to other people. Someone is always going to be doing a better job than me, or appear to have it more together than I do. I can see now why you're fighting so hard to protect me from looking like a fool. I don't want to look like a fool either. You're right: I am a bit of an imposter as well. I have faked things before and have told white lies to make myself look better to others. Thank you so much for pointing these things out to me and for working so very hard to keep pain at bay." Having expressed this, check in and see how the critic is feeling now. It may have calmed some or not at all; simply check in.

Debrief this part. Offer a loving confrontation to gently show this part some of its blind spots: "*And*, if I do screw up, it's true that that will hurt. But you know, I'm a pretty well-resourced person these days. I've been doing a lot of healthy work on myself lately, developing emotional intelligence, developing my meditation practice. I have good people in my life who love and support me. I'm pretty sure that I'll be able to bounce back from any hurt that might come of that, should I screw up. And you know something else? If we look back at my previous failures, they actually taught me a lot and pushed me to reach for some life-affirming things. Even if I do look like a fool, I might end up being better for it in the long run. And, even if you don't buy any of that because I've been so wrong in the past, maybe you can see that, when you yell at me like this, it makes it more likely that I'll screw up. When you yell at me like this, I lose sleep, I get nervous, and I become preoccupied, and this is all creating pain instead of helping me avoid it. The thing is, you and I are actually on the same side. I don't want to get hurt or fail either. What can I do so that we can begin to work together instead of against one another?"

Apply, Rinse, Repeat

I generally find that it takes two or three rounds of this process to help the inner critic to calm down. This is a part of you that has become incredibly mistrusting of you, so don't be surprised if winning it over takes some work. After your first round, check in with the part again. Has there been any shift in the thoughts you're experiencing or the way your body feels? If you need to complete the DAD steps again, then patiently and kindly do so.

Once this part of you has softened, check in with your emotions and see what's there. You may find calm or relief, or it's entirely likely that you'll notice some feelings that are more vulnerable in nature, such as sadness or hurt. You are now experiencing the exiled part of you the inner critic was defending. In either case, check to see if self-energy is more available to you now; that is, see if you can feel some warmth, empathy, or curiosity in your inner system as well. You can offer some of that warmth to the exiled part, you can choose to just rest here and breathe a while, or you can simply say goodbye to your parts for now and transition from your practice.

15

Putting It All Together: Integrating Buddhist Meditation with Parts Work

There is a teaching that says that behind all hardening and
tightening and rigidity of the heart, there's always fear. But if
you touch fear, behind fear there is a soft spot. And if
you touch that soft spot, you find the vast blue sky.

—PEMA CHÖDRÖN

I AM SITTING on the coast of Ecuador as I write this, not far from
the lazy surfer town of Montañita. To get here, I needed a ride
from Brooklyn to John F. Kennedy International Airport, a ticket
to fly to Bogotá, Colombia, another ticket to fly into Guayaquil,
Ecuador, and a hired driver to show up and bring me to the bun-
galow I had reserved. As I sit and watch the waves roll in, grateful
for the reprieve from the constant cacophony of noise and bustle
that is New York, it occurs to me that this moment is a product
of many variables both coming together and somehow flowing
smoothly enough for my safe arrival.

Together, we have arrived at a similar moment in this book
and the practices we've developed. Our final practice incorporates every element of each of the meditations explored so far. By
adding in the option to practice either maitri or tonglen at the
end of our parts work, we are thus arriving at a true integration
of Eastern and Western practices. The prospect of healing our
lives is firmly in hand.

It has been said that meditation and psychotherapy are com-
plementary, like two sides of a coin. What one does, the other
cannot, and vice versa. To paraphrase Buddhist psychotherapist

Jeff Rubin, meditation is excellent at training us to be present for our lives but terrible at giving us the means to delve into the histories that have molded us into who we are today. Conversely, psychotherapy gives us the means to excavate the past but is lousy at helping us to become truly available to our experience now.

I see it differently. In my experience, these two practices are more like a Venn diagram: two complete, intersecting circles with a large area of overlap between them. Within that overlap lies the final practice laid out in this book: using self-directed parts work combined with mindful emanation of the heart's deepest energies. To my knowledge, this has not been done before or, if so, not in this way. We stand at the cutting edge of a new understanding together—right here, right now.

The practice that follows is identical to the Parts Work Meditation we explored before (page 223–26), except you will have the option to extend maitri or tonglen to the target part you are working with. This is powerful work, and I've seen it shift things for people who encounter parts that are stubbornly silent and do not wish to engage. I've also seen it help people reach new depths in their relationship to hurt parts they were already working with. The only thing I need to highlight before we begin is this: whether you practice maitri or tonglen is not up to you, it's up to the part. In the practice, we will check in with the target part and ask if they'd rather have some of their burdens lifted or if they'd rather bask in the sun of lovingkindness. Which road you take is entirely up to your unconscious.

Practice: *Parts Work with Maitri or Tonglen*

Sit upright and take some time to review the points of posture. Check in with yourself. Invoke somatic awareness by scanning the body. Balance your system with breathwork as needed.

Then let your attention land in the center of the heart and feel your breath rising and falling there, allowing it to find its natural rhythm, honoring the spaces between breaths.

Think of a situation from recent history that upset you. Please don't pick a traumatizing event but something mildly intense. Choose a time when your feelings were hurt or you were worried, ashamed, or angry. Don't worry too much about finding the "perfect" scene. It's all connected anyhow. Once you settle on a scene, allow it to play out in the theater of your mind's eye.

Let the feelings come. This is a safe space for them to emerge, and they are welcome here. Notice that they arise not only in the mind but also in the body. What are the sensations present, and how do they manifest? Heavy or light? Sharp or dull? Pulsing or constant? Warm or cool? Feel into the somatic dimensions of this emotion, allowing the story in the mind to fade away.

Acknowledge that this is a part of you and not the real you. It's a part of you that is just like another person. Check to see whether there's any space between you and this part or whether you feel like you're "in" it. Notice how quickly you blended with this part. In a friendly manner, begin unblending from this part, as if you're taking two steps back from another person. It might help to say to this part, "I'm not going to push you away or beat up on you—I would just like to get to know you."

Take all the time you need here. If unblending is all you work on with the rest of your allotted meditation time today, fantastic. This much alone is a tremendously useful skill.

Once there's a feeling of space between you and the part, notice how you feel toward this part. Hate it? Ashamed of it? Sick of it? Wish it would go away? Get honest. It's perfectly logical for you to be averse to unpleasant feelings. And at the same time, I want you to ask these other parts if they would simply relax and stand to the side. They don't have to go away but rather move aside. This may take a few tries. A friendly tone helps. It might also help to let these other parts know that you're perfectly safe and that you're simply trying to get to know what I'll now call the "target part."

Notice whether there are any residual negative feelings toward the target part. If so, simply keep asking these other parts of you to relax and stand to the side. Spend as much time as you need to on this step.

If one of these other parts of you—whether it's numbness, anger, shame, or something else—has come front and center and doesn't seem to want to go anywhere, we want to honor the wisdom of your system. Make this insistent part the target part. First take a moment to make sure you're unblended from it, and then continually ask any negative feelings you have about this part to relax and stand aside.

Look for a place inside of you that feels kind of clear, perhaps warm and kind, and open to working with this part of you. You might already be leaning in, really curious about this part, or you might be feeling empathy for this part and it's struggles. If you can't find this natural state, your Buddha nature, keep asking anything else that's in your way to simply relax and stand aside.

Once you have recovered the energy of your true nature, discern whether this is a hurt part that you've exiled or a defensive part of you that's trying to keep you safe in some way. What comes next will be determined by the type of part you are meeting with and the intuitive sense you get of its reaction to you.

If this is a defensive part of you (which is most likely the case, but not necessarily), can you see how hard this part of you has been working on your behalf? Can you find any gratitude, any respect? Can you see how you've had a misinformed relationship with this part of you all along? If so, express those feelings and revelations to this part, and see if you can sense its reaction, which might come as a subtle change in how you feel, or it may come in words. Take your time. Then, with the attitude and tone of a good friend, express to this part that you would like to meditate for it, and ask if this part would prefer for you to take away some of its burdens and offer compassion, or if it would simply like to feel your loving intentions for it. It might be subtle, but you will get a sense of this part leaning toward one more than the other. If the answer is tonglen—to experience compassion and a relief from suffering—begin breathing in the thick black smoke of this part's upsets and exhaling the golden space of compassion. If the answer is maitri, or lovingkindness, begin emanating your heart to this part with phrases such as, "May you be happy. May you be healthy. May you feel safe. May you be free."

If this is a hurt, exiled part of you, approach it as if it were a child who is freaked out, alone, and afraid: with tenderness. Acknowledge that you see that this part is hurting. Check to see if any empathy, compassion, or remorse is arising in you. If so, express this toward the part and see if you can sense any sort of response—perhaps a softening of the body, a shift in how you feel, or perhaps the part seems to be "saying" something in response. Then, with the attitude and tone of a good parent, express to this part that you would like to meditate for it, and ask if this part would prefer for you to take away some of its burdens and offer compassion, or if it would simply like to feel your loving intentions for it. It might be subtle, but you will get a sense of this part leaning toward one more than the other. If the answer is tonglen, begin breathing in the thick black smoke of this part's upsets and exhaling the golden space of compassion. If it is lovingkindness, begin emanating your heart to it with phrases such as, "May you be happy. May you be healthy. May you feel safe. May you be free."

When it is time for the meditation to end, either because you are out of time or because it just feels right for any other reason, say goodbye and express your thanks to all your parts, to your entire system, for being willing to work with you today and for all that they do for you always. Take a deep breath and let the practice go.

Settle back into the space of your breathing heart for some

time. End your practice with a big, stupid smile or some calming breathwork, or both.

Transition gently out of your practice. Now go do something supremely kind for yourself. You've earned it.

Conclusion

I WAS IN LINE to board a roller coaster the day it hit me that terror and excitement are actually the same feeling. I've always had a mixed relationship with roller coasters. My dad once humiliated me to no end when I was all but six years old because I was so scared of them. The mental association never faded. That doesn't change the fact that they look damn fun. The advertisements showing us the cliché images of riders raucously screaming and laughing and carrying on are indeed effective. So, when my friends invited me to hop on a bus to Six Flags in New Jersey, I took it as an opportunity to rewrite the story my dad had left me with.

There was one feeling tone to every experience of that day: adrenaline rush. Yet, I stood there in each line, vacillating between dread and desire about what lay ahead. The part of me that hated the idea of being strapped to a chair and surrendering all control called the adrenal feeling "anxiety," "fear," "terror." The part of me that has always dreamed of soaring through the air called the feeling "exhilaration," "suspense," "excitement." There was only one feeling in me, and yet my experience of it danced between two poles. In moments when I found myself averse to a ride, I recoiled. In moments when I was attracted to a ride, I experienced giddy anticipation. Strapped into a seat, ascending that first gigantic incline, everything in me would scream, "*No!*" Flying weightlessly down the same incline, my whole being echoed, "*Yes!*" That is to say, as my relationship to what was happening shifted, the quality of my experience followed suit.

Question: What's the difference between a romantic gesture and a creepy one?

Answer: Our relationship with the person making said gesture.

If someone we're in love with were to surprise us by showing up at our office with a poem they've penned and a box of pastries, we'd be flattered, endeared. If someone we find to be the social equivalent of a bag of rocks with halitosis were to make the same gesture, we might just call the cops. Same poem, same box of pastries, different relationship, and thus a different chain reaction of experiences.

This is a hopeful truth. It points to the fact that we are never stuck in this life. Our experience is forever workable, made malleable by our relationship to it. We might not be able to change the circumstances we find ourselves in, but the option to shift our relationship to what is happening, and thus to change our experience of it, is always available. This is especially true of how we experience ourselves: our mind, our emotions, our self-worth. We might consider ourselves to be a bag of rocks with breath one can smell from across the room, but the power we have to take a different mindset means we might just be able to discover our inherent loveableness after all.

Life is but a series of "if/then" propositions. *If* we are averse, *then* reality appears one way. *If* we are curious, *then* things open up in a different way. There are endless iterations of this.

We have the opportunity to see this for ourselves in the practice of meditation. When we relate to our thoughts with care, acceptance, and respect, we find that what we once beheld as irritating is actually alive with lessons and insight. We find it's been asking us to look beyond surface appearances all along. By relating to other beings with generosity, we graduate into the realization that we belong to one another—that your joy is my joy, that our well-being is bound up with one another's. We see that those whom we once mistook for objects are actually living reflections of ourselves. We find that the earth is not dead but has actually been hounding us with its gravity, tugging on us to let go of everything we neurotically cling to; asking us to shift from a state of tension to one of relaxation, openness, and clarity.

Relating to our emotional parts with compassion, we start to see that they have been working hard on our behalf all along. They have been either holding our pain for us or fiercely vying for safety. In shifting toward the growth mindset, we discover that the disruptiveness in our life is actually a calling to look beyond the superficial and to reach for deeper satisfaction. All the dragons and paper tigers in our lives merely want to see us act with beauty and courage. Let us not miss the opportunity. Let us proceed with honesty and earnestness. Let us discern correctly that the longing we so often mistake for loneliness is indeed a hunger and a thirst for awakening. What we learned to call pain is actually a calling to come home to our deeper nature.

What if loneliness and anxiety are just indescribable joy wearing a different mask?

May we not back down. May we never give up. May we persevere despite the comfort of the cocoon. May each of us keep going. Ever onward, ever deepening. May we not ignore our precious and fleeting chance to taste the true sweetness of things, not just the menu. May we recognize that openhearted living is the true courage. May we employ our inherent power toward justice and the end of all cruelty. May we pierce every veil of misunderstanding, shatter every dead-end story we've been told. May we come to unconditionally cherish one another, our world, our experience, and ourselves, moment by embodied moment, for the time that these have been entrusted to us. May each day be lived as a celebration of possibility. May we discover our deepest inspiration and purpose for being here. May we unapologetically howl this gospel of possibility from the very rooftops.

Acknowledgments

I bow my head to . . .

. . . those who made this book possible:
Lodro Rinzler, Dave O'Neal, Susan Piver, Matt Zepelin, KJ Grow, Katelin Ross, Audra Figgins, all at Shambhala Publications, Dr. Miles Neale, Ethan Nichtern, Miranda Ganzer, Gretchen vanEsselstyn, Adreanna Limbach, Janae Ewald, Keith Curts, Anna Lindow, Ann Sensing, Erin Dolak, Sarai Schneider, Lynne Desilva-Johnson, Jennifer Darling, Melissa Valentine at Sounds True, Hisae Matsuda at Parallax Press.

. . . those who have fostered opportunities for growth and expansion, those who inspire to no end:
Acharya Eric Spiegel and everyone at Shambhala Meditation Center NYC, Ajna Rae, Alexandra Ariadne, Allison Wilner, Amanda Schnedel, Ambyr D'amato, Andrew Richdale, Ani Gregorians-Beddow, Arianna Bickle, Arusha Baker, Ashley Aplin, Ben Chapman, Betsy Babinecz, Bonnie Pipkin, Brigid Huntoon, Britta Plug, Chera Finnis, Dan Sieling, David Evans, Deborah Brewer, Elizabeth Martinez and everyone at Graham Windham, Ellie Aaron, Ellie Burrows, Erika van Gemeren, everyone at Maha Rose Healing Center, everyone at Spirit Rock Meditation Center, everyone at the Daily Dharma Gathering, Heather Adams, Heather Coleman, Jack Kornfield, Jacob Kyle, Jennifer Jones and New Love City, Jennifer Dopierala, Jessica Stickler and everyone at Jivamukti Yoga Center, Joe Mauricio, Josh Korda, Karen Chadwick, Karen Rosand

and all at Won Dharma Center, Karina McKinney, Kate Barrow, Kathy Cherry, Katie Down, Katy Hansz, Katy Otto, Leslie Guyton, Lila Donnollo, Lilia Mead, Lisa Levine, Maddy Gerrard at Insight Timer, Mata Amritananda Mayi, Mark Beddow, Michael Hewett, Michelle Hansen, Morgan Murray, Nathan and the staff at Esme, Nathan Feiles, Neil McKinlay, Nickie Tilsner, Norman Elizondo, Olivia Marlow-Giovetti, Patricia Pinto, Peter Criswell and all at Omega Institute, Rebecca Greenfield, Rebecca Paul and all at Embodied Philosophy, Reggie Ray, Samantha Yurkosky, Sandy Levine and the staff at NY Open Center, Sarah Seely, Shannon Iverson and all at Kripalu, Sharon Rudeman, Sharon Salzberg, Stephe Psyckes, Steve McKinney, Sue Pincusoff, Sydney Faith Rose, Tania Ryalls, the clinician family at Maria Droste Counseling Services, the gracious staff at Dharma Ocean, the MNDFL fam, Victor Costa, Vinny Ferraro and the good people at Against the Stream SF, every single person who has passed through the doors of my therapy room or classroom; all the rabble-rousers, yoga teachers, dharma proponents, and professional helpers of the world; and those I have so mistakenly forgotten.

. . . my family:

Sally De La Rosa, Tillie Real, Kelsie Johnson, Leslie Fernandez, Danny Fernandez, Micah Fernandez, Mila Fernandez, Bailey Seay, Martin Peña, Lonnie Johnson, Pinkie Anderson, Leyton Anderson, Chris De La Rosa, Jesus De La Rosa, Laura De La Rosa, Monica Garcia, Tencha Garcia, my extended relatives, and all who are gone but not forgotten.

Notes

INTRODUCTION

1. Nancy Colier, "How to Live Peacefully with Repetitive Negative Thoughts," *Psychology Today*, March 8, 2017, https://www.psychology today.com/blog/inviting-monkey-tea/201703/how-live-peace fully-repetitive-negative-thoughts.
2. Sakyong Mipham Rinpoche, in-person teaching, Karme Chöling, Barnet, Vermont, October 2008.
3. Laboratory of Neuro Imaging, "Brain Trivia" (n.d.), September 30, 2017, http://loni.usc.edu/about_loni/education/brain_trivia.php.
4. H. H. Dalai Lama and Howard C. Cutler, *The Art of Happiness* (New York: Riverhead Books, 1998), 47.
5. Merriam-Webster (n.d.), https://www.merriam-webster.com /dictionary/monkey%20around.
6. American Psychiatric Association, *Diagnostic and Statistical Manual of Mental Disorders*, 5th ed. (Washington, DC: Author, 2013).
7. Tad Friend, "Jumpers," *New Yorker*, October 13, 2003, https://www .newyorker.com/magazine/2003/10/13/jumpers.

CHAPTER ONE: TAKING RESPONSIBILITY FOR YOUR OWN HAPPINESS

1. Matthew A. Killingsworth and Daniel T. Gilbert, "A Wandering Mind Is an Unhappy Mind," *Science* 330, no. 6006 (2010): 932, doi:10.1126 /science.1192439.
2. Thomas M. Heffron, "Insomnia Awareness Day: Facts and Stats," last modified March 9, 2018, Sleep Education, http://www.sleepeduca tion.org/news/2014/03/10/insomnia-awareness-day-facts-and-stats.
3. "Insomnia: Symptoms and Causes," last modified March 4, 2015,

Sleep Education, http://www.sleepeducation.org/essentials-in-sleep /insomnia/symptoms-causes.

4. Elijah Wolfson, "The Rise of Ambien: Why More Americans Are Taking the Sleeping Pill and Why the Numbers Matter," *Huffington Post,* July 8, 2013, https://www.huffingtonpost.com/elijah-wolfson- /ambien_b_3223347.html.

5. American Society of Hypertension, "New Research Shows What Raises and Lowers Blood Pressure: Cell Phones, Salt and Saying Om," *Cision PR Newswire,* May 15, 2013, https://www.prnewswire.com/news -releases/new-research-shows-what-raises-and-lowers-blood -pressure-cell-phones-salt-and-saying-om-207508571.html.

6. Carol Dweck, *Mindset: The New Psychology of Success* (New York: Ballentine Books, 2007), 12.

7. Statist Brain Research, "Lottery Winner Statistics," *Statistic Brain,* July 12, 2017, https://www.statisticbrain.com/lottery-winner-statistics.

8. Tyler Curry, "Op-ed: Call Me Crazy, But Here's Why I'm Thankful for Being HIV-Positive," *Advocate,* June 4, 2014, https://www .advocate.com/commentary/tyler-curry/2014/06/04/op-ed-call -me-crazy-here's-why-i'm-thankful-being-hiv-positive.

CHAPTER TWO: THE MAGNIFICENT MISMATCH

1. Fabienne Picard, "State of Belief, Subjective Certainty, and Bliss as a Product of Cortical Dysfunction," *Cortex* 49, no. 9 (2013), https:// www.ncbi.nlm.nih.gov/pubmed/23415878.

2. Russel D. Fernald, "The Evolution of Eyes," *Brain, Behavior, and Evolution* 50 (1997): 253–259, doi:10.1159/000113339.

3. William James, *William James: Writings 1878–1899* (New York: Library of America, 1992), 228.

4. Ivana Buric, Miguel Farias, Jonathan Jong, Christopher Mee, and Inti A. Brazil, "What Is the Molecular Signature of Mind-Body Interventions? A Systematic Review of Gene Expression Changes Induced by Meditation and Related Practices," *Frontiers of Immunology* 8 (June 16, 2017), doi:10.3389/fimmu.2017.00670; Linda Carlson et al., "Mindfulness-Based Cancer Recovery and Supportive-Expressive Therapy Maintain Telomere Length Relative to Controls in Distressed Breast Cancer Survivors," *Cancer* 121, no 3 (2014), 476–84, doi:10.1002/cncr.29063.

Chapter Three: Befriending the Body in Meditation

1. Bessel van der Kolk, *The Body Keeps the Score: Brain, Mind, and Body in the Healing of Trauma* (New York: Viking, 2014), 173–185; Peter Levine, *Waking the Tiger: Healing Trauma* (Berkeley, CA: North Atlantic, 1997), 13–22.

2. Reginald Ray, *Touching Enlightenment: Finding Realization in the Body* (Boulder: Sounds True, 2014), 1–5; Reginald Ray, "Reggie Ray: Buddhism, Trauma, and Healing," talk presented at Nondual Conference at the California Institute of Integral Studies in San Francisco on March 4, 2016, CIIS Public Programs podcast, March 28, 2016.

3. Daniel Siegel, *The Mindful Brain* (New York: W. W. Norton, 2007), 30–33.

4. Kalila B. Homann, "Embodied Concepts of Neurobiology in Dance/Movement Therapy Practice," *American Journal of Dance Therapy* 32, no. 2 (2010): 80–99, doi:10.1007/s10465-010-9099-6.

5. John Suler, *Contemporary Psychoanalysis and Eastern Thought* (New York: SUNY, 1993), 45–52.

6. Mary Oliver, "The Summer Day," in *New and Selected Poems.* (Boston: Beacon Press, 1992), 94.

7. Reginald Ray, "Earth Descent" (guided meditation), Dharma Ocean, accessed November 12, 2017, https://www.dharmaocean.org/meditation/learn-to-meditate/learn-to-meditate-foundational-practices.

Chapter Four: Evolving the Monkey's Motivations

1. Rick Hanson, *Hardwiring Happiness: The New Brain Science of Contentment, Calm, and Confidence* (New York: Harmony, 2013), 68.

2. Lisa Wimberger, *Neurosculpting for Stress Relief: Four Practices to Change Your Brain and Your Life*, audio book (Boulder: Sounds True, 2014).

3. Greg Boyle, "No Matter Whatness," June 3, 2016, YouTube, https://www.youtube.com/watch?v=Pc6IpqTyFL8.

4. Kelly McGonigal, *The Willpower Instinct: How Self-Control Works, Why It Matters, and What You Can Do to Get More of It* (New York: Penguin, 2013), 27–28.

5. Daniel J. Siegel, *The Mindful Brain: Reflection and Attunement in the Cultivation of Well-Being.* (New York: W. W. Norton, 2007), 25–28, 33–47.

6. Rod Meade Sperry, "That Time David Bowie Almost Became a Buddhist Monk—and What He Said (and Sang) about That Time," *Lion's Roar*, January 15, 2016, https://www.lionsroar.com/that-time-david-bowie-almost-became-a-buddhist-monk.

CHAPTER SIX: OUR MONKEYS, OURSELVES

1. Solange Akselrod et al. "Autonomic Response to Change of Posture among Normal and Mild-Hypertensive Adults: Investigation by Time-Dependent Spectral Analysis," *Journal of the Autonomic Nervous System* 64, no. 1 (1997): 33–43.
2. Daniel Kahneman, *Thinking, Fast and Slow* (New York: Farrar, Straus, and Giroux, 2011).
3. Rick Hanson, *Hardwiring Happiness: The New Brain Science of Contentment, Calm, and Confidence* (New York: Harmony, 2013).

CHAPTER SEVEN: HOW YOU BREATHE IS HOW YOU FEEL

1. Andrew Weil, *Breathing: The Master Key to Self-Healing* (Boulder: Sounds True, 2001).
2. Pierre Philippot and Sylvie Blairy, "Respiratory Feedback in the Generation of Emotion," *Cognition and Emotion* 16, no. 5 (2010): 605–27.
3. Weil, *Breathing*.
4. Herbert Benson, *Relaxation Revolution: The Science and Genetics of Mind Body Healing* (New York: Scribner, 2011), 54–70.

INTERLUDE: THE STORIES WE TELL OURSELVES

1. A. D. Craig, "How Do You Feel? Interoception: The Sense of the Physiological Condition of the Body," *National Review of Neuroscience* 3, no. 8 (2002): 655–66, doi:10.1038/nrn894; "James-Lange Theory," Oxford Quick Reference, accessed January 22, 2017, http://www.oxfordreference.com/view/10.1093/oi/authority.20110803100017783.

CHAPTER EIGHT: HOW WE GET STUCK

1. Steve Connor, "The People Who Can't Feel Pain: Scientists Discover Cause of Rare Inherited Condition That Turns Off Pain Sen-

sors," *Independent UK*, May 25, 2015, http://www.independent.co.uk
/life-style/health-and-families/health-news/the-people-who-cant
-feel-pain-scientists-discover-cause-of-rare-inherited-condition-that
-turns-off-10274604.html.

2. "Sigmund Freud Quotes," Brainy Quote, accessed December 12,
2017, https://www.brainyquote.com/quotes/sigmund_freud_151781.

3. Judith Herman, *Trauma and Recovery: The Aftermath of Violence—from
Domestic Abuse to Political Terror* (New York: Basic Books, 1992), 35–47.

4. Rick Hanson, *Hardwiring Happiness: The New Brain Science of Contentment, Calm, and Confidence* (New York: Harmony, 2013), 20–27.

5. Laura A. Baker, Serena Bezdjian, and Adrian Raine, "Behavioral
Genetics: The Science of Antisocial Behavior," *Law and Contemporary
Problems* 69, no. 1–2: 7–46, accessed December 24, 2017, https://www.
ncbi.nlm.nih.gov/pmc/articles/PMC2174903.

6. Daniel J. Siegel, "Toward an Interpersonal Neurobiology of the
Developing Mind: Attachment Relationships, 'Mindsight,' and
Neural Integration," *Infant Mental Health Journal* 22, no. 1–2
(2001): 67–94, doi:10.1002/1097-0355(200101/04)22:1<67::AID-
IMHJ3>3.0.CO;2-G.

Chapter Nine: What We Lose When We Lose Empathy

1. Nancy A. Shadick et al., "A Randomized Controlled Trial of an Internal Family Systems-based Psychotherapeutic Intervention on Outcomes in Rheumatoid Arthritis: A Proof-of-Concept Study," *Journal
of Rheumatology* 40, no. 11 (2013): 1831–41, http://www.jrheum.org
/content/jrheum/40/11/1831.full.pdf.

2. "B.C. Wildfires Map 2017: Current Location of Wildfires around the
Province," *Global News*, September 28, 2017, https://globalnews.ca
/news/3585284/b-c-wildfires-map-2017-current-location-of
-wildfires-around-the-province.

3. Qinjian Jin and Chien Wang, "A Revival of Indian Summer Monsoon
Rainfall Since 2002," *Nature Climate Change* 7, no. 8 (2017): 587–94,
doi:10.1038/nclimate3348.

4. Umair Irfan and Brian Resnick, "Megadisasters Devastated America
in 2017. And They're Only Going to Get Worse," *Vox*, January 8,
2018, https://www.vox.com/energy-and-environment/2017

/12/28/16795490/natural-disasters-2017-hurricanes-wildfires-heat
-climate-change-cost-deaths.

5. Chögyam Trungpa Rinpoche, *Cutting Through Spiritual Materialism* (Boston: Shambhala Publications, 1973), 97.

Chapter Ten: The Challenge of Self-Love

1. Sharon Salzberg, *Lovingkindness: The Revolutionary Art of Happiness* (Boston: Shambhala Publications, 1995), 20–21.

Chapter Eleven: The Monkey Is a Mensch

1. Charlie Morely, "The Three Happiness Paradoxes," January 28, 2012, YouTube, https://www.youtube.com/watch?v=oOZjn2T2a_E.

2. Bethany E. Kok et al., "How Positive Emotions Build Physical Health: Perceived Positive Social Connections Account for the Upward Spiral between Positive Emotions and Vagal Tone," *Psychological Science* 24, no. 7 (2013): 1123–32, doi:10.1177/0956797612470827.

3. David J. Kearney et al, "Loving-Kindness Meditation for Posttraumatic Stress Disorder: A Pilot Study," *Journal of Trauma and Stress* 26, no. 4 (2013): 426–34, doi:10.1002/jts.21832; Sarah Bowen et al, "Relative Efficacy of Mindfulness-Based Relapse Prevention, Standard Relapse Prevention, and Treatment as Usual for Substance Use Disorders: A Randomized Clinical Trial," *JAMA Psychiatry* 71, no. 5 (2014): 547–56; D.P. Johnson et al., "A Pilot Study of Loving-Kindness Meditation for the Negative Symptoms of Schizophrenia," *Schizophrenia Research Journal* 129, no. 2–3 (July 2011): 137–40, doi:10.1016/j. schres.2011.02.015.

4. Elizabeth A. Hoge et al., "Loving-Kindness Meditation Practice Associated with Longer Telomeres in Women," *Brain, Behavior, and Immunity* 32 (August 2013): 159–63, doi:10.1016/j.bbi.2013.04.005; M. E. Tonelli and Amy B. Wachholtz, "Meditation-Based Treatment Yielding Immediate Relief for Meditation-Naïve Migraineurs," *Pain Management Nursing* 15, no. 1 (2014): 36–40, doi:10.1016/j. pmn.2012.04.002; James W. Carson et al., "Loving-Kindness Meditation for Chronic Low Back Pain: Results from a Pilot Trial," *Journal of Holistic Nursing* 23, no. 3 (2005): 287–304.

Interlude: Love, Level 10

1. Yongey Mingyur, *The Joy of Living: Unlocking the Secret and Science of Happiness* (New York: Three Rivers Press, 2008), 7–10.
2. Yongey Mingyur, "Joyful Wisdom," lecture presented at Shambhala Meditation Center, New York, NY, June 23, 2009 (event description at https://ny.shambhala.org/program-details/?id=19844).

Chapter Thirteen: The Family Within

1. Sandra Ingerman, *Soul Retrieval: Mending the Fragmented Self* (New York: HarperOne, 2006), 78–83.

Resources

RECOMMENDED READING

Barrett, Lisa Feldman. *How Emotions Are Made: The Secret Life of the Brain* (New York: Mariner, 2018).

Earley, Jay. *Self-Therapy: A Step-By-Step Guide to Creating Wholeness and Healing Your Inner Child Using IFS, A New Cutting-Edge Psychology, Second Edition* (Larspur, CA: Pattern System Books, 2012).

Ensler, Eve. *In the Body of the World: A Memoir of Cancer and Connection* (New York: Picador, 2013).

Herman, Judith. *Trauma and Recovery: The Aftermath of Violence—from Domestic Abuse to Political Terror* (New York: Basic Books, 1993).

Kahneman, Daniel. *Thinking, Fast and Slow.* (New York: Farrar, Straus & Giroux, 2016).

Kornfield, Jack. *A Path with Heart: A Guide Through the Perils and Promises of Spiritual Life* (New York: Bantam Books, 1993).

Levine, Peter A. *Waking the Tiger: Healing Trauma* (Berkeley, CA: North Atlantic Books, 1997).

Ray, Reginald A. *Touching Enlightenment: Finding Realization in the Body* (Boulder, CO: Sounds True, 2008).

———. *The Awakening Body: Somatic Meditation for Discovering Our Deepest Life* (Boulder, CO: Shambhala Publications, 2016).

Rinzler, Lodro. *Love Hurts: Buddhist Advice for the Heartbroken* (Boulder, CO: Shambhala Publications, 2016).

Schwartz, Richard C. *You Are the One You've Been Waiting For: Bringing Courageous Love to Intimate Relationships* (Center for Self Leadership, 2008).

Siegel, Daniel. *The Mindful Brain: Reflection and Attunement in the Cultivation of Well-Being* (New York: W. W. Norton and Company, 2007).

Strayed, Cheryl. *Tiny Beautiful Things: Advice on Love and Life from Dear Sugar* (New York: Vintage, 2012).

van der Kolk, Bessel. *The Body Keeps the Score: Brain, Mind, and Body in the Healing of Trauma* (New York: Penguin Books, 2014).

williams, Reverend angel Kyodo and Lama Rod Owens. *Radical Dharma: Talking Race, Love, and Liberation* (Berkeley, CA: North Atlantic Books, 2016).

Recommended Listening

Gangaji and Larson, Hillary. Podcast. *A Conversation with Gangaji.* gangaji.org/radio/episodes/a-conversation-with-gangaji/.

Hanson, Rick. Podcast. *Being Well with Dr. Rick Hanson.* rickhanson.net/multimedia/being-well-podcast/.

Kornfield, Jack. Podcast. *Jack Kornfield Heart Wisdom Hour,* Be Here Now Network. beherenownetwork.com/category/jack-kornfield/.

———. "Take the One Seat." Recorded lecture. September 3, 2007. soundcloud.com/jack-kornfield/take-the-one-seat-september.

Nichtern, Ethan. Podcast. *The Road Home,* Be Here Now Network. beherenownetwork.com/teachers/ethan-nichtern-road-home-podcast/.

Piver, Susan. *The Susan Piver Podcast.* itunes.apple.com/us/podcast/the-susan-piver-podcast/id679834668?mt=2.

Ray, Reginald. "Episode 178: Physical and Emotional Pain Part II." Podcast. *Dharma Ocean Podcast,* April 19, 2017. dharmaocean.org/episode-178-physical-and-emotional-pain-part-ii/.

———. "Episode 170: Making Friends with Ourselves Part II." Podcast. *Dharma Ocean Podcast,* December 20, 2016. dharmaocean.org/episode-170-making-friends-with-ourselves-part-ii/.

Rinzler, Lodro. Podcast. *MNDFL Meditation.* itunes.apple.com/us/podcast/mndfl-meditation/id1285190149?mt=2.

Sattin, Neil. Interview with Richard Schwartz. "Episode 26: How to Get All the Parts within You to Work Together (and with Your Partner) with Dich Schwartz." Podcast. *Relationship Alive,* February 15, 2016. neilsattin.com/blog/2016/02/26-how-to-get-all-the-parts-within-you-to-work-together-and-with-your-partner-with-dick-schwartz/.

Salzberg, Sharon. Podcast. *The Metta Hour Podcast.* sharonsalzberg.com/metta-hour-podcast/.

Tippett, Krista. Interview with Brené Brown. "Strong Back, Soft Front, Wild Heart." Podcast. *On Being with Krista Tippett*, February 8, 2018. onbeing.org/programs/brene-brown-strong-back-soft-front-wild -heart-feb2018/.

About the Author

RALPH DE LA ROSA is a psychotherapist in private practice in NYC, specializing in trauma-focused care. He began teaching meditation in 2008 and leads workshops and retreats on utilizing meditation and contemplative processes for psychological healing and growth. Ralph began meditating in 1996 within the bhakti yoga tradition and has studied Buddhism since 2005. He currently studies in the Dharma Ocean lineage of Tibetan Buddhism. Ralph himself is a depression, PTSD, and addiction survivor. His work is inspired by the tremendous transformation he has experienced through meditation, yoga, and therapy. Ralph is also a musician and storyteller, currently residing in Brooklyn, New York, with his two cats, Emma Goldman and Henry.